SECRET

COURTS

Child Protection?
..or Child Abuse?

How and why 'the system'
is failing our children!

Joe Burns

SECRET COURTS
Child Protection or Child Abuse?

ISBN-13: 978-1-906628-76-5
Published by CheckPoint Press, Ireland

First published in eBook format in December 2014 and released on Gumroad.com under the title: 'Secret Courts: Ireland's next scandal waiting to be exposed'.

CHECKPOINT PRESS, REPUBLIC OF IRELAND
EMAIL: EDITOR@CHECKPOINTPRESS.COM

WWW.CHECKPOINTPRESS.COM

CheckPoint
Press

SECRET
COURTS

Child Protection? ..or Child Abuse?

Joe Burns

How and why 'the system' is failing our children!

In the Irish interpretation by Van Nost, erected in 1751, it was said by Dubliners;

"The Lady of Justice

Mark well her Station

Her face to the Castle

And her arse to the Nation!"

' Justitia' as she is known, is often represented by a blindfolded lady, as Justice is supposed to be blind. In most interpretations her sword is held down or in a more forthright stance. Our Irish Justitia is admiring hers.

When she was erected above the arch, she was placed facing into the Castle with her back to the City of Dublin. She is perhaps an accurate reflection of Irish Justice today where there are two different systems of Justice, one for those who can afford it and one for everyone else

DEDICATION

I would like to dedicate this book to the many children who have died in the "Care" of the State and to those who have been trafficked into sex slavery, those who have been denied the right to be raised by their parents, those whose suffering was so immense that they chose to end their life because they felt they had no other way to end their pain.

I also dedicate this book to the hundreds of parents and children who put their faith in my colleagues and myself, who in the face of pain and adversity had such courage to fight such an unfair fight for their children.

To the parents who risked prison, suffered intimidation and never gave up fighting for their children. To the many who asked me to be their voice when they are gagged and cannot speak for themselves, I will not fail you.

To my esteemed colleagues around the world, many of whom do not wish to be named, I say 'Thank You' on behalf of the many children who are being raised by their parents today, and that your work has inspired me.

To the many who have lost their children forever, and yet continue to help others, to lend support and a listening ear, to fight to protect other families, to educate the public, to lend your voice, I say 'Thank You'; your work is having an impact and the tide is slowly turning in favor of the children.

To my own Parents and Family, who raised me and taught me the value of "Biology", To my Cousins, Aunts and Uncles, many of whom I only see every few years, and yet still embrace me as Family as if time and distance had no bearing on the inseparable bonds of love and belongingness that only Family can understand, I say 'Thank You' for being my safety net and giving me the courage to be who I am.

To the loyal supporters of my blogs and readers of this book, I thank you for keeping an open mind and for challenging me to keep me on the right path. I don't pretend to have all the answers or to be the man I set out to be; I am constantly humbled by your support and dedication to the cause of helping children. The proposition of Science is that we should always keep an open mind and not accept anything on Blind Faith alone.

We can only build a man or a system by constantly challenging them and they become more robust by that challenge or fade into the sands of time. I welcome any challenge to what I have said in this book, there are uncomfortable conversations that we need to have and if we are ever to protect children, we need to have these debates constantly and not be afraid of challenging our beliefs or the sacred cows of 'Child Protection'.

It is not my intent to defame any individual, organization or profession. Time and time again I see good people with the best intentions whose faith in a system is misguided and misplaced but good intentions is a road to Hell that leads us nowhere. Children deserve the best protection that Society can afford them and unless there is constant scrutiny and evaluation, we will continue on a road to Hell 'in good faith' that our system is working and later, pay the price to society.

No evaluation of the system can ever take place and no benefit to children can ever be measured or demonstrated in a Secret Court.

Joe Burns

REVIEW

"The child protection 'industry' in Ireland is out of control and has long-since lost its moral compass. When unfounded and unproven allegations by anonymous sources can be brought against otherwise decent parents; and when those allegations are given weight and credit in 'secret courts' by reckless, unqualified and amoral agents of the State; and when children can be kidnapped and families destroyed... then clearly, there is a problem here that needs to be tackled urgently. Joe Burns knows his stuff. This book is essential reading for anyone who claims to genuinely 'care' about our children."

Stephen T Manning PhD.

Author and founder of the Integrity Ireland Association

CONTENTS

CHAPTER 1

"I CAN'T GET MY HEAD AROUND THIS"

If I told you that there were secret courts operating in Ireland for many years, courts where you are presumed guilty until proven innocent, courts where the Public may not enter, courts where you are punished regardless of innocence or guilt, would you believe that they exist?

Would you believe that you are not entitled to know what evidence will be used against you, you and your family can be punished and in order to prove your innocence, you must prove it beyond all reasonable doubt? Or that Psychology is used instead of hard evidence for fictitious mental illnesses that do not exist?

Did you know that agents of the State might enter your home and tell you how to run your life under threat of punishment if you do not co-operate? One parent could be told to leave the home or face the removal of your children. You do not have to be accused of any crime but you could lose your child until the age of 18 without anything more than accusation.

The Agents of the State are not Police and have no statutory authority without a judge having granted an order. The Order can be granted "Ex-Parte" which means without you being present in court. Much of the time, the law is broken when an "Apprehension" takes place. Children are fraudulently removed without a court order and Police, Social Workers and Judges are complicit in this illegality. You are gagged both legally and under threat of punishment that your relationship with your child can be terminated or severely restricted.

You may wonder what legal basis exists for these miscarriages of justice to take place. In truth there are no grounds that allow for much of what takes place. If such practices took place with rapists and murderers, Civil and Human

Rights groups would be up in arms at the injustice of it all, and yet, this is allowed to be perpetrated on children and their parents, in secret courts.

Because all of this takes place in total secrecy, nobody is allowed to know what happens. Victims may not talk to their family and friends and even the children are gagged. When people appeal to higher courts, the secrecy is still maintained. The secrecy is the In-Camera Rule, there is no statutory law named the In-Camera Law. People are charged and jailed in secret for up to 2 years without benefit of a jury, the critical eye of the public or the media being present.

Most people including Police and those caught up in the system have a poor understanding of the system. I wrongly believed that children were only removed on the basis that children have been harmed and a crime has been committed. Most people don't understand that in cases of suspected abuse or neglect there are two parallel investigations. If the criminal investigation is not prosecuted or Police do not find enough evidence, the cases are still prosecuted in a Family Court. In the UK there are special family courts, however the magistrates may also hear other cases such as traffic courts or minor offences. In Ireland there are no family courts as such, District or Circuit Court judges hear them, the same judges hear traffic and criminal cases.

When people are accused of crimes, they have a reasonable chance at justice. The criminal justice system is supposed to be predicated on the belief that ten guilty men should go free before one innocent man is punished. Even though the State may have 60 people involved in prosecuting you and have unlimited budgets and even though you may only have a Legal Aid lawyer that you met 30 minutes before the trial, you still have a reasonable chance at justice, as the system is supposed to have checks and balances.

The family court is predicated on the belief that 184 innocent people should be prosecuted before one guilty parent is prosecuted. Very few people who lose their parental rights are ever convicted of any crime; most are not even accused but severely punished anyway. The system is geared towards destruction of the family rather than fixing broken families. The system has gone beyond "Risk Aversion"; it has now surpassed total avoidance of any risk to "Shoot first and ask questions later".

After the death penalty, the most severe punishment that can be inflicted on a human being is to remove their children. This punishes not just the parent, but the child as well. The parent grieves for the distress that the child is being subject to and the child suffers also. As this is a Child Protection System, there is no support or care for the parent involved. The system destroys families and has no obligation or duty to parents. The child is not just the primary consideration it is the only consideration. Many of the cases I have been involved in meet the standard of the United Nations, of Torture.

When parents are thrown into this netherworld of a system, very few know how to navigate through it and are at a loss to know what to do. People hire solicitors only to find that many do not give proper representation. Rather than presenting a defense for their clients, they advise to co-operate fully and not to fight the system.

If you are charged with a crime, Police investigate, Prosecutors prosecute, judges will judge and punishment is carried out by the Prison Service or Probation Service. In Family Court the whole system the same people investigate, prosecute and punish. Many would say they also judge, as judges are reluctant to go against Social Services. Judges almost never refuse an application to take a child into care. They usually grant the orders without hearing any evidence and the punishment without crime, or even evidence of a crime, starts right away.

In a recent case in Scotland, social workers were charged with contempt of court for failing to comply with the judge's direction, that the parents have contact with their child. The social workers and their unions disagreed with the judge citing that they had an absolute duty to protect the child and felt that it was in the "Best Interests" of the child to have no contact with the parent. Their union also supported this position. Essentially, as the social workers had investigated, prosecuted, judged that they knew better than a judge and punished the child and the parents, they have set themselves up as Judge, Jury and Executioner. Far from this case being an anomaly, social workers rarely follow the dictates of the judge. It is highly unusual that social workers are ever prosecuted, certainly not in Ireland, but in the UK many are struck off the register every year for fabricating reports, perjury and neglect.

In some cases, there is a Case Conference and Police, Doctors, Teachers or other involved parties would be present to discuss the plan of action. Parents are rarely present at these meetings. In many other cases, no conference is held and the child/ren are taken illegally in some cases.

When the decision is made to remove a child, placement with other family members should be considered first, for the sake of the child. An aunt or Uncle or Grandparent should always be considered under guidelines and Best Practice. The problem is that Best Practice is rarely followed. I know of cases where newborns were removed shortly after birth, social services refused to allow for breastfeeding or bonding. It is the right of a newborn baby to be breastfed and bond with its mother, however, social services don't necessarily follow any rule unless it is on a statutory footing. Even then they don't always follow court orders or even the law.

I have an audio recording of an HSE Manager saying he had no intention of following the Children First Guidelines, Human Rights Conventions or anything that is not on a statutory footing. Even the Social Work Handbook is thrown away in many cases and the rules invented as time progresses.

I came upon this topic quite by accident 7 years. I have no children of my own but have raised and been a stepparent to many and I have never been personally harmed by the system. I have no declared interest in this topic and I do not benefit financially for taking the position I take on this topic.

Before I delve further in, you are probably wondering about my motivations and my perspective on the issue. I have been interviewed by journalists and on the radio many times. One of the first questions I am often asked is; "how can you help child abusers?" This is a loaded question and presupposes that the people whom I help are criminals who abuse and neglect children. I respond that I have never helped in a single case where the parents are actually charged with child abuse and never will. Most people are taken aback at this but it is the truth, the vast majority of people who lose their children to this system have never been charged with any crime in relation to their children. I have never become involved in any case where a parent was a substance abuser or where their baby was born an addict, not once in hundreds of cases I have been involved in.

The inference that some journalists want to make is that "you are either against child abuse or you are for it". Any criticism of the system is seen as support for child abuse. If you criticize Foster Care or Adoption or ask questions about Children's NGO's, you are seen as attacking sacred cows that are beyond all criticism, and apparently beyond all scrutiny. This is heresy and blasphemy. One of the first questions interviewers want to ask me is; "Why are you assisting child abusers?" My answer is that I have never helped a child abuser, ever.

For most people, their position is based on blind-faith that the system works. They cannot claim to have knowledge of the system as law forbids them to know what happens. As the Ryan Report destroyed the faith that many had in their religion, surely this new religion of Child Protection will suffer a similar fate when Ryan Report Two convenes? The children mentioned in the Ryan Report fought for years to let the public know that they had been abused, as people's faith didn't allow them to believe it. People asked when the truth came out; "how could this happen and why didn't the previous generation do something about it?" My questions to you are why are you ignoring the abuse that is currently happening today? And why are you ignoring the mounting evidence that the system is "not fit for purpose" to use a quote from a government report? If my assertions in this book are even 1% correct, shouldn't that prompt another Ryan Report?

I recently watched a documentary where a solicitor had some issues with people who help in these cases. It was stated that we didn't have access to social services or police reports and they believed that we were operating in a deficit of information. In truth, McKenzie Friends as they are known as, have far better access than most lawyers and unlike the lawyers; we actually meet the children in most cases. You would have to wonder is a solicitor who represents Guardians ad Litem has ever met any of the children that they purport to represent? Unlike lawyers, who often meet their clients 30 minutes before a court case and don't have the luxury of picking their clients, McKenzie Friends get to pick and choose cases and will tend to pick cases where the parents are completely innocent of any wrongdoing. You also have to wonder in the €30 million a year of legal cases, if any of the State lawyers have met any of the children that they want to separate from their parents?

As children very rarely appear in family courts it would be an exceedingly rare event that the lawyers would meet the children they supposedly represent. In Law, it seems astonishing that the children who mostly want to stay with their parents, have no voice and are represented third-hand by a solicitor they have never met. People will say that the children are represented by the Guardian ad Litem, but in my experience the GAL is another social worker working against the family, and the GAL who is paid €125/hour, is represented by a solicitor for €225/hour. It would be extremely rare for a GAL to go against the social worker. For earnings of up to €330,000 a year, would you go against the grain of your industry?

When I talk to people about this system, I find that the majority makes assumptions that the parents are bad parents and although there are certainly some bad parents out there, I don't help these people. There is a huge disparity between the numbers of children removed from parents and the crime statistics. If child abuse and neglect is a crime, which I believe it is, why isn't it punished as a crime?

For example the HSE claimed in 2011 that there were 541 "Confirmed" cases of sexual abuse of children in Ireland, and yet the Director of Public Prosecutions only had 39 prosecutions, mostly of historic cases where the child victims were now adults. Does that mean that the HSE let off 500 paedophiles a year? Or that they have "confirmed" 500 cases of sexual abuse that never occurred?

When you look at statistics in this system, the numbers just don't add up, on one hand you have social services claiming that abuse of children is at epidemic proportions on the other hand you have crime statistics that show that child abuse and neglect prosecutions have not increased in decades, but the size of the Child Abuse Industry has doubled in one decade? Because there is no scrutiny, there is no public outcry. I doubt that anyone would disagree with me when I say that anyone who sexually assaults a child should be punished. People affected are doubly gagged, once by the court that you cannot say "anything to anyone" and again by social services that they will cut or terminate access to your children if you don't do as they say, regardless of what the judge thinks.

We often hear of the bad parent stories but almost never hear of the stories of where the parents are completely innocent. For example you never read about the case where social workers went to the wrong house and removed the wrong child for months before the mistake was discovered. A doctor on the witness stand looked at photographs of a child and declared; "this is not the child I examined". You will never read about these cases because the parents are gagged under threat of imprisonment. Journalists wont cover the stories either as they could face jail. Nobody in the system will talk about the injustices or the mistakes.

The turnover in Child Protection is extremely high, but it is not because of high caseloads, poor pay or shortage of staff. Many lawyers wont take cases against the authorities but will gladly take cases of parent versus parent. In a competent system, how is it possible to remove the wrong child for months before the mistake is discovered? If police made this same mistake would there not be a big media event and public outcry?

I have assisted many researchers for TV and Radio shows that you see in the UK and introduced them to parents affected by the system, some of them on the run. I eventually became involved in cases around the world, particularly medical cases where I could use my training and experience in cases where children were misdiagnosed and assisted parents wrongly accused. I did this with assistance from many of my colleagues, all of us unpaid, and all trying to restore justice for the children affected by this.

For almost 4 years continuously I worked full time with my colleagues throughout the world. Buoyed by our great success, often against teams of lawyers, some paid €3,000 a day, we became victims of our own success. In my own case I have depleted my savings and need to return to work.

My colleagues and I have been threatened and intimidated, physically and verbally attacked, we have spent a lot of our own money, had corrupt HSE (CFA) lawyers try to jail us, have been the subject of secret meetings of HSE lawyers, had our website visited every day and scanned for any hint of a violation of the In Camera Rule by government departments. Our webpages and many of the opinion pieces and blogs that I have written have been produced in courts around the country as "Evidence" that we are "anti-state" or "anti-system" when in fact the opposite is true. We are anti-child abuse, especially when the perpetrator is the State. We are not anarchists or activists; we are simply people helping people. We work within the law for the benefit of the children we help. The only protest that I have ever attended in my life was a protest against the HSE to get an inquiry into the deaths in State "Care".

Fortunately many judges are as unhappy with the dysfunctional Child "Protection" System as we are and I have been complimented on my analysis more than once by many judges. Some judges have been around long enough that they have witnessed "Inter-generational Recidivism", they saw children taken into "Care" years ago and now see the children of those children coming before them have fallen afoul of the law or social services. Their parents were taken into "Care" to prevent them becoming dysfunctional adults, but the experiment in Social Engineering has been a dismal failure. A woman who has spent any time in State "Care" is statistically 66 times more likely to have her child removed and placed in "Care". That dreadful statistic should be ample evidence of a system that does the complete opposite of what it purports. In future chapters I will delve into "care" in far more detail.

Some judge's love seeing my colleagues in court, a few don't. They know that we take cases where we believe the parents to be completely innocent and that we come to court very well prepared with case law which makes the judges job easier. Case law includes previous decisions, usually of higher courts and the judge must follow the law or risk having their decision overturned. In one case where I was not present the CFA produced printouts of our webpage and used this as an argument as to why we shouldn't be allowed in the court. The judge refused to see them, as he was a regular reader of our page and complained that we had a dead link on the page. I had recently added a few pages and only a regular subscriber would have known that the link no longer worked. I believe the page was one of our pages on Case Law, which was widely used by solicitors and barristers in Ireland.

We ended up shutting down our web page as it had served it's purpose and plan on a new and improved website in the future.

Over the years I have been in contact with colleagues who have never been personally harmed by the system and yet spend a great deal of their time fighting to improve the system. I have spoken with many people who have dealt with Child Protection issues for years. Ian Josephs, a millionaire businessman who lives in Monaco has dealt with these cases since the 1960's in the UK and never lost a case. I have interviewed social workers at great length in several countries and discussed how they operate compared to the UK and Ireland and even they find it shocking at what is happening here. I will publish some of their opinions later in the book and compare the systems. It took me years to understand how this system functions and why it doesn't, and will never work as it should. I will try to fairly represent the views from people affected, to the decision makers who run the system. I don't pretend to be an expert or even a writer but I will explain the situation as best I can.

I will start off with a problem statement as I see it,

- We are asking social workers to do a job that they will never be capable of doing.

- We have an attitude that it is acceptable to wrongly take 100 children into "Care" on nothing more than suspicion in order to prevent the 1 in 100 or 1 in 1,000 being the victim of child abuse and neglect.

- If the system is working, why don't the care recipients have far better outcomes in life?

- We have allowed our system of Justice to become corrupted by having different standards of justice where you can be innocent in one court but still punished in another.

- We have allowed Psychology and Sociology to become integrated into our government and court system, both are products which are over-sold and neither one is robust enough to be used as evidence to the minimum standard of justice.

- We have blindly supported without question, a system of protection that historically has never worked.

- We are taking children from the frying pan and placing them in the fire. We take children with no evidence of harm and place them at higher risk in "Care" where they are virtually guaranteed to have bad outcomes.

- We have ignored far better models of Child Protection around the world but instead choose to follow the worst example possible from the UK.

- The system does far more harm than good.

- The profit motive of the Child Abuse Industry drives the system. The system is expensive and is designed to be adversarial and profitable.

- There is no upper management in child protection and no government management. Unions have far more influence than Ministers.

- The In Camera Rule has been perverted to protect the system.

- "Best Interests" doesn't protect or benefit most children.

I could continue on with a considerable list of issues but the top three reasons should be more than enough to concern people. When you break down the system into its component parts and examine each system, you find that nothing works, as you would expect. When you compare the systems in other countries where the system works better, you'll see why it doesn't work in Ireland or the UK.

Could you imagine a Policeman going to a judge and asking for an arrest and detention warrant based on nothing more than suspicion that the suspect may (or equally may not) at some point in the future, may rob a bank or commit murder? If this happened in a criminal court the policeman would be laughed out of court and civil and human rights groups would be up in arms at the human and civil rights abuses. And yet, this is exactly what happens in secret family courts in Ireland and the UK every day and it's happening to children.

One day in court, I was assisting a parent. After our case was heard, Solicitors for Social Services approached the judge to grant an Emergency Care Order. In the short time it took me to quickly grab my papers and coat and walk to the door, the order was granted for 3 children. No evidence was presented, the parents were not present and the entire process took less that one minute.

If such an event took place in a criminal proceeding, the media and public would be outraged.

You should also realize that for me to disclose this incident to you, I am (technically) breaking the law. I have not identified any child or the people involved but it is nevertheless a crime under the law to disclose "anything to anyone" that occurs in these secret courts. How do you write a book about a topic that you are not allowed to discuss? Ireland has now become the most draconian family law system in the world because even Sir Justice Munby, the president of the UK Family Courts, has decreed that the secrecy has no place in law. No such decrees have been forthcoming from the Irish Judiciary who are long overdue restoring justice from those who have perverted it for their own gain.

When Police are looking for a search or arrest warrants, they need Probable Cause or some form of evidence before a warrant would be granted.

The question this raises for me is why are criminals more deserving of human and civil rights than children and their innocent parents? The reason that human and civil rights groups are not involved is because this happens in secret with no scrutiny of these courts, very few written decisions exist and none are published and case law only exists in higher courts or other jurisdictions. In the alternate universe that the family court has become, anything is possible.

In any organization there is a tendency to grow, it is a survival imperative. Small enterprises become big companies and employ more people and make more profit. This tendency exists in Government also; new laws will generate more control and more people falling afoul of the law and more revenue being generated. The difference however with private industry is that it must compete in an open marketplace. It must consistently turn out a good product at a fair price in order to remain competitive and profitable. No such controls exist for protecting children although many other government departments have seen their budgets slashed and have had to do more with less. In a decade in Ireland and the UK the budgets and numbers of children in "Care" have doubled even though neither the crime statistics nor the demographics can support or justify such growth.

For years while Ireland was suffering from austerity measures, the Child Abuse Industry has been the only growth industry in Ireland. In 2011 the HSE took 3.7 times more children into "Care" on a per-capita basis than the UK, and the UK had a record-breaking year also. Nobody asked why, but the explanation offered by the government is that the number of complaints of child abuse and neglect has dramatically increased over the years, in Ireland now 40,000 calls a year. Despite "calling social services" as being the weapon of choice for vindictive neighbors or relatives, nobody is ever prosecuted for this crime. I know this because I have tried without success to get social workers to make formal complaints.

If police received double the amount of complaints, would it follow that the conviction rate would also double? What is often blamed for the increase is the "Baby P Effect" but the truth is that although this death had an impact, it wasn't the cause of more children being removed, it was however used as an excuse.

I have blogged and written opinion pieces, been interviewed on the radio in several countries and nobody wants to have the debate. The usual excuses are trotted out; "lessons will be learned", "we have put measures in place", " these decisions are never made lightly", "we cannot discuss individual cases" and my favorite; "think of the children". I have toyed with the idea of writing a Public Relations Manual for social workers and departments. After you have heard all the sorry excuses for a long time you tend to mouth the well-worn phrases in sync with social care providers.

Social Work and Child Protection has come under the spotlight a lot more in the last decade. The result of the public scrutiny is that child protection social workers have become the most hated profession especially in the UK. To counteract the entire bad PR from failures that have come to the public attention, the response has been to prop up the profession. PR Guru Max Clifford was hired in an effort to boost their public perception. Councils had difficulty getting staff and job turnover increased. The use of agencies increased to fill gaps and the support from the UK Government increased. Max Clifford was convicted of child sexual abuse but this PR failure was not big news outside the profession.

New PR terms started creeping in to the profession such as "damned if we do and damned if we don't". This was mostly in response to the Baby P fiasco, which I will deal with in more detail later. After Baby P, the media started paying more attention, but like Ireland, were severely restricted by the secrecy of the family courts. Many cases did come to the media attention, mostly because of Social Media breaking the silence and putting the information in the public domain. Facebook became the bane of social workers but later they learned to use it as a tool against parents. But because of the growth of the Child Abuse Industry, far more parents were being affected and a small percentage of them were brave enough to post their stories. This encouraged other parents to come forward and eventually hundreds of anti-social services groups started popping up. My own page on Facebook received an astronomical number of hits during the Children's Referendum.

Where the media failed in its duty to be the "Watchdogs of Society" and keep an eye on the government, the public sought it's own news on the Internet. Eventually the Media started paying attention and doing their own investigations and although some were less than balanced, at least the discussion was out there in the public domain. In the UK, even though I am Irish, I have been contacted by many researchers and producers from all the major TV and Radio stations, talk shows and helped them with research and putting them in contact with parents, McKenzie Friends and other interested parties. I have declined to be interviewed myself due to time constraints. I have done a few interviews on radio in other countries but few in Ireland, I don't get asked.

Ireland has always followed the UK policies on Child Protection, if only 5 to 10 years after. When Ireland announced that the Media would be allowed to enter the family courts, of course at the discretion of the judge and report certain details of the case, again at the judges discretion. Since the same announcement was made in the UK, it has never resulted in any controversial case being reported in the media, I predicted it would have the same effect in Ireland. Journalists don't have the time to sit for a week in case of social services versus parent and would not take the risk of spending a week on one case and then not be allowed to report anything.

The only time the "opening" of courts has had any impact is when the journalists were tipped off to attend the High Court where cases are usually dealt with in hours rather than days. Even then, they will over cover the points allowed by the judge. In one high profile case I had a small part in, Gardai used their Armed Response Unit to break into an empty house, which was reportedly ransacked. They were acting on behalf of the CFA social workers that had illegally obtained the wrong type of court order in a District Court, which was contrary to a High Court order not to interfere with the family until the High Court matter was decided. Essentially this was an attempted kidnapping by social workers aided by armed police contrary to a High Court order. Newsworthy?

The entire break-in of the home was captured on a house security camera of the Gardai breaking into an obviously empty house. The reason the house was empty at the time was because the parents were in the High Court against the CFA. The video, which I edited and posted on Facebook, received over 20,000 hits. Even though the episode was mentioned in the High Court and the media were present, the story of the break-in, ransacking and attempted kidnapping did not appear in Irish media. Other attempts to interest Irish media in other stories have met with indifference. On the rare occasion that Irish journalist dig for a story, or a granted freedom of Information requests, they do occasionally come up with interesting stories. I suspect that when Ireland catches up with the UK in 5 years or so, that TV and Radio will catch up also and do some documentaries as the BBC have done, even doing stories in Ireland.

The social media and the mainstream media are totally out of sync. The views and opinions online don't necessarily reflect the overall public opinion but the gap appears closer than before as more people become literate with technology.

At the present time, the public is acting in a deficit of information as one lawyer put it. We have courts that are so secret that you can be jailed for saying "anything to anybody". You have a public on a drip-feed of government press releases that are an exercise in cheerleading a clearly dysfunctional system. You have nearly 30% of Irish children living in consistent poverty and over 700 children homeless, meanwhile you have a billion a year Child Abuse Industry with a seeming unlimited budget and all the time more children are dying, being raped, abused and neglected in complete secrecy and I have only scratched the surface so far.

CHAPTER 2

A RECIPE FOR DISASTER?

I have never been much of a cook; I probably inherited that from my mother. I used to joke with her that she could burn water. My mother wasn't a bad cook, just not very adventurous. Like most Irish Mammies at the time, was severely restrained by budget and other factors. Fortunately I also inherited her sense of humor.

I have tried, but struggled with recipes. I have a friend who is a chef and can do amazing things even with a bare cupboard. The difficulty I have always had is that the recipes are so vague. I am more accustomed to scientific recipes where all the variables are accounted for. The scientific process is rather simple, if you boil water to 100*C at atmospheric pressure, the experiment is repeatable anywhere.

The difficulty I have is when try to cook food is the recipe says;

- A sprinkle of…
- A Dash of…
- A whiff of…
- A sifter of…

The instructions are so vague that if I make pancakes and I end up with rock cakes. Cooking from frozen gives me chills, as I don't want to undercook and end up eating poison, I never eat anything past the sell-by date. On one hand I want to balance my diet on the other to eat healthy.

Please forgive my departure here into a diversion. I do have a point I wish to make and my thought processes works by way of analogy. I have a tendency to compare apples to apples and find the irony in situations. There are many facets of life that are absurd and sometimes we don't realize them until we see a Stand Up Comic or critical thinker who will point them out to us. I have often wondered why more comedians don't cover the topic of Child Protection.

Cooking is an art, referred to as the Culinary Arts. Rather than having one universal recipe for spaghetti, cooks and chefs have great latitude to make their creations pleasing to the palette and a visual delight, or not depending on the cook. I recall the worst spaghetti I ever had was in Rome and the best in Cancun, the worst curry in Madras and the best in Kerry. The biggest issue is consistency even though the raw ingredients are very similar.

Producing food on a grander scale is an entirely different matter. In the kitchen of a restaurant chefs are managers and have to balance so many factors at once in an environment with more pressure than an operating theatre. Not only that but they have to able to deliver under budget consistently, order the right ingredients at the right time and right quantity. Highly skilled and talented chefs are highly sought after, must be artists and managers of people at the same time.

When you get to the scale of mass-produced foods, for example a can of fruit cocktail, you need to have everything down to a science and every detail from fruit picking to canning and shipping must be worked out in the minutest detail. If cherries cost more that pears or apples this year because of a bad crop or season, the producer must finely balance the amount in each can or the company will be out of business from one bad shipment or by adding too many cherries to each can and going bankrupt in the process.

In the world of fast food, restaurateurs have had to develop specialized equipment for manufacturing, to automate the production of food. They found it necessary to standardize the processes. If you look closely at the equipment you will see instructions, which make the entire process foolproof;

1/ Place Burger Patty on plate A and press button B.

2/ When green light appears burger patty is cooked.

The computer touchscreen of the operator produces the order in the kitchen with instructions for the burger flipper to follow the instructions. We have eliminated thought from the process, follow your checklist and let the machinery make all the decisions for you, which eliminated human error. There are probably vending machines in development now that will supply the most delicious hamburgers you ever tasted made exactly to your taste. These machines will replace cooks and servers.

Years ago when I drove into a fast food restaurant drive through in Arizona and placed my order. I had difficulty hearing the person on the other end and making my order known to the operator. I found the cause was because the drive through was being routed through the bad Internet connection to a call center in India.

The advantage of this automation and systematic approach is not just economic, consistency in fast food is paramount for the customer. You may have tasted better taco's or burgers elsewhere, but at least you know in advance the food will always be consistent whether you have your burger in Dublin, London or Rome. The training required by staff is minimal and new staff can be productive with only a few hours training. The training is even automated and the staff member will watch a video, read and understood the process and signed a contract. If the staff is low paid and has a high turnover, it doesn't matter much to the owner or franchisee, as qualifications are almost unnecessary.

Henry Ford developed far more than the first standardized motorcar, the Model-T, he invented the very concept of mass production. He said the car was available in any color you like, as long as that color was black. The model T had few variations and parts were interchangeable from one to the next. He had developed a system where engine builders only built engines and had no clue as to the intricacies of installing the steering, seats or axel. Ford also inadvertently started the Aftermarket and Wreckers Yard Industries.

In the 1940's, the concept of Standardized or Best Practice helped form the International Standards Association. Without standardization every nail manufacturer could manufacture a 4-inch nail but they would vary significantly from one manufacturer to another. One could make their nail as thin as a needle to save money on material which would bend with a 2 pound hammer or make them so thick that they would not bend, but also split the wood that they were intended to keep together. There would be different types of steel and different qualities; some nails would be sharp and some dull. Without standards there would be anarchy and our lives are much improved thanks to visionaries like Henry Ford.

The International Standards Association (ISO) also developed standards that could be applied to almost any field of endeavor, initially these were known as ISO2000 and later ISO9001 and beyond. The purpose of these standards was to drive consistency by developing auditing measures and practices that guaranteed a consistent result. We can be very grateful for these standards as most of them keep us safe. You don't need to unplug your TV every night as Electronics Manufacturers are no longer allowed to make TV's that blow up or catch fire. If the manufacturer made a consistently bad product, the Success Criteria would be met for every product they make. If the product was consistently bad, it was the auditing system and the success criteria that was at fault. It's virtually impossible to initiate standards of practice for every situation unless every single variable is factored into the equation and followed to the letter of the recipe. But consistency and quality only happens under certain circumstance when the standard of training for all employees meets a minimum requirement, when the employees follow a standardized plan and when all variables and contingencies have been accounted for. Keep it simple, document a procedure for everything, and ensure that everyone is working together and that the different systems interact with each other. No system is foolproof as Nature is constantly working on building a better fool.

Many people have pointed out over the years that if private industry operated the same way as governments, that they would be bankrupt in a week. Companies cannot raise the cost of services or goods in the same way that government can raise taxes by raising taxes. If you price yourself out of the market another competitor will fill the void quickly. There has to be a constant evaluation and implementation of scientific principles and shrinking and growing to meet the needs of the consumer. Manufacturers don't do downsizing or upsizing; they do "Right-sizing" and Flexibility Models.

Governments have repeatedly tried to implement the culture of private industry with varying results, but mostly met with failure. Successful implementation depends on the culture of the organization and the willingness of the participants to participate. Change doesn't happen overnight and doesn't happen at all unless the participants participate and recognize the need to change. You can't fix it unless people recognize it's broken.

Betting Shops must know the outcome of an election or referendum better than the pollsters and governments, they must hedge their bets and manage their risk. Where gamblers are gambling on an outcome, the betting shop must also take a managed risk if they want to make a profit. Insurance companies hire statisticians, mathematicians and work from actuarial table. If you drive a 2,000 cc motor your rate of payment will reflect many factors depending on whether it is a sports car or a people carrier. Insurance companies don't take risks; they manage risk and make a profit. It is a survival imperative, adapt or fail, fail and cease to exist.

Compare this to the world of Child Protection and you are comparing a system that must be efficient to survive, to a system where virtually no quality standards exist. There is no standardization and no quality control. There are no consequences for failure and no attempt to measure success. The entire system operates as hundreds of different organizations with no connection to upper management who are not allowed by law to know what is happening on the front lines. It is a massive ocean liner and there is no connection between the Captain on the Bridge and no idea what happens below deck.

When you look at any aspect of how the system operates you can see why the system fails. We put more thought into Fast Food than the protection of children.

Science: Although Sociology and Psychology are presented as sciences, albeit "soft sciences", it does not follow the basic principles of science. There is no standardization, no success criteria, no accountability and no auditing. There is no blood test, x ray to validate a diagnosis. Theories are based on the beliefs of the Theorist and the Theory doesn't exist independent of the Theorist. Psychologists are Cognitive or Behavioral, Freudian or Jungian. Psychology doesn't have a single blood test, x-ray or lab test to prove the existence of a single condition. Psychology is only branch of Medicine that that has never "Cured" a single patient. None of the psychological conditions exist in medical journals and psychologists have had to invent their own book, the Diagnosis and Statistical Manual of Disorders. It only takes the consensus of 4 Doctors, who do not need to be Psychologists, to have a disorder listed.

Budget: Social Services are not required to keep within budgets. The legal budget for the CFA has been exceeded from €10 million consistently for years and has run to €30 million. Despite attempts by the governments and departments to keep within budgets, no control has ever been successful. The HSE budgeted €3 million to set up it's own legal department and yet the practice of using private law firms continues unabated. Frances Fitzgerald when she was Children's Minister suggested that social workers could be trained in the law to reduce it's legal budget but this was resisted strongly by social workers and their unions. The DCYA noticed that McKenzie Friends were winning cases against highly paid solicitors and barristers, some of them "Hired Guns" brought in when they were losing cases. The HSE and DCYA sent out a team on a fact finding mission and discovered that the McKenzie Friends had no funding or formal organizational structure, but still were far more successful than barristers paid €3,000 a day. In reality, the people at the top of the organization are not in control of the people on the front-line and have little idea of what is happening. In effect, there is no control over the budgets and the €650 million a year budget will continue to be over-spent. As there is no control of the legal process, the private law firms have been "stretching out" cases for as long as possible to maximize their profits. The lack of control and scrutiny has lead to the CFA legal budget being overspent by 200% for the past few years.

Training: It has only been in recent years that standardization of qualifications of social workers has come into play. Many of the HSE's staff was recruited from the UK after minimum standards were implemented there. It has only been since 2012 that the registrations of social workers came under a statutory footing in the form of SORU but at the time of writing in 2014, there are no Fitness to Practice Committees and no mechanisms to punish rogue social workers, even when they break the law. The In Camera Rule allows such secrecy that "anything said by anybody" cannot be repeated outside the courtroom. Even judges in higher courts were not allowed to hear details of what occurred in lower courts. The HSE knowingly used unqualified staff for years, many times by getting Agencies to fill the gaps. These agents were not social workers in many cases and there is documented evidence and witnesses to show that they have used nurses, retired persons, students and anyone the agencies could find to fill gaps. There are no standards for Guardians ad Litem and many earn in excess of €300,000 a year and have not even been vetted by Gardaí.

Quality Auditing: As I write in 2014, the Children First Guidelines are not on a statutory footing. Even though this document is the standard of practice, albeit a very vague one, there is no legal requirement for the CFA to follow it. I have an audio recording of an HSE case manager stating that he had no intention of following Human Rights Law, the UNCRC, Children First or anything that was not on a statutory footing. HIQA, the Health Information Quality Authority only recently were granted the power to audit the children in Residential "care", their powers do not extend to Foster "Care" and their mandate is only to audit that the basic needs of the children are being taken care of. They have no authority to investigate why these children came into "Care" and don't follow up on these children when they turn 18 and are dumped on the streets in most cases.

The Minister for Children, the upper management of the CFA, the DCYA and all the "Experts" have no entitlement to enter a secret family court and observe the proceeding. If the Minister for Children were to have knowledge of a case, they would also be guilty of offenses under the Standards in Public Office by intervening in cases. Enda Kenny as Taoiseach intervened in a case and was informed by Justice Minister Alan Shatter that he could not intervene or even know the details or circumstances as "sitting minister. Essentially, nobody is in charge as it would be against the law for anyone who is not party to the proceedings to have knowledge of the case.

If a member of a Children's "Charity", a Politician, the Justice or Children's Minister, the head of Tusla, DCYA or the CFA ever say that the system is working, they cannot say this from an informed perspective because they simply are not informed and cannot enter a secret court. There is no quality auditing, as even High Court judges cannot know the details of a case. The only possible mechanism would be another Ryan Report and the judges being granted immunity to violate the In Camera Rule. As long as the In Camera Rule exists, there cannot be a system of quality assurance. So essentially, the law harms children instead of protecting them.

Accountability: In Ireland in a decade from 2000 to mid 2010, 260 children died in State "Care", 196 of those deaths were investigated. In the same decade, 500 went "missing" from State "Care". Nobody was ever held accountable. There is no record anywhere of a social worker in Ireland ever being struck off for any infraction even though there is considerable evidence against them. I know of a Psychologist who has perjured himself in court and was caught on tape, but never prosecuted, he is still in the employ of the CFA and only produces damning reports tailored to make the parent look unfit. I also know of unqualified "Experts" who have lied or exaggerated their qualifications, but are still being used as weapon against parents. No mechanism even exists for this to be investigated and no prosecution is possible under the current law.

Consistency: In my own experience, which is based on helping families and having unprecedented access to secret courts and family homes, I can safely say that the two worst areas in Ireland to raise children are Cork, Cavan and Meath. Social services in these three regions are the worst in the country in terms of miscarriages of justice and a system completely out of control. I recently read a story where a Full Care Order was granted, which was being appealed to the High Court, and the judge didn't even give reasons for granting the order. Can you imagine someone being given a life sentence and not being told what crime they were guilty of?

A look at the court statistics for Ireland shows the disparities in all regions. In some areas judges will grant 100% of requests for Emergency Care Orders in others slightly fewer. In some areas there are higher rates of Full Care Orders being applied for and granted. Some areas will have a disproportionate number of applications against foreign nationals than others but in general, the numbers of children of foreign nationals coming to the attention of social services is far higher that that of Irish children and parents.

What passes for protection in one area would be substandard in another area and it has only been in recent years that any attempt was made to address these issues. There doesn't appear to be any successful attempt to standardize practices to the point where it could be shown scientifically that the system works equally in all areas. We have Gardai and other government bodies and for many years have been very consistent in their approach. Gardai also work under a veil of secrecy but yet can maintain a reasonable standard in any town and village as they can in large cities.

Where Bookies Shops have to maintain a consistent standard of quality, why cant Child Protection? Is it because Bookies have consequences for their failures where there is no consequence for social workers? If a Garda Superintendent in charge of a division yearly result were less than adequate, how long would they remain in their position?

Success Criteria: In the field of Child Protection, there must be an assumption that when the State steps in and removes a child from a parent who is failing in their duty to that child, that the outcomes in life for that child would be considerably better than if the child had been left with the parent. The fact is that no such success criteria exist.

How can the public be reassured that the system is working? It appears that the public at large believes that the system is competent and for the most part, actually works, despite all the evidence to the contrary. When the State takes a baby at birth and looks after that child until their 18th birthday, wouldn't it be reasonable to assume, given the horrendous cost involved, that the child would become a Doctor, Scientist, Accountant, be highly educated and go on to do great things with their life? So why do these children have far poorer outcomes? Is anybody even paying attention to what happens to these children? Does the public care what happens? Or is the public being fed a lot of misinformation? I will deal with many of these issues in greater detail later. The facts speak for themselves, children of foster and residential "care" have far worse outcome in 80% of cases. There is no Quality Control, Success Criteria, Accountability or any standards and the outcomes for "Cared For" children prove beyond all doubt that the system is not working.

Essentially we have a system that has evolved from the previous failed system of orphanages ran by religious orders. As bad as the system was then, there was very little issue of bad outcomes, at least not on the scale we see today. In fairness, they did not have the issue of drug addiction although alcohol addiction was rife. Crime was rare then compared to today and children could be taken into "care" for relatively minor reasons. For the most part children were looked after by the church to a high standard except that many were physically and sexually abused. At the time in Ireland abuse of children by their parents was rife compared to today. Teenage pregnancy was also rife but the penalty for a young girl being raped or abused, would be that her child would be taken from her and sold for Forced Adoption. The girl would then have to serve for three years as a penitent or prisoner in a laundry or other enterprise unless her parents paid £100, the cost of a house at the time, to "take care of the problem".

I am not defending the actions of the religious orders, these issue were dealt with during Ryan Report and the Redress Board. It was a different time in a land long ago and should be taken in that context. It could be fairly said that most of the children were well cared for by the standards of the day excluding those who were abused, and most had good outcomes in life if they were not abused. The incidence of paedophilia was not statistically higher in the clergy than it was in other sectors. Of course the clergy need to be held to a higher standard as they themselves, had set themselves to a higher standard than everyone else. It was this betrayal and the subsequent cover-up that remains to this day, that most infuriated the public. The attitude of some in the Church is that sexual assault of children is a sin, but is it a crime?

The children who were "cared for" by the State in Reformatories or Religious institutions were better cared for and had better outcomes given the context of the time. Many people applied to the Redress Board but many more did not and were grateful that someone stepped in to rescue them. The vast majority of priests and nuns did their best, just as I would say today, that the vast majority or social workers, foster carers and judges today do their best and are honest. The question is however, why don't children today have far better outcomes given the lessons learned from Ryan Report, the advances we have made in society and the seemingly unlimited budgets thrown at Child Protection?

My own father and my aunt were sent to an orphanage at a young age, it was a topic that neither wanted to discuss but it would appear that they were very grateful for the care they received and both were devout Catholics for the remainder of their lives, never uttering a harsh word against the system. My grandmother took to her bed for almost the remainder of her life when her marriage failed. Although she was fairly wealthy before her marriage, she was left a broken woman in poverty for the remainder of her life. I have talked to many other people who were cared for by the State and few had anything harsh to say about their treatment. I have also talked to many children of the current system and they are less that glowing in their praise.

The fact is that I cannot prove with statistics that the children cared for by the religious institutions statistically had better outcomes and it would be foolhardy of me to go against the findings of the Ryan Report, there are virtually no statistics from that time. Nor am I trying to defend the actions of the church. The context of the time is important and we cannot fairly judge what happened by the standards of today.

I can prove however that children who are cared for today in the current system have dismal outcomes and that Ryan Report and the Redress Board should have closed that chapter in Irish history. Not that we should forget what happened but rather learn from past failings and commit to building a better system.

It appears that the church ran institutions were ran by individuals rather than rules that were clearly defined. There didn't seem to be a need for standards and a scientific approach or even success criteria, and yet, for the most part the system worked very well. Even the Reformatory System, essentially Juvenile Justice seemed to be more geared towards Reform and many of its alumni went on to do great things with their life. The original Borstal Boy Brendan Behan went on to international success and acclaim and his work still stands today as some of the best Irish literature and plays. The influence of his "Reform" at a young age is testimony to the system, which obviously left an impression on him. Of course Brendan died a hopeless alcoholic and a troubled man and we have to wonder if his time in "Care" affected this outcome?

There are a few other success stories from that time, but I have to wonder how many successes since the children were removed from orphanages and placed in foster care. I believe it is an important question but one where there is little research available and many of the Care Alumni of the Church don't want to talk about it. There are also stunning examples such as Boystown in the USA which had been a success for many years with very little controversy. The founder of Boystown, Fr. Flanagan visited the Irish institutions at the time and was appalled at what he saw. He tried to speak out publicly but the media wouldn't cover the story as the church dictated that he be ran out of Ireland and not quoted by anyone. If Father Flanagan had spoken out publicly, would we see 60,000 children who were born in these Irish Mother & Baby Units looking for answers of how they became victims of Forced Adoption?

Orphanages in most countries have been abandoned and those that existed until recently have been the topic of horror stories. Many of the issues came from former Soviet Republics such as Romania, which were decried internationally. But I have to ask, is the Orphanage better in terms of outcomes for children than Foster Care? It's a legitimate question, I don't have any biases either way, I simply want to get to the bottom of which is the best method of caring for children if the State deems that their families have failed in their duty of care. Most people would instinctively say that Foster Care is better, but if this is true then why don't the children of foster care have better outcomes in life?

There is of course a far better way of children having better outcomes in life and it's a recipe designed by Nature, the Family. Even when a parent has failed in their duty, the child still has another parent and extended family on both sides. In many countries, their culture dictates that if the parents are not capable of looking after their children, that the duty of care falls to the extended family, this is done without the need for courts and in many countries there are no social services or a dedicated child protection system.

Kinship Care is a term gaining popularity in the last few years, it is simply that the kin of the children care for the children when the parents cannot. It seems a bit odd that we have to have a name for when family takes care of it's own. In many cases extended family can look after children and frequently do. For single parents if they become ill or incapacitated the grandmother is often the first port of call to step in if social services are not involved. Often when children are removed by social services, the first actions are to place the children with people who are strangers. I will deal with the issue of "Care" separately as it is the most important issue in this book. I will deal with whether children are actually better "cared for" by the State and if the children would have been better off without the intervention.

One of the most dangerous assumptions we could make about the field of Child Protection is that the system actually Protects Children. Historically in Ireland we have not accomplished an adequate system of protection, the Ryan Report should be testimony of the States ability to parent any child.

What should we do with bad parents? We take their children from them and raise the child properly, so what can we do when the State **is** the bad parent?

What is supposed to happen when suspected abuse is alleged is that an assessment of the parent takes place. All aspects of the child's care are looked at and a decision is made as to whether the child will be cared for to a minimum standard at least and that the child will be better off for the intervention.

In this book I have laid out my arguments for and against the practices used to protect children. I have placed myself in the role of doing a parenting assessment on the State and I make no apology for being self-appointed. Nor do I have any formal qualification in the field but what I can offer is a unique perspective gained over seven years of researching the topic. Where many people who are seen as experts in the field, I can safely say that I have seen the system as few people have. I have worked with children from toddlers to adults, before, during and after their "Care" by the State and still do today. I have been involved in cases before Social Services became involved, got to know the children, have fought in the courts with their parents and picked up the pieces of shattered lives when the State had no further interest.

It is not my intention to simply criticize the Child Protection System only, although I frequently do. Criticism alone is of no value unless you build a better model. I have no issue with "tarring everyone with the same brush" as long as the people involved won't speak out for the victims of this cruel and unjust system. I have a tendency to be brash and cut to the heart of the matter sometimes to the detriment of the point I am trying to make. I make no apology for being passionate about this topic because as I see it, we have an issue that demands our urgent attention.

My analysis of the current situation doesn't take into account the feelings of persons or individuals, this issue is not about individuals or about me, it's about a System Failure which is far bigger than any individual, career or organization. It is not my intention to defame any individual, people have the best intentions, but "Best Intentions" don't always translate into Best Practice or even the Best Interests of Children. I would ask people to work as a team where there are no individuals, for the betterment of children and to put their biases and filtering aside and recognize that we have a serious problem that we all need to work together as a team to resolve. I don't pretend to have all the answers but as a problem solver I can certainly spot problems and use a systematic approach to solving them.

To solve a problem, we must first recognize that we do have a problem and move on from there. I have often said that if I am even 1% right about what I have said about the system, that we have a very serious problem on our hands. As I see it we need to have another Ryan Report just to understand the seriousness of the problem.

We have a system that has evolved into a Recipe for Disaster and if it continues unabated, will harm far more children than it helps. Because of a lack of Science and a systematic approach and because there is no auditing or even a system of auditing, it just blusters it's way from bad to worse. There is no scrutiny as the biggest barrier to auditing is the In Camera Rule. The people running the organization have little idea of what is happening and no legal right to know. This is a huge ocean liner that has left port with no Captain on board or a Mental Institution ran by the inmates, nobody is in charge. Money, above all else is the driving factor but even if a Minister for Children wanted to fix the system, they would have no knowledge and no legal right to intervene. The majority of what the public have been told has been nothing more than Press Releases and a carefully orchestrate Public Relations campaign. The media are terrified of the topic because their Legal Departments wont allow these stories to be published. Journalists, who are supposed to be the "Watchdogs of

Society", know that if they speak a word or put a foot wrong that they will be jailed or fined. Even when the dysfunction in the system comes to light, it has usually been the effort of an individual who had the courage to do something. On the rare occasions where journalists get Freedom of Information requests granted, they don't ask the tough questions and even when a horror story comes to light, the public seemingly have little interest in acting on behalf of children.

The real question is; "Do we cherish all the children of Ireland equally?" or do we continue to bury our heads in the sand? It doesn't affect me so why should I be bothered? Even though you may not have an interest in Politics, doesn't mean that it doesn't have an interest in you. Throughout history, people have failed to notice when governments became tyrannical until it was too late and failed to act. It is because the Irish and UK citizens are not paying attention that governments can get away with almost anything. People whine for a while and it's all forgotten by the time the next Shock/Horror story comes out next week. The issues and problems of Child Protection wont be solved in a week and perhaps if this book has an impact, it will be very short lived and forgotten about quickly.

If your children are really your most important and valuable "possession", if you really want to give your children a better life than you had, if we want to progress as a civilization, then why doesn't everyone put children at the heart of all our issues and work towards building a better future for them? Is it not true that you can tell the health and level of civilization of a country by how well it looks after it's children?

Perhaps it's my arrogance, but I believe that everyone should read this book and fully understand it. It's an uncomfortable conversation we need to have with ourselves, even if we don't have any children. It is an instinct in all older persons to look out for younger people. It's an instinct that is being driven out of us by the hysteria and the misinformation. Even a toddler looks at a newborn and wants to take care of it, even animals have that instinct. With the hysteria around child protection adults are afraid of children, they will cross the street to avoid them in groups for fear of their own reputations. Judges will grant Child protection orders to protect children and their own reputation because of the fear and hysteria that the Child Abuse Industry has created. We are living in a Moral Panic, not much different from the Salem Witch Trials and the many other Moral Panics that have come and gone since. We need as a society to take the message on board that myself and others are trying to impart. Heed the lessons of history or be doomed to repeat them. We can standby and remain silent because it doesn't affect us yet and by the time it does affect us it will be too late to do anything.

When you look at any aspect of the topic of Child Protection you can see huge problems, from every perspective the system is a failure. It all begins with planning and a systems approach, using Science rather than subjective opinion. When the system fails as any system does, you need to go back to basics and the scientific approach. You wont get a scientific approach from using Social Science, you need a Statistician rather than a Social Worker, you need an Engineer rather than a Judge and you need a Parent rather than a Surrogate State Parent, because at least the parent will make their decision based on love for their child. The Statisticians can tell you where the system is failing and the Engineer can build a better system. Instead what we have is a system that runs on nothing more than subjective opinion.

Psychology can be a wonderful tool where a skilled therapist can prevent a depressed person from committing suicide, it can also be used as a weapon to take a newborn baby away from it's mother. Social Work and Sociology can be a wonderful tool when it is used to help people such as the disabled to improve the quality of their life or to help a person coming to the end of their life to deal with all the necessary issues that will give them and their family Acceptance and Closure to ease their suffering, or it can be used as a weapon to damage children and their parents forever. A question I will pose in this book is whether Psychology or Sociology are robust enough as "Sciences" to tear families apart and whether both can be used to improve Society?

I hope to prove in this book that the current system is a Recipe for Disaster and to help build a better model by getting people to have that uncomfortable conversation first with themselves and then with others. I will go into as much detail as I can or is necessary to state the problems in the hope that the system will change. I also hope that if the System and the Industry isn't willing to change, that the public and the media will be the change that they wish to see in the system.

I originally finished writing this book three years ago and sent it to a publishing agent and the feedback was very enlightening. She said that she rarely read a book from cover to cover, in order. She found the topic very compelling even though she had no particular interest or knowledge of the subject. She also said that the book made her very sad, this was not a topic that the public would be comfortable reading, but one that people should read it because they needed to even if they didn't want to, because it was a good resource for Human and Civil Rights activists and parents. But, she said, that some people would not read past the first chapter as they might find it more frightening than a horror novel, truth is stranger than fiction. Essentially, I was preaching to the converted and she knew that this was not my intention.

If I had published 3 years ago I would have sold a lot of copies but mostly to people in the industry or people who were victims of the system. I struggled for 3 years to present my arguments is such a way that I could walk into a church and announce to the congregation that there was no God and have them believe me. I thought that maybe if I softened my arguments and understated the problems that maybe people would be more open-minded. I realized though that being an "Elephant in the Room" was not a solution. I have been that elephant many times in court and at social services case conferences and have had limited success, I have had always been more successful with a more brash and logical approach.

As an example I was arguing in court where a judge allowed me to speak, which doesn't always happen but has become more frequent as some judges have found that I do better research on cases than the majority of lawyers. The social worker argued against the proposition of allowing the newborn to be breastfed and had experts to show that breastfeeding would not be in the "Best Interests of the Child" (I'm not joking). She didn't want the baby to bond with its mother as she felt that ultimately the child would be forcibly adopted. I turned to the judge and asked; "Judge, who is this baby supposed to bond with?" A very compelling argument for the Human Right of the baby under Article 8 of the Human Rights Act. I also had a stack of Case Law to show that judges in other courts had always supported the right of the newborn to bond with it's mother and the judge had little choice but to follow the law as the needs of the child are paramount.

I eventually came to the realization that nobody was going to write a book that proved beyond all doubt that the system was a failure and I would never convince all the members of the congregation that there is no God. This was arrogance on my part that I could convince anyone of anything. I am just a person with an opinion. I have a unique perspective because unlike judges, lawyers and experts, I know the children that I help represent in court, I have met them, played with them, talked to them and asked them what they wanted. I have asked their parents the tough questions, looked in the cupboards to see if there was adequate nutrition, looked in their bedrooms and playrooms to see that they were being adequately cared for and brought in other parents to help the family. This is a unique perspective that few can claim. Many people who decide for children have never even met those children. Many politicians who make laws for children have never set foot inside a family courtroom. Many experts have only studied the topic from one perspective and are completely ignorant of what happens, even if they do have the best intentions.

I came to the conclusion that there was no "right time" to publish the book and that the longer I delayed, that more children would be harmed. I am only one man with an opinion and a messenger who has tried faithfully to understand the problems from all perspectives. Nobody can sit on a fence for long; you have to choose which side of the debate you are on. I choose the side of the children who are being harmed and I speak for some, but not all of them. During the Children's Referendum the Minister for Children said; that "some children do have a good experience of care". I cannot refute that statement, I can only say that the other 80% of children who don't have a good experience or good outcomes in life are my only concern and that any system with a success rate of less than 20% needs to be under public scrutiny as a matter of urgency.

If you find this book depressing as the literary agent predicted, I would urge you to struggle on and keep an open mind on the topic. Nobody can reasonably argue that the system is working and the penalty we pay as a society is that children are dying and being harmed, we can prevent this. The governments and experts have said the system is not fit for purpose, but there have been no significant improvements since Ryan Report. Even if this book doesn't have an impact or be a catalyst for improving the system, I can only claim to be a messenger, a person with an opinion and at the very least get the topic on the table and people talking about it, as uncomfortable as it may be. Read on.

CHAPTER 3

"IF IT'S NOT BROKE, LETS FIX IT!"

I had my first introduction to Child Protection 7 years ago. I was asked by a friend and work colleague to attend a case conference. I wasn't told much beforehand other than social services had taken the couple's children into care.

My initial reaction was that obviously the parents have done something terribly wrong; social workers don't take children away from parents for no good reason. I decided I would attend and support the couple, as I had known him to be a very honest man for years, in fact too honest. I decided that either he or his wife were guilty of some terrible crime against their child.

I woke up that morning full of hope that we could resolve this and that I would help my friends in any way I could. Up until that point in my life I believed that we lived in a reasonable, free and democratic society. Sure, the police and judges occasionally made mistakes but most of the time the system worked and is fair. I was shocked and dismayed that without any evidence, that parents could lose their children forever and never be accused of a crime.

In my naivety I thought that a judge would never sanction this and that any good lawyer could sort this out quickly. I also thought the case was an anomaly and that there was something they weren't telling me or that I had missed something. When I started investigating the murky world of Child Protection I quickly discovered that there is an alternate world of Justice that the public is not allowed to see. I learned that the incompetence and injustice I saw in this case was not uncommon at all, that thousands of families in Ireland and many more in the UK are affected by this. I also learned that the system is incredibly incompetent, it doesn't protect children as it purports but actually places children at far higher risk.

I researched the topic and talked to many, many people from all perspectives. I have interviewed children as young as three and many who grew up in the "Care" System, social workers, charities, lawyers and even a few judges. As I learned more I started to see patterns emerging that were quite disturbing. Much of the dysfunction stems from the secrecy with which this system operates. You would think that journalists and the media would be all over this issue and the public would be enraged at what is happening to Irish children. Children are removed from loving homes and placed at a far higher risk.

I even began doubting my own instincts thinking that I was missing something, but the more I delved into this, the more it confirmed my beliefs. When I am faced with the prospect that I am missing something, I tend to delve further in and try to understand the issue from all perspectives. What is of particular interest to me is the motivations of why people do what they do and it is important to me that I try to understand the issue from all sides.

The more people I talked to, especially parents affected by this issue, the more I found that I could help people affected by passing on information or introducing them to others who are affected and they could help each other. After a while I appeared with them in court or helped their solicitors prepare the case.

The case conference itself was quite remarkable, there were 16 people present which I thought boded well, many hands make light work. The meeting started off with a report on the children from 3 different people. I have a habit at meetings of writing; it helps me think about complex issues on many levels at the same time. I listed the points that each made. The overall report of all 3 was that the children had been saved from these awful monsters of parents and were happy and thriving in their new homes.

I noticed that the 3 people gave 3 conflicting accounts of what I thought were relatively unimportant factors. One said that when the child saw his father that he went running and smiling to him with excitement, another said that the child cowered away as the father invaded the personal space of the child almost as if the child expected to be hit. There were many other points that made no sense and nothing that had been reported amounted to Evidence of any wrongdoing. Before this meeting I had seen the family as had another colleague who had attended and neither of us had ever witnessed anything to make us believe that this couple were anything but the best parents that any child could have, I have seen far worse.

Also in the report was mentioned that the child did not have ADHD as the parents had alleged. Having chaired many meetings, particularly when it comes to solving problems, I could see the meeting was turning into a bitch session against the parents and that nothing was being done to resolve the situation. They were united in their beliefs and there was a lot of head nodding and "acting" of exaggerated body language.

I had only experienced such a display once when out of curiosity I had attended a Baptist Church and while a preacher performed with such religious fervor that his congregation reveled in their rapture and cheered him on shouting out AMEN! And Halleluiah! It was what you might see on the Oprah show. These Saviors of Children were "washed in the blood of the lamb" and it seemed that nothing was going to change their unshakable faith. **Enter the dragon**.

I interjected; "tell me, what have you presented to these parents to resolve this situation?" The main social worker threw her book on the table and threw her hands up in the air, as if to God, and in her best condescending tone asked; "what have you heard in this meeting?" I answered; "well frankly I listened to 3 conflicting reports and frankly, your report was so negative that it lacks any credibility". There were gasps around the room, shuffling of papers, an uncomfortable silence, but also a few doubts in the minds of some of the attendees. The Chairperson tried to take control but I wasn't having it. "Answer my question please, how are you going to repatriate this family?" The social workers clammed-up as most do when they are cornered, especially in court. She looked at her boss to bail her out but I persisted.

The father then interjected, "they have done nothing and your report madam was very negative". I said "ok, lets look at the issue of ADHD, the parents say their child has ADHD, have YOU, now pointing the finger assessed the child?" Another silence and more uncomfortable squirming. The Chair now turned his attention to the Child Psychologist and after a few seconds he answered; "I will do it very soon, before the next conference". It appeared that they never had any intention of assessing the child, had not covered all their bases and any good lawyer could tear them apart in court. They were turning from "Child Protection Mode" to "Self Protection Mode".

What we later learned was far more disturbing. What wasn't mentioned in the conference is that the foster carer of the child called the social workers and said "there is something seriously strange about this child's behavior". We found that he had been taken to a GP and a Paediatrician by the social worker to be assessed for ADHD. Neither would have been qualified to make a Psychological diagnosis. We also found out much later that the child, at the age of 6 had contemplated suicide but did not know how to terminate his life. In foster "Care" he had done some very dangerous things such as climbing on walls and very risky behaviors, which rightly the foster carer reported right away. The social worker and the GAL ignored these signs, which is fairly typical. They were presenting a lie that the child was in fear of his father and had been abused; the child on the other hand was suicidal and wanted to go home.

The younger child was taken into "Care" at 6 months as a breastfeeding infant, he was no longer allowed to breastfeed and not weaned off gradually. When he came out of "Care" many months later, all of his milk teeth were rotten. I took a photograph after he had been home for a few days. I also attended the next case conference after the HSE lost their case in the District Court and the matter of the rotten teeth was discussed, this time with a much smaller audience.

The infant experienced some pain and discomfort and when the parents discovered the rotten teeth, they immediately took him to a dentist. The dentist said that this case was far more serious than could be handled in an ordinary dental surgery and the child needed specialist intervention by a paediatric dental surgeon. After visiting several dentists, they finally found one who would accept the case. Some were not paediatric specialists and the assistance of a paediatric anaesthetist would also be required if they decided that surgery was necessary. At the case conference as the parents explained the whole issue, the social worker then turned to the case manager and asked; "is this not shopping for doctors? Like Munchausen's?" I laughed, as did the parents. You can see the mindset of social workers here; they are always looking for "evidence" against a parent and will pick up on the most inane things as evidence to remove a child from their parents.

At the meeting my thoughts were if the parents had discovered the rotten teeth within hours of the baby coming home, why didn't the foster carer? I remained quiet during the meeting because the tone this time was completely different. At the previous conference the parents begged and cried and pleaded with all the people in the room; "please, tell us what we have done wrong and how we can fix this?" "Tell me what you want me to do and I will do it", "Please, give my children back to my wife and I will leave them, never see them again, the children need their mother". The situation had changed completely, now the parents had the upper hand and the HSE were only holding the conference because they were required to and the father insisted on having the conference.

I also recorded both meetings on a recording device. The father had recorded every single interaction he had with everyone involved in the case, made transcripts, documented everything carefully and in the many months his children were in "Care", had become a "Jailhouse Lawyer" and both of us learned everything we could about this system.

In court, the HSE had applied for a Full Care Order. In their minds they had built a case against the parents, as far as they were concerned these parents were not capable of looking after children and it would be in the "Best Interests" of the children if they never saw these monsters again. This was the final hearing and everything would be decided in 2 days. To the dismay of the HSE, the original judge involved in the case was no longer involved; he had been taken off the case and replaced. This wasn't going to be the "Rubber-stamping" exercise they thought it would be and they would have to prove their entire case all over again.

We discovered that the original judge had broken the law by allowing the children to by taken into "Care". By his reputation and the accounts of many who were unfortunate enough to have come before him in court, this judge was a racist who didn't like foreign nationals and had previously told a mother that she was a witch and should go home to her husband even if he did beat her and see other women. The woman eventually fled Ireland and raised her children alone. In this case when the father first spoke in court and the judge heard the foreign accent, he called on Gardai to arrest the couple and prove that they were in Ireland legally. He clearly had a bias also when he first saw the parents, and scowled at the father and accused him of being an abuser before he had even heard any evidence.

But now the new judge wasn't interested, he wanted to hear the entire case again from the start and had no interest in what the previous judge had decided. I should also mention at this point, that if parents have sufficient evidence against a judge that they should write a letter to the President of that court outlining their concerns. If they have witnesses, especially lawyers who are officers of the court, they should name them and also give any supporting evidence and documents to the President. Judges are supposed to judge "without fear or favor" and not pre-judge any situation without hearing evidence. They also have an obligation to follow the law, to the letter of the law regardless of their personal feelings.

The usual social worker evidence was trotted out endlessly and a physician testified far beyond the level of his training and competency. The star witness was a Forensic Psychologist from outside of the Republic. He had interviewed the parents, given them tests and testified to the effect that these people were monsters who shouldn't be allowed to own pets, never mind raise children. Fortunately for the parents they had hired one of the best solicitors and barristers in the country at very considerable expense.

The testimony of the psychologist seemed absolutely damning. At first the barrister encouraged the good doctor to spew his vile diatribe against the parents and shook his head in support, then he started asking him to expand on his answers. He asked for example if the doctor knew that the father had adult children from a previous marriage, all who had graduated university and had successful careers? The Barrister expanded on questions and asked one particular question; "did you ask the parents…." To which he replied he had not and would never ask such a question. The barrister persisted; "I'll ask you again and remind you that you took an oath on the stand and also took an oath as a doctor". The doctor insisted he had not but he seemed less sure of himself this time.

The barrister then turned to the judge and announced that the father had secretly recorded the psychological assessment and the recoding was available to the court with a transcript if the judge would allow it to be entered into evidence. The judge in his infinite wisdom decided that he would recuse himself and let the lawyers fight it out among themselves, much to the consternation of the HSE who, rather than seeking justice as you would expect a prosecutor to do, they tried objecting that the recording was illegal even though they could not cite any particular law opposing it. They listened to the recording and it proved beyond all doubt that the Forensic Psychologist had blatantly lied on oath. The good doctors and the HSE were now squirming and clearly out of their depth.

The father, although he may appear odd to many people, is one of the most intelligent people I have ever met. He is also very well educated in many disciplines and an excellent parent.

When the judge returned, he himself questioned the doctor and let him off prosecution for perjury and his testimony now on the fitness of the parents was worthless regardless of what he said after that point. The barrister now focused on other details and established that the children were in fact kidnapped by the social worker contrary to the law. The original judge cared little for the law and had himself broken the law by allowing the children to be kidnapped.

On the basis of a 3-minute conversation with the father on the doorstep, the social worker, backed by Gardai removed the 2 children. The gist of the conversation was that the father said, "who the hell are you to come to my home and tell me how to raise my children, I'll do what I like". As the father is a very quick thinker and intelligent, few people could argue with him, he is never aggressive or threatening in any way but he's not a person who suffer fools gladly and not afraid to speak his mind.

The social worker however felt she had the power even if she didn't in law and had the full support of unwitting Gardai to do whatever she liked. She was going to protect these children regardless and nothing was going to stop her in her mission. The Gardai snatched the baby from the mother's arms and took the children away while two Gardai backed the father into a corner and was told to calm down and everything would be all right. How could everything be alright? They were taking his baby and young son, the child seeing the parents distress was also severely distressed and frightened and driven away by strangers. The child remembers that incident to this day but can only verbalize it as the terror he felt and not by what happened.

I have seen this situation repeated many times and I have always advised parents to record the "Apprehension" on video and post it widely on the Internet. Every day I see new videos of babies and children being snatched, many at birth but then the videos will quickly be removed but not before a few thousand people have watched them. It's barbaric to remove a newborn from the breast of their mother is not something you would even witness in the animal kingdom. Sometimes it is of course necessary because there are simply people who should not be allowed to have children.

In this particular case, it was clearly a kidnapping. The social worker did not have an Emergency Care Order and took the child based on a 3-minute conversation with no evidence. She had set herself up as Judge, Jury and Executioner. The children were driven away and the social worker phoned the HSE lawyers and said she had performed a Section 12 removal. Section 12 of the Childcare Act allows a member of the **Gardai** to remove a child from anywhere at anytime if they reasonably believe the child to be in danger of harm. The actual harm must be established in a report and the Garda should testify before a judge to establish that the threshold to intervention had been met and the actual danger to the child had been established in this case, it hadn't.

The Garda involved didn't even realize that they had performed a Section 12 and a social worker has no such power under the law to invoke a Section 12. We found this out later and reported the Garda who himself was perplexed at the whole incident. Many Gardai are not familiar with the law and whenever they are challenged on Section 12, as we have done many times, the Gardai are forced to retreat and uphold the law.

In Ireland Section 12 is one of the most misused and misunderstood sections of the law. Social workers have tried to invoke section 12's in delivery rooms and often are aided by unwitting Gardai. Under the Act, the actual danger must be established to the satisfaction of the police officer but Gardai are rarely called to testify before judges who allow these kidnappings. A Hospital could never be considered a place of danger for a newborn surrounded by doctors and nurses but yet newborns are removed from the mother's breast illegally every day in Ireland.

In our case, the HSE applied for an Emergency Care Order the following day and this was granted Ex Parte, which means without the parents present. The barrister presented this evidence that the children were in fact kidnapped and had the court documents to prove it. As the case against the parents further degenerated the judge became angry and had heard enough. The judge turned to the father and asked him how much he had spent on legal fees and then turned to the HSE and asked them "how much they had spent torturing this family?", they answered close to a million. The judge said he wanted these children home NOW and also took the unusual step of ordering the HSE to pay the families legal bill which was over €120,000 even before an order of costs was requested. It was a spectacular defeat for the HSE but no journalist was there to witness it.

Later the father would defeat the HSE again in the High Court but it took years to accomplish and again, occurred without any scrutiny of the public or the media. But when I say "defeat" I am exaggerating slightly. Even though the State agreed damages and paid the lawyers involved far more than the compensation they agreed to pay the family, they later decided to challenge the matter in the Supreme Court, knowing full well that they could tie the case up for years and never pay a penny, except of course to the lawyers.

What I learned from this case was invaluable. Law forbids me to speak about "anything to anybody" under the law. Even though I have not identified a single child, I could fall afoul of the law or this book could be censored by the courts and banned in Ireland. I am not concerned that I could be prosecuted by the State as such a prosecution would need to be held in an open court and I would need to call many witnesses. If another tribunal such as the Ryan Report is ever held I will present all the evidence that I would not be able to cover in this book.

The Psychologist continues to practice, he was never charged with perjury and never faced a Fitness to Practice hearing at the GMC. Because of the in camera rule, a prosecution could never take place because "anything said by anybody" could not be used in evidence against him. In fact, **the same psychologist, who the HSE knew he had perjured himself in an Irish court, was used again by the same HSE lawyers to testify against another family in the same courthouse**.

Essentially the CFA or HSE use "Experts" who they know will lie on their behalf and give false and damning reports on parents, which have no basis in fact or in truth. This is not the only case that I know of where this has occurred, I have evidence of the CFA using "Hired Gun" experts who are unqualified, not known to any professional bodies and who have testified in many other cases in Ireland and the UK. In the case of this particular psychologist when he was used again in the other case, the father testified about his previous perjury.

In many of these cases the parents will be told that they require an assessment from a certain "Expert", even though the court has not requested it. Often parents are told that it must be Mr. or Ms. X and that nobody else is qualified. If the parent goes to X the parent is not entitled to know the outcome of the assessment and the expert does not necessarily have to appear in court. In criminal courts such nonsense would be dispensed with quickly. Essentially the social workers can hire a "Hired Gun Expert" who is not qualified, sometimes the "Expert" has never even met the parents and the parents are not entitled to know what evidence will be used against them in court.

In a post-script to the case of the 2 children, I was involved with this family for years after and spent a lot of time with the children. For 3 years after being taken into "Care" at the age of 6 months, the infant had nightmares and would wake up screaming from an afternoon nap or in the middle of the night that the bad people were going to take him away from his parents and brother. By the time he was 3 years old he could verbalize his experience, albeit in the words of an infant. He distinctly remembered having two mammies but apparently only one of them had breasts. He remained very clingy to his parents and brother and of course his "Uncle Joe" for some time after. I was the only babysitter that both children had for some time after and got to know them well. The older child has been on medication since I raised the issue at the case conference.

At the next case conference that was held after I attended, the social workers again gave glowing reports about how the children were thriving and the older one didn't want to go home. The Guardian ad Litem who works for a major "charity" also sang from the same hymn sheet but as we learned, the older child was actually suicidal having been separated from his parents and brother. Even the Principal of the child's school gave a glowing report of how well the child was doing but his report didn't match the school records that were later released. A late attendee to the meeting was the HSE Child Psychologist who had assessed the child. Not having heard the glowing report from the social workers, the good doctor then presented his report and said that not only did the child have ADHD but also had comorbidity factors and needed urgent help. I wish that I had that conference on video to show you, the silence was deafening until the parents spoke out. Even then, the HSE said that this didn't prove anything and they were going to go ahead with their plans for a Full Care Order. The "evidence" of the Forensic Psychologist would be enough to split this family up. Even if their child suffered from ADHD and needed to be medicated, it still didn't prove that the parents were capable of looking after houseplants, never mind house-pets.

There are even more disturbing factors in this case and I feel it is important that people know about them and the Modus Operandi of social workers. During their initial investigation both Gardai and social workers investigated. Gardai quickly concluded that no crime had taken place and that they didn't even need to refer the matter to the DPP for a decision. Gardai were apparently told that the father was a brutal monster who beat his wife and children so a Superintendent investigated due to the seriousness of the allegations. Some time later when we tried to get the Gardai reports the Superintendent couldn't understand why the entire case didn't end there, no crime was committed, the initial report came from a vindictive neighbor allegedly because the father refused to have sex with her. Her account of an alleged beating that took place was an outright lie as it would have been impossible.

You may wonder at this point how Gardai, who concluded their investigation in a matter or hours and decided that no crime took place, and yet the HSE, the parents and children "Tortured" to quote the judge, prosecuted the case in a parallel "investigation" which took 8 months to conclude? Welcome to the alternate universe of Child "Protection". You are only beginning to understand the illegality, the lack of Human and Civil Rights and the fact that the system harms more children than it helps.

What also occurred was that the social workers, knowing that they didn't have much evidence, went from door to door in the neighborhood asking people if they had any "dirt" on these parents. They broke the In Camera Rule and violated their own secrecy by telling neighbors that the father had physically assaulted the child and the mother. At one point in the case the social workers started "working" on the mother and used a common tactic that I have seen many times. They told the mother that if she admitted that her husband beat her, that they would give her the children back. They said that she had to move into a Women's Shelter and get a Barring Order against him. The next time they appeared in court they had proof that the mother was so abused that she had to leave her husband and move into a Women's Shelter. The father though had already sought a Barring Order against himself and moved out so that his children could return to their home with their mother, even if he could never see them again, at least the children would be home with the mother.

Of course when it came time to give the children to the mother, they said that she was unfit as she allowed herself to be abused. Gardai asked for the medical records of the parents at an early stage and the records showed no injuries whatsoever to support the accusation of Domestic Violence. The neighbors never complained of any noise from the home and there was no indication anywhere that these parents were anything other than upstanding citizens who paid their taxes, had never came to the attention of Gardai and loved their children.

When word of the physical abuse of the child spread around the neighborhood, the father was set upon by a group of vigilantes and suffered a heart attack, many cuts and bruises in a brutal assault. Social workers, even if they didn't prove their case, certainly left their mark on the father. The mother was also physically assaulted by a group of women because she wouldn't listen to the advice of the social workers. She appeared at a case conference with a black eye but nobody asked how it occurred. Of course they already knew.

A few year s later I was shocked to learn that a teenage girl asked the father if he was still "diddling" his son. The local legend started by the social workers grew into a fable of epic proportions and had now been upgraded to sexual abuse. One person asked me how I could be involved with these "criminals"? I answered that if they were criminals, wouldn't they be in jail? Five years after he initial intervention and after the family had been vindicated in the District and High Court, the father was assaulted again when more false allegations were made, even though the family were vindicated, the vindication was in a secret court and the public will never know or even believe the truth as I cannot identify them. Until these children both turn 18, there will be no vindication.

This is only one of hundreds of cases that I have been involved in and despite all the criminality nobody is ever punished. Ireland has now surpassed the UK in terms of secrecy. The secrecy benefits the system far more than it benefits the children. People's faith and belief in this system is unjustified in my opinion. You have to wonder why the "experts", the lobbyists, the Children's NGO's, the Human Rights organizations and even why many of the people affected are not speaking out? The fact is that many people are speaking out as individuals and people who work in the industry would have no vested financial interest or obligation to say anything other than the system is broken and we need to throw more money at the problem. Even many of the lobbyists, the educators, the NGO's have no real idea of what happens in secret courts and have to rely on the PR and press releases that they are being fed. By law they can't talk to people affected and those who are affected are not only gagged by the judges, they are gagged again under threat of having their children removed. This simply can't continue.

CHAPTER 4

"I'M DOING THIS IN YOUR BEST INTERESTS."

I remember getting spanked by my father many times and being threatened many times by my mother; "wait till your father gets home". The wonderful and talented comedian and singer Brendan Grace did a sketch about this. Every child in Ireland had the first same name when they were in trouble, "Hugh". "Hugh, come here till I knock your block off!" Over 50's can relate.

At the core of Child Protection is the Best Interest Principle (BIP). Written into the United Nations Convention on the Rights of the Child, is the BIP. Anything done, for and about children are done to this standard of quality. No other guiding principle on how the success of the intervention exists.

A few years ago a judge listened to the arguments of both sides and said we have to act in the child's best interests and everyone nodded in agreement. I asked the judge to please give me a Legal, Scientific and Moral Definition of Best Interests. The judge was stumped as many are when you ask for a definition, however it has been defined many times, perhaps best by Hilary Rodham (Clinton), she defined it as;

"An empty vessel into which adult prejudices and beliefs are poured".

As a standard of quality, BIP is nothing more than a slogan, a weapon to beat parents with. If you look at the horror stories, you have to ask,

Was it in the best interests of?

- 196 children who died in State "Care" in a decade?

- 500 children who went missing from "care" in the same decade?

- The children who were left at the mercy of social workers for 11 years in the Roscommon House of Horrors?

- Baby P who was visited 60 times before he was murdered?

- Daniel Pelka who was starved to death by his parents?

- The 3 children of Mark & Nicky Webster who were forcibly adopted because their parents were wrongly accused of a crime?

In the case of Danny Talbot, Tracy Fay, Daniel McAnaspie and many others who died in Irish State "Care", in each case the judge decided that taking them into "Care" was in their best interests. But the question is; did these children benefit from their experience? Obviously not, but in a system where the standard of quality is a vaporous term with no Legal, Scientific or Moral Value, the operation was a complete success even though the patients died. The quality criteria were met, even by the ISO2000 standards. The auditing system did what it was supposed to do, the justice system did what it was supposed to do and the child protection system did what it was supposed to do. No wonder then that the supposedly "Independent" panel that investigated didn't find a single person responsible.

In the 3 cases I mentioned above, I also did my own investigations and came to a completely different conclusion. Where the "Independent" Panel concluded that the system was "Not Fit for Purpose", my conclusion was that we need to scrap the Best Interest Principle as a matter of great urgency as the lives of children depend upon it.

There must be a presumption, an expectation in fact, that when the State steps in and decides that a parent "has failed in their duty", that when the children are taken away, that they will be placed in a far better situation and have a far better outcome in life. If this is not the case, then why take children at all?

The Child Protection Service is proving a service to the citizens, they are the Service Providers, and the children are the Service Users. If you went to a Doctor and that doctor gave you a warning that 80% of their patients didn't actually get better, most got worse, you would run screaming from their office. You could report the incident to police; the Medical Council and you could go to the media and tell your story. If you were raped in the waiting room you could report the rape to police. If a similar incident happened with the Police, there are similar courses of action you could take.

If you are a child taken into "Care" you have no mechanism to deal with any of these issues. You have no voice because your voice is provided for you in the form of a Guardian ad Litem who is just another social worker working against you. You are gagged from speaking out and you will be punished and your visits with your parents taken away or restricted. When I have talked to children in "Care" or who have left "care", I have never heard a single child from "Care" who didn't hate social workers, judges and lawyers. When children are abused or raped, they have no mechanism to speak out. If they walk into a Police Station, the Police cannot investigate. Only Social Services investigate Social Services.

I know of a case where the complaint was against an HSE manager. The manager was also the investigation officer for the area. When he received the complaint against himself, he found himself not guilty of any wrongdoing.

Some people will say that no system is perfect; human beings are not perfect and are subject to human error. To my earlier analogy in chapter 2, I used the Food Industry as an example. The consequence of an error in the food industry is that people could die from food poisoning. There are many controls and standards and regular auditing, laws and penalties to protect the public, even then, some people will get food poisoning, no system is fail-safe.

The EU bring in new laws and regulations every week, 3,000 a week, so many that Members of the European Parliament don't have time to read every law that they must vote on. You have 30,000 words on the regulation of bananas and no regulations, no auditing, no standard of quality and no quality control of a system that purports to protect children. There are of course laws, one being the UNCRC and I will discuss the UNCRC in greater detail later. Our most important resource is our children; they are our future, quite literally. While we have many rules and regulations and standards of quality for things such as a child's education, health and standards and laws that parents must obey, there is nothing to hold the State accountable for their failures. In theory we have the European Court of Human Rights, in reality, a child will already be an adult before the ECtHR hears the case.

If Child Protection had a Failure Rate of 1%, this would mean that 650 children are currently being harmed, nobody could argue that this is not a very serious issue. But as the Failure Rate is closer to 80% by most estimation, I believe we have a national crisis on our hands. You could certainly understand why any government, "Charity" or Child Advocate would want to maintain the secrecy and pretend that the system is working. The only problem is for the government and the Child Abuse Industry is that these "protected" children are growing up and the evidence is mounting.

If there are 6,500 children in State "Care" at the present time and they were removed supposedly because their family failed in their duty, when the State fails who is the actual "parent" and who will be held accountable to the same or higher standard as a parent would? On mere suspicion a child can be taken away from a parent, but who will take the child away from the State?

In one case I was involved in, a baby had been taken at birth. The social worker and the GAL who worked for a "charity" didn't want the baby to be breastfed or bond with the mother. We took the case to the High Court as an abuse of the Human Rights of the baby and the judge granted generous contact for breastfeeding. The social workers argued that the mother was harming the baby by breastfeeding as they have done in many cases before. The HSE brought in experts who claimed the baby would be harmed by breastfeeding, the judge didn't buy it, but these are the typical ridiculous arguments we often hear in court.

The baby would arrive at contact after being fed and sometimes vomited or burped as babies often do. Sometimes the baby didn't want to feed as it had been fed shortly before contact. We also found out that baby was being fed the wrong food that was not suitable for a baby of that age. The baby also suffered a severe nappy rash and was prescribed a prescription topical cream medication. The mother had to breastfeed in what she described as a broom-closet and she had to do this under the glare of several "professionals" who scrutinized her every move and made extensive notes. Apparently if you answer your phone while breastfeeding you are a bad mother. We often hear stories of mothers trying to breastfeed in public places and are thrown out of restaurants etc., you should try breastfeeding your baby in "Care".

On one visit the mother phoned me, frightened, her baby was crying loudly in the background that I knew something serious was afoot. I asked the mother to describe what she saw; the baby was drawing their legs up to their chest, obviously in serious pain. The nappy rash looked extremely painful and it appeared that the baby was in serious condition. I told her to hang up, dial 999 and ask for Gardai, this baby needed to be taken immediately to hospital. When the Gardai arrived they were sufficiently concerned that they removed the baby under Section 12 of the Childcare Act from the HSE. This is the only documented case I know of where Police removed a child from State "Care". The foster "carer" was force-feeding the wrong type of food, which caused abdominal pain and also refused to use the medication prescribed by the doctor. The baby had also arrived at contact covered in dog hairs and wrapped in a blanket smelling of dog urine; such is the level of "care" for newborns in Ireland.

This incident and many others brought me to the realization that child "protection" isn't really about the protection of children. Social workers in this case were more concerned with punishing the mother than they were with the needs of a newborn. As I said in an earlier chapter "whom is the baby supposed to bond with?" If the whole issue is the protection of the baby and keeping it safe from harm, why isn't the system Child Centered rather than being centered on the wishes and whims of social workers, many of them recent graduates with no children and no life experience?

A 23-year-old "Care" recipient who spent her life in "Care" made one of the most stunning observations about the system to me. **She observed at the age of about 8 years old that she believed that social workers magically transformed into Psychologists at the age of about 25. In her 18 years in "Care", she had never met a social worker over the age of 25 and that all the other professionals were older.**

To use another analogy, to compare social protection teams to soldiers, I think is a particularly good analogy when you look at the similarities. Because the turnover in Child Protection is so high, typically the average social worker is under 30; most are not married and have no children and no life experience. There are no other jobs available for new graduates and many people have remarked that the "good" social workers get out of child protection as soon as they can, to work in other areas of the practice. Social workers can do great things working with the disabled, the elderly and in specialist areas they can improve the quality of life for their clients. There is no vilification of social workers in other areas but child protection social workers are the most hated profession today. They have overtaken Parking Enforcement Officers in terms of "most inflexible civil servants that ever existed".

Why are child protection social workers so hated? They protect children from bad parents? They prosecute and punish child abusers and keep our children safe, so why are they so hated? You would think that such an important role would be highly valued in society and that we would have "Social Worker of the Year" Awards. You could also reasonably expect to hear about all their great success stories, Ireland has 6,500 children in "Care", surely at least there are hundreds of harrowing tales that could be turned into Hollywood movies of how a brave and determined social worker fought the system and saved a child? Not even one success story? Your hear stories of Police Officers charging into burning buildings and rescuing babies from certain death, why not even one story of one success from social workers? If Haringey social workers who visited Baby P 60 times before he died, had actually saved him it would have raised the profile of social workers. If the Irish social workers in the Roscommon House of Horrors had saved the children on their first visit, the children would not have had to suffer for 11 years and would not have had to save themselves.

Equally you hear stories of high caseloads and how tough Child Protection is. You hear social workers crying the blues and yet, why is it that the children in their "Care" die at a higher rate, why is it that the suicide rate of social workers is not 10 times the national average as it is their clients? Why is it that you never hear of social workers being killed on the job at the same rate as Firefighters or Police? Is it really such a tough job taking other peoples children?

In my analogy if you look at the Armed Forces, you see young men, idealistic, forthright, desperately wanting to do an important job and save humanity. An opportunity to be a hero and to be a patriot and give your life in the service of your country. I really respect soldiers and admire their courage; I pay my respects to those who have gone before us for their service to humanity. A few years ago I toured the Green Fields of France and was humbled and stunned into silence looking at a sea of white crosses, countless white crosses. I spent a great deal of time looking at the names and ages of the fallen heroes; many were barely out of childhood and died too young.

I believe that war is just organized murder, mass insanity and pointless. That however does not take anything away from the heroes, who had the most altruistic intentions and made great sacrifices on our behalf. The highlight of my visit to Omaha Beach was to meet 4 very old American Veterans who had returned, probably for the last time to remember their fallen comrades. I was deeply touched and very proud to shake the hands of these men, I thanked them for their service to all mankind and I shudder to think of what the world would be without soldiers and armies. I warmly shook their hands they beamed and said Thank You and You're Welcome.

Armies, right or wrong are a necessary evil. The world has not yet become sufficiently civilized and a trillions a year industry and many jobs depend on conflicts breaking out. When you look at the demographics of armies or the ages of those who died in conflicts, you see that the majority are young idealistic men, mostly working class and many come from socially deprived areas. Soldiers are not born, but broken down and then rebuilt and reborn to an ideology of absolute obedience. Men over the age of 35 don't make good, obedient soldiers. They have sufficient life experience, knowledge and education that for most, you could place a high-powered rifle in their hands, but you could not convince them to kill another human being at the request of a politician. They are wise enough to know that the sons and daughters of the politicians will never be placed in any danger and cynical enough not to trust the government. I know career soldiers that enjoy the work and the career, most of them work in Search & Rescue and I can say that I have never met a group of people so opposed to war as the older career soldiers.

When you look at the demographics of Child Protection Social Workers, you see the Career Child Protectors, mostly in the role of taking children away from parents. By now many people have seen videos of babies and children being taken, it is extremely painful to watch. Many people wonder about the motivations of a social worker that could wrestle a newborn from the arms of a mother. It's barbaric to witness. Some people often make the analogy of prison guards at Auschwitz screening people arriving by train and choosing who will live and who will die. At the Nuremburg Trials, many of the senior leaders pointed out that they had never killed another human being in their life and most of them could claim that they have never even met any of the Jews, Gypsies and others who were systematically slaughtered by the lower ranks. Many defendants also tried the "Nuremberg Defense", "I was a mere soldier following orders". Naturally none of these strategies succeeded and the guilty were given the death penalty.

In my own work I have seen young social workers, mostly under 30. I am fascinated by the fact that those who rose through the ranks are not involved in the process of physically grabbing a child from a parent and placing that child in "Care". Although social work tends to be over-represented by women, 86% in some cases, the men tend to have managerial roles and tend not to get their hands dirty by physically taking children away. Others like Ian Josephs have also noted that the younger "foot soldiers" doing the "dirty work" tend to be the younger ones.

In a campaign launched by Barnardos Ireland called "Saving Childhood Ryan" one of the guest speakers was a UNICEF Special Rapporteur who incidentally is a Professor of Social Work from Hungary. She also made the observation that social work managers are unleashing young graduates who have no children and no life experience and yet are put out in the front lines of the battle to protect children. The older ones that I have met have no role in removing children and tend to be in areas such as After-Care or cleaning up the messes of their younger colleagues.

So my questions are why are child protectors vilified, and if the role is so rewarding, as you might expect it to be, then why is the turnover so high?

I don't accept that caseloads are too high or that there is a shortage of social workers, the evidence doesn't support this, the numbers of criminal prosecutions for child abuse and neglect have not increased in decades although the size and budget of the Child Abuse Industry has doubled in a decade.

For years we have heard the excuses of high case loads and shortage of social workers, however when Ireland added 260 new social workers to the already 4,000 in 2010/2011 the result was that they took 3.7 times more children into "Care" than the UK, who also had a record year at 10,000. Nobody asked what the justification was for this increase. During the Children's Referendum I mentioned this to every major news outlet in Ireland, nobody asked questions and nobody reported it. Did we suddenly become a nation of child abusers?

I have noticed the drip-feeds of press releases in the last few years are again leading up to another announcement that there is a "shortage of social workers". The Industry is quick to point out that on a per capita basis, the Republic has less social workers than Northern Ireland. What they are less quick to point out that Northern Ireland has more social workers per capita than the rest of the UK and also have more children in "care" per capita than the rest of the UK. In the area of Policing, crime rates go down when more police officers are added which proves that better enforcement reduces the incidence of crime. When Police go on strike, the crime rate soars. So why is it than when you put more social workers into an area, that the "crime" rate soars? You would think that putting more social workers in an area would mean that more social workers are available to help vulnerable families and eliminate the necessity to remove more children?

Since Baby P, social workers are more likely to remove children than to work with families. They have shifted from being "Risk Aversive" to totally eliminating any possibility of risk. No evidence is needed, "shoot first and ask questions later". An accusation alone is enough "evidence"; the evidence can be gathered or fabricated later.

A trend that I noticed in many cases is that the reason for an Emergency Care Order (ECO), will change by the time the Interim Care Order (ICO) is applied for and by the time the Full Care Order (FCO) is applied for, the entire story has changed entirely to the extent that you are not talking about the same family. When they fail to prove one thing they will move on to the next. They will use "Hired Gun Experts", some not even qualified or use them knowing full well that they have previously perjured themselves in court.

During Access or visitation to your children, you will be carefully scrutinized by someone with a clipboard, It's like taking a driving test and many parents have told me, just a stressful. Nothing positive is going to be reported in these notes, having seen enough of them, it's very hard to find any positives. These are the type of notes I spoke about during the first case conference I witnessed. Once a child is in "Care", it's no longer about repatri-ating the family. The child is in "Care" based on a suspicion and the objective is to turn that suspicion into evidence. In more than one case, Psychologists have made 300 page reports on children based on these notes; none of the psychologists had ever met the parent or the child. Can you imagine a witness testifying against a bank robber when they have never been to the bank and didn't witness the robbery?

Judges love paperwork and a 300-page cut and pasted report can be quite compelling, even if it is a work of fiction. The parents are not entitled to know the contents of the report before it is presented in court. The Prosecution have a copy and will not use the expert if they have something nice to say about the family. When you challenge the "Expert", they will say it's just their profes-sional opinion. They can apparently appease their conscience by saying it's just their opinion and the parents can get another "Expert" opinion, except they cant in most cases. You also don't get to pick and choose the expert and sometimes you never meet them. Can you imagine this being allowed in an open Criminal Court?

I am not the only one to note the phenomenon of Hired Guns or unqualified "experts", In 2009 the UK government asked Professor Jane Ireland to assess the reports used in family courts. Professor Ireland found that 70% of these experts were unqualified and many were not in current practice, they make their living solely from family courts as experts and command huge fees. I know of another case in Ireland where the HSE used a woman who was retired, had exaggerated her qualifications, was not registered by any professional body and did a report on a psychological condition that does not exist. Even though the judge discounted her testimony, she was paid €40,000 for her report. The same "expert" testified in a case in Northern Ireland and commanded a similar fee. When we tried to report her for practicing without a license, we were told that because she was not a member or a professional body, that they could not take any action. Also because the "fraud upon the court" was held in a secret court, the Police and Gardaí could not investigate.

These are examples of "Best Interests" in practice. Everything that is done in Child "Protection" is done in the best interests of children. If a social worker or a psychologist lie or exaggerate or if a judge turns a blind eye, it all based on the best interests principle, but is the BIP actually working to the benefit of children?

Social Worker Charles Pragnell was probably the first person to criticize the Best Interests Principle. Charles has extensive experience of many years, written many scholarly articles on the topic of Child Protection. In the social work community he is well known and respected for his analysis. Charles noted that BIP is not measurable and not demonstrable and has suggested that BIP be replaced by the standard of,

"To the Demonstrable and Measurable Benefit of the Child"

Under this standard, the entire face of child protection would change forever. If it were within my power to only change one thing in social work, justice or law, I would removed the BIP and replace it with Charles's standard which is easily defined Scientifically, Legally and Morally. If the child does not benefit and if the standards of "Care", Justice and Protection are not measured or demonstrated, then the effectiveness of the system cannot be measured or demonstrated. In simpler terms, if it's not working then why do it?

Not that anyone is interested in measuring or demonstrating its effectiveness; we only hear the horror stories and not the successes. The social work community and the Child Abuse Industry have fought any attempt at scrutiny. They cannot relate any success stories because there are none. They hide behind the PR of "we cannot speak of any individual cases". There are no children coming forward thanking the State for having rescued them. Not a single NGO or expert or lobbyist has ever been a whistleblower for any of the horror stories that we have heard about. In truth there have been whistleblowers but they tend not to be given one column inch in the media. I will talk about one in particular later.

I'm sure in my father's mind that every time he spanked me that he did it out of love. I'm still undecided if I benefitted in any way but I cannot say that I was harmed by it. On the other hand, I was also beaten with the strap and received "6 of the best" many times by "Christian" Brothers and sadistic teachers in school for relatively minor infractions, many times beyond my control. What I learned from the experience is to always question Authority and a strong sense of Social Justice that I have had since being a child and boldly looking up at the faces of sadistic teachers without giving them any indication that they had made any impact on me. It didn't make me hate education as I spent many years after at night school and incessant reading and study. I'm strongly opposed to corporal punishment but only because it may have an unintended consequence but I am equally opposed to criminalizing parents for relatively minor infractions. I believe that spanking causes harm to the child/parent bond and that the evidence shows that it simply doesn't work.

When the intervention by social services is far worse than the alleged harm that may be caused by a parent raising their voice, administering punishment or teaching their child Life Lessons, I would say that the child would benefit more than if the social services had not intervened. At least when the parent intervenes its done out of love for their child. If we are really serious about protecting children, we must do away with BIP and demonstrate and measure the Benefit of our actions in every case for every child. The next time you hear someone say Best Interests, ask them for a definition.

CHAPTER 5

"HOW'S THAT WORKING FOR YOU PHIL?"

Dr Phil McGraw, aka 'Dr Phil' has been heavily involved in Child Protection for many years. He and his wife are members of CASA and he works with children in "Care". Phil has stated on his show "he would rather see 1,000 children taken (into "care") than see 1 child swinging in the breeze". He believes that it is ok to take 999 children from innocent parents if it saves ONE child.

He is not alone in his thinking; it is in fact the very Modus Operandi by which the system operates in some countries, but would not be tolerated in others. When the social worker keeps changing the reasons for applying for the court orders from the ECO to the ICO to the FCO they are struggling from one to the next and when they lose the case and the child is returned, it's assumed that no harm is done, and this is exactly Dr Phil's thinking. Phil's other mistake is in thinking that children are returned when the parents are innocent.

It's not about being Risk Aversive, it's about trying to eliminate risk entirely. As there is no particular term for this strategy of child "protection", I will call it, "Shoot first and ask questions later". This strategy is wrong for many reasons,

- It harms 999 children.

- It goes against Human Rights Law under several sections.

- It is illegal under the Irish Constitution and the laws of many countries.

- It's 999 times more expensive than the system needs to be.

- It takes social workers away from the role of helping families.

- It makes caseloads 1,000 times higher than necessary.

- It harms far more children than it helps.

- It cannot be justified in Law or Justice.

- It is a prime example of how Witch Hunts operate.

The learning from the Baby P case supposedly created the "Baby P Effect". Rather than 1 child "swinging in the wind', take every child on the basis of Risk and if the parents are not guilty, the child goes home and no harm is done, supposedly.

The fact is that considerable harm is done to the child by the system, which purports to protect them. It also destroys the family and leaves many parents, unemployed or unemployable, bankrupt from having to take time off work to see their children during the office hours that the system operates in, and many parents are left emotionally shattered and sometimes dysfunctional.

Next to the death penalty, the most draconian punishment that can be given is to remove a child from a parent. It harms the child as much as the parent. Earlier I gave you an example of where 3 children were taken into "Care" in the space of less than a minute without any evidence being presented and the parents not allowed to present their case or protest their innocence. I struggled to get my head around this incident after I left the courtroom. I sat in my vehicle in the parking lot of the courthouse. After a few hours the judge came out in his Armani suit and strolled happily to his classic car. I was tempted to ask him what was going through his mind at the time he made this decision but fact was that he was accompanied by 2 Gardaí and escorted to his classic car. It's also important to remember that I could have been jailed there and then for up to 2 years in a secret court proceeding and nobody would know, simply by asking the judge.

While the judge was happy that he had finished another day's work, I could only focus on 3 children crying for their parents and the distraught parents at their wits end trying to get their heads around to why their children were taken without due process of law. I also struggled with why this troubled me so much but apparently not the judge? Unlike the judge I get to meet these children, sometimes after their 18th birthday when they are dumped on the streets. I wonder how many of these children that the judge meets? Maybe the unidentified young beggar on the street, the young prostitute or the young criminal who has come before him for stealing food because he was hungry?

In my experience in District Courts, I have sat there waiting for cases to be heard and heard these DC judges handing out fines for litter and driving offenses and minor infractions of the law. In most cases it's assumed that the perpetrators are guilty when they appear before the judge and they will try to justify their actions or mitigate the case. Any Police Sergeant could handle many of these cases and in many countries do. But then the In Camera sign goes on the door and the courtroom is cleared, the legal team for the social workers and GAL's, the "Experts" in their Armani suits will fill one side of the courtroom while a parent or couple and their Legal Aid solicitor, whom they just met for the first time only 30 minutes before, will be relegated to the other side. It's a totally unbalanced scene, like a football match with 2 or 3 people on one side and I have seen as many as 15 on the other side.

Justice is supposed to be predicated on the belief that 10 guilty people go free before 1 innocent person is convicted. In reality, this hasn't happened much since the time of the Magna Carta, but there has to be a presumption of Innocent until Proven Guilty, and a person should only be found guilty Beyond all Reasonable Doubt. In Family Court you and your children are punished first whether you are guilty or not, you are not entitled to know the evidence being used against you, you are doubly gagged, once by the judge who will jail you for saying "anything to anybody" and gagged again by the social workers that if you don't jump through all their hoops, they will take away visits with your children.

In a criminal court you are innocent until proven guilty but because the proceeding is public, you have some chance at justice. The Prosecutor who is independent of the State decides which cases to prosecute and have a reasonable record of prosecutions, in the 90% range. Sometimes guilty people will get off, but equally, miscarriages of justice can take place as the system is far from perfect.

The balance between how Family Courts operate versus Criminal courts is so removed from the principles of fairness and justice, that the two systems are almost the polar opposite of each other. In Criminal Law you have the Gardaí to investigate, the DPP to prosecute, the judge to decide on innocence or guilt and the Prison System to punish. In the Family Court System you have the judge and the social workers.

What few people don't understand about this system is that if you are accused of child abuse or neglect, there are two parallel systems under which you will be Investigated, Prosecuted, Judged and Punished. The most important thing that people need to realize, that if you are deemed innocent and Gardaí drop their investigation, that you are investigated again by people who have no training in investigation, you are punished in a secret court as are your children, the quality and mercy of Justice that you receive is of a very low standard and is judged by lesser qualified judges under a lower burden of proof. You are guilty without evidence and not entitled to know the evidence against you and you are punished regardless. The Prosecutor has no legal duty to put Justice first, they are not Independent, and they are hired by the State whose only goal is to take every child for any reason. The "Prosecutors" are private law firms and the system is incentivized for the prosecutors to "stretch-out" the case as long as possible to make more money.

Baby Peter Connolly was 17 months old when he died. He lived a miserable existence and had 18 life-threatening injuries when he last visited hospital and was sent home without being examined and died shortly after. His case was widely used as an argument as to why we need more social workers and to make the public believe that child abuse and neglect are at epidemic proportions. Social "Scientists", all singing from the same hymn-sheet, to the tune of "shoot first and ask questions later", have written many books.

I believe that the Baby P case is a stunning example of why Social Work, Psychology and Sociology will never be capable of protecting children. I realize that this is not a learning that the Child Abuse Industry want to take, as it doesn't support the case for more or earlier intervention, it is in fact quite the opposite.

What should have been the principle learning from Baby P is that social workers can visit the home of an abused child with horrific injuries, not once or twice, but visit the home 60 times and not see the threshold to intervention being met.

What is interesting is that I have talked to a police officer in the area and they said if Child Protection had been the role of Police that Peter would never have died. The officer said that they would have investigated the very odd guy who lived upstairs with 2 Rottweiler dogs, who if they had, found that he was previously investigated for abuse of infants. The Police had indeed visited Peters home on another matter but for some very odd reason, it seems that Police have no duty to serve and protect children in Ireland or the UK when in fact other countries police forces at the hub of child protection.

The Manager of Haringey was Sharon Shoesmith, even before Shoesmith, Haringey was failing children. This was just a long line of failures that continues to this day with many other controversial cases and controversial managers who seem incapable of protecting children. Baby Peter wasn't the first and wont be the last. In fact the Baby P case would never have come to the publics attention at all if it hadn't been for whistleblowers and courageous journalists willing to penetrate the armor of this secret world.

What is not widely known about the Baby P case is the chaos and dysfunction that existed in Haringey Council in the time leading up to Peter's death. Nevres Kemal who worked there and tried to blow the whistle but was ignored. Nevres was not directly involved in Baby P but worked in the same office as those who did. She blew the whistle on Haringey 6 months before Baby Peters death but was largely ignored by the Department of Education. She was eventually booted out, supposedly over another issue. After Baby Peter died, the press started to listen, as did the government but the government handling of the situation led to Sharon Shoesmith being reinstated on grounds of wrongful dismissal rather than her handling of the case. Recently another book written by a Prof of Social Work tried to shift the blame for Baby Peters death away from the social workers.

People can argue that the Media and the Government did wrong in the Baby P case and they can distract us with other issues, but the bottom line is that social workers claim that they can protect children, they claim to have crystal balls like Psychology and Sociology and that they, any only they, can protect children. They can claim that they did everything by the book and when the child dies, they ask; "why are you blaming us?" They can't see that they have a duty to protect the child, that's what we are paying them for, and that's why they are vilified when they don't protect the child. With the benefit of hindsight, I would say that Baby P would still be alive if Police had the role of protecting him. Either the brother and his Rottweiler's would have left the home or Baby P would have been removed.

How the entire Baby P fiasco was handled, is testimony to a broken system and testimony that everyone who Peter came into contact with in his short life, had failed him at every opportunity. There were over 50 people involved and any ONE could have saved him. Where Social Work has hijacked this case to their own benefit, the facts speak for themselves. Even in death, Baby Peter is still being failed today, as the lessons have clearly not been learned. The number one finding should have been that social work could never protect children and that social workers should have no role whatsoever in removing children. If child abuse and neglect is a crime, then why isn't it investigated by Police, prosecuted by the DPP or CPS, as they are known in the UK, why are lower court judges allowed to administer the most draconian sentence imaginable on children and parents? Social work has no basis in Science and subjective opinion is not robust enough to be used for punishment without crime.

What we should have learned from Baby P is that social workers are being asked to do a job they will never be capable of doing. Psychology and Social Work are a product that has been over-sold to a gullible and adoring public, judiciary and government.

John Hemming MP in the UK has summed it up very well in his analysis; "This is the Thought Police approach to protecting children".

Ian Josephs has equally stated the problem well in regard to the law he says this is, "Punishment Without Crime"

As Social Worker Charles Pragnell points out that there is no system of quality and that we need to replace Best Interests with;

"To the Demonstrable and Measurable Benefit of the Child"

Social workers don't do investigations and receive no training in a systematic and scientific approach to problem solving. They don't investigate; they do 'assessments' from a tick-box checklist that is so vague and subjective, that it could be used to remove any child from any parent. As no evidence exists in the vast majority of cases and because 70% of children are removed on the basis of "Possible Risk of future emotional harm."

Is it any wonder then that by my own estimation, that for every 186 cases where Irish social workers are granted an order, that only ONE parent will be charged with a criminal offense? How is this even possible under that law? How can you be tried twice for the same "crime" under two different burdens of proof?

It is indeed the very system that John Hemming and Ian Josephs describe; it is also the very Modus Operandi that Witch Hunts are conducted. But the system is far worse than this, once "protected"; the children are placed at a higher risk in "Care". You may wonder why I use quotation marks around the word and I have devoted a whole chapter to the topic.

If you compare the child protection system to other systems, you should see that social workers are being asked to do a job that they will never be capable of. Nobody can predict future outcomes for children, but it is a scientific fact, that children "cared for" by the State will have poor outcomes in life in over 80% of cases.

Where we used to talk of "children in need", the term "Children at Risk" has now replaced it. 70% of all children removed in the UK are removed on the basis of "Risk of Future Emotional Abuse". The theory that something may, or equally may not, happens at some point in the future. How can children be removed from parents on the basis of future crime? It is exactly as John Hemming described, the Though Police approach to protecting children. How is this ethical or legal? The fact is that it is not legal under Human Rights Law; it is as Ian Josephs says, "Punishment Without Crime".

This is not to say that there is no mechanism of protecting children, the systems used in other countries work very well and you tend not to hear the horror stories you hear from Ireland and the UK. The difference in how different countries operate child protection is simply that a social worker alone has no power to remove a child and the decision to remove a child should never be decided by a judge in less than one minute as it could in Ireland and the UK.

In Ireland, we had a case that was worse than the Baby Peter case in many ways, but fortunately the children did not die. This case was known as the Roscommon House of Horrors where children were subjected to the most severe neglect over a period of 11 years and were sexually assaulted. The mother herself at her criminal court hearing said that she was the worst mother in the world.

During the corrupt Children's Referendum many politicians used Roscommon and 17 other cases of where parents had failed their children. But many of us on the No side of the debate used it as a stunning example of how the State had failed in its duty to protect these children. By cherry picking of arguments, they mentioned that a misguided person helped the parents get a court order preventing the Health Board social workers from intervening. What the cherry pickers neglected to mention was the fact that the social workers were involved with this dysfunctional family for 11 years and had not seen the threshold to removing the children as having been met. The judge accepted the argument that as the social workers had been involved for 11 years, they had ample opportunity to put any measures they felt necessary in place but had chosen not to. The social workers also had the opportunity to challenge or appeal the case but never did. Nobody was ever punished for such an obvious dereliction of duty.

Social workers feel they should not be held accountable for their failures but will pick on every single nuance of a parent and use it as evidence to remove a child. If you left your children at home with a babysitter and the child was harmed or died in their care, you would accept nothing less than Justice. When a child dies in the care of social workers, nobody is ever responsible or held accountable. Why do we accept a lesser standard of parenting from the State and the children in their "Care"? One reason is the In Camera Rule, the parents are not entitled to copies of all evidence held against them and they are gagged under threat of prison.

The children in the Roscommon case would regularly be seen trudging through the streets carrying alcohol for their parents. Neighbors were calling Gardaí and reporting that the children were rummaging around their garbage bins for food. Many others raised concerns with Gardaí which were passed on to social workers and in the end, it was the children who decided to save themselves. Nobody was ever punished and no lessons were ever learned. It is shameful that these children suffered for 11 years under the nose of social workers and Gardaí. The locals did their job of reporting but it is quite astonishing that the State uses this as example of where parents abused their children when the children were further abused by people who had a statutory duty to act on behalf of the children. The Roscommon case is also widely used as an example of why social workers should remove children on nothing more than suspicion rather than leave one child swinging in the wind, when in fact it is a prime example of why social workers are simply not capable of detecting child abuse.

At any stage in the Baby P or Roscommon case, police could have stepped in and saved the children. In Ireland Gardaí can act under Section 12 of the Childcare Act and remove any child from anywhere without needing to obtain a warrant. As long as the Garda reasonably believes that a child is in danger, they can enter any building or structure without a warrant, they can use any reasonable force and they can remove any child to a place of safety. I have used S12 against the HSE myself to remove a baby from the "care" of the HSE. They only caveat is that that they are required to establish the danger that exists. This does not stop them from investigating and removing the child, but if they can't establish the actual harm, they can't keep the child. Similar laws exist in most countries.

You may remember during the referendum a solicitor who said that the laws are such that "a parent can literally have their hands around the neck of a child and throttle that child within an inch of it's life before the State can intervene". Clearly Section 12 of the CCA strongly disputes this. Also the fact that there are 186 Orders of the courts for every criminal prosecution clearly disputes that the State has no power to intervene and protect children when necessary. Many judges have also said that the State has always had adequate laws and that any Constitutional change was unnecessary. Judges have held court in their kitchens at 2 in the morning in cases where it was necessary to protect children. In cases such as offspring of Jehovah Witnesses receiving blood products no child has ever died at the hands of a parent as a result of inadequacies in Irish Law, but hundreds of children have died at the inadequacy of Irish Law to protect children who are in the "Care" of the Irish State because the In Camera Rule forbids reporting of child abuse or neglect to Gardaí. Only the CFA investigate the CFA.

Section 12 as a tool to protect children is frequently misused by social workers that have no legal right to invoke any law without the directions of a judge and a written court order. Many times the social workers show up with court orders, but the orders have not been signed or stamped by the judge or clerk of court. These are clearly kidnappings and I have seen documents where children were removed on a Friday afternoon but the order was not stamped and signed until Monday. Corrupt CFA lawyers and equally corrupt judges frequently break the law and nobody is ever held accountable.

What frequently occurs when children are kidnapped is that social workers show up at a Garda station and request backup for an "Apprehension" as they call it. Gardaí don't ask to see their warrant and in the process, are unwittingly used as accomplices to kidnapping. When they arrive at the house they might make their decision based on a 3-minute conversation as I wrote about in the first case. They tell the parents they are taking the children and don't show a court order to Gardaí or the parents. Once they speed away they call the corrupt CFA lawyers and say they have invoked a S12. The lawyers then go before a judge and say that the children were in such danger that Gardaí had to remove them. The Garda doesn't even know that he or she has performed a S12 and the corrupt judge doesn't ask and grants the order in less than a minute. It would be difficult to estimate how many kidnappings there are in Ireland every year but I would estimate it could be as high as 800. An audit of court records would show that a large number of children have in fact been kidnapped and I would place the blame fairly on judges for allowing this to occur.

It would appear that Gardaí believe that they have no duty to protect children and almost always "pass on their concerns" to social workers, who only work business hours, children are poorly protected out of hours. Rather than Gardaí properly investigating these cases, they abrogate their responsibility to serve and protect all the citizens of Ireland under the age of 18.

One such example was the Monageer Case. It involved a young family with two toddlers. The father was going blind and was suicidal. As is common in cases where people are seriously going to attempt suicide, they often go to the trouble of making all their final arrangements before the act of suicide. People will give away property, visit people before the act for the last time and arrange for everything so as not to be a burden on the people left behind.

Having talked to people over the years that have reached this stage, there are warning signs that every professional should know in order to prevent suicide. For many people living a life of pain, they see no other way out and many have told me of the great relief they feel and the calmness that they experience when they take the decision that suicide is the only way to be free of their pain. Many people have a strong belief in God or an after-life and hope that they will be free of pain in death because life was not bearable. Quite often with suicide there is a dark depression that few could even begin to comprehend, never mind explain. When you talk to these people you often find that the cause of their pain is a temporary condition. Suicide does not solve the problem; it prevents any chance of the problem being solved. It is a very permanent solution to what is often a temporary problem.

Suicide is a huge problem in Ireland with more people taking their lives than are killed from vehicle collisions. What everyone tends to say after their loved one has passed that it was such a waste and that they would have given anything to save the life of the person. Suicide is an area where social work and psychology can be life saving. A skilled therapist can cut to the heart of the matter and resolve the situation in the majority of cases. I would urge anyone contemplating ending his or her life to talk to anyone, especially those specially trained. Every professional should learn the warning signs and not fail the victim.

In Monageer the young family walked into an undertakers and selected caskets for their children who were very much alive. I can't think of a more overt call for help than the act of selecting caskets. It was a call for help that the Undertaker understood loud and clear and did everything in their power to get help for this young family. The local Gardaí were warned straight away but failed to save the family. As is customary for Gardaí, they tried to get a hold of the on-call social worker and had great difficulty. Eventually Gardaí got a hold of the local priest, maybe not the first person that would come to mind in a mental health emergency but the priest did his best and was reassured that everything would be ok and left it there for the moment. Later when they checked on the family they found the parents and children dead from an apparent murder/suicide.

Of course "lessons were learned", "we have put measures in place" and all the usual rhetoric was rolled out. Gardaí could have removed the children at any time under Section 12 and could have possibly sectioned the parents under the Mental Health Act. The law was more than adequate and a judge would have gladly got up in the middle of the night and erred on the side of caution and protected this family. Of course hindsight is 20/20 but no lessons were learned. Everyone blamed everyone else and if the same incident occurred today, it's likely that the same results would occur. Nothing has changed substantially, social worker only work office hours and Gardaí still pass on concerns rather than doing their job of protecting citizens, even the ones under 18.

Whenever a failure analysis is done in these cases, nobody is ever fired or suffers any consequences for their actions or lack of action. Not that we should play the Blame Game but we should learn from these systemic failures that as long as social workers are at the hub of child protection, that children will not be protected. In a system that is a recipe for failure with no checks and balances and no success stories to share, we cannot have any confidence that when needed that the system will work. Only by following the examples of other countries can we be reassured that Best Practice is followed. The UK model that Ireland follows is the worst possible system in the world.

Until every Garda in Ireland fully understands Section 12 of the Child Care Act, nothing is going to change for the better. Until Garda Management implement policies that S12 will be used and only used by Garda Members who must then testify in court and give their compelling reasons and establish the actual harm, the Gardaí cannot claim to protect children adequately. I believe that judges need to be held accountable for the kidnapping of children that they have allowed.

For too long judges have abrogated their responsibility because they wanted to protect their own reputations. One judge put it quite succinctly; "put yourself in my position, somebody believes the child to be in danger, what am I supposed to do? You would do exactly the same thing." Actually I wouldn't. I would not impose the most draconian sentence on a child as to remove them from their parents without first being shown some evidence of a crime having taken place. I would also want to hear from the parents and if the child were old enough to talk, would want to hear their views. When social services inevitably fail these children or the child dies in "Care", the judge is absolved at least in their own mind that they are not to blame. Judges in most other countries have the power to investigate and it would not be unusual for a judge to leave the courtroom and visit the family home.

Dr Phil also mentioned on his show that children in "Care" suffer from Post Traumatic Stress Syndrome. They are twice as likely to suffer as troops returning from combat zones such as Iraq and Afghanistan. They also suffer in the order of four times more severe. Nobody disputes this. What is in dispute is the cause of the stress. While many believe that the children were "damaged" before being taken into "Care", the evidence simply doesn't support this theory. What is far more likely is that the very process of grappling a child from the arms of their parents, dragging them away kicking and screaming and placing them with strangers for months or years is extremely damaging to the child.

Having witnessed it myself in the case of a baby who was taken at 6 months and spent about 8 months in "Care", I can say that PTSD even in babies is a real phenomenon. I have heard many times from parents telling me stories of how their children wake up in the middle of the night with flashbacks of the trauma of being removed and placed with strangers, away from everything that makes the feel comfortable and safe. I would never have believed that a baby of 6 months could be so traumatized by the experience and still recall the events later at the age of 3, which was the first time that he could verbalize with his apt description of having "two mommies". The entire intervention in the case of this child was unnecessary, a kidnapping and a testament to everything that is wrong with the system. While the other child was old enough for therapy, all that could be done for the baby was constant reassurance.

Education is a product that is bought and sold. Colleges must compete and remain competitive and few have the budget to keep up with technology or advances in science. While many colleges have relationships with large companies to fill in for what they lack, social workers largely work as Civil Servants and colleges have partnered with government. It's not unusual to see social work students in family homes as part of their work experience. Few of them will have the opportunity to go into other areas of the practice and Child Protection is seen as entry level because the turnover is so high. Many graduate social workers go into other areas and never practice social work.

The basis for Sociology is Psychology, the only branch of Medicine that has never claimed to have "cured" a single patient. Both as products are oversold and misrepresented as "Sciences". For psychological conditions there are no blood tests, no x rays or other scientific tests that prove that any psychological illness exists. The Manual of Psychiatric Disorders, known as the DSM requires the consensus of only 4 psychologists to list a new disorder. The latest version of the DSM has been widely rejected by psychologists and psychiatrists everywhere, mostly because they have now listed every human emotion as a psychiatric disorder.

The profession of psychology is under fire, not just because it has been misrepresented and over-sold but because it purports to be a science even though it doesn't use any known scientific principles or methods. Psychology has worked its way into all areas of our life. In advertising, human resources, education, even manufacturing. The biggest customer of psychology and sociology is Government. Psychology is used in courts and presented as a science, some judges wont work without them, they are used for sentencing reports for offenders, but is it robust enough to be used as evidence Beyond All Reasonable Doubt? Many psychologists themselves don't believe it is and the list is growing.

Governments have used Psychology and Sociology in an attempt at social control. Eugenics wasn't invented in Nazi Germany; it had been used many years before in the USA. It was used before Psychology was even in its infancy.

Eugenics went beyond birth control, it was felt that the poor could be eliminated altogether and that humans could be bred, as animals are bred and negative traits could be eliminated. The rich and the industrialists were ardent fans. Eugenics only fell into disrepute when Hitler tried to create the Aryan Race. But Eugenics lives on today under the name of Social Engineering and social workers and psychologists are at the forefront of the battle to control society.

Psychology has limited its value by coming a magic pill to solve every issue. It's being exposed as a fraud in courtrooms everywhere. The prosecution brings in one psychologist to say one thing, the defense has another psychologist who's opinion is 180* opposed, who do you believe? This is not how Science works, a proposition either IS or ISN'T, yes or no. In the family courts the report of Professor Jane Ireland commissioned by the UK government should have been a wake up call for courts but had little impact. A book written by Psychology Professor Margaret A Hagen entitled "Whores of the Court", should have been a wake up call for the entire profession. The subtitle of her groundbreaking book was, "The Fraud of Psychiatric Testimony and the Rape of American Justice". Her book is available to download free. It's a difficult read but worth the effort.

Psychology can be a life saving discipline for many people. A skilled therapist can quickly get to the heart of the issue and improve the quality of life for the patient. But when the craft of Plumbing is represented as Brain Surgery, it can never deliver on its promise. Psychologists can make you buy more products or save an advertiser millions, they can talk suicidal people off ledges and bridges but what they cannot do is diagnose any patient with 100% certainty or cure that patient with a 100% success rate. They can render an opinion but they cannot claim that their diagnosis is 100% accurate and judges cannot claim that their opinion is any more than a subjective opinion. In my own experience I have seen the HSE using liars and whores of the court who will prostitute their good name for the highest bidder and destroy the lives of children for money. At least with Plumbing you can use scientific methods. Pipes come in standard sizes and building codes dictate best practice. Plumbers have to be professional and competitive and their results are predictable. And many can command fees rivaling Brain Surgeons.

When Tony Blair took office in 1997, he had 28 social workers in his party. Since 1997, social work and psychology have taken off. Tony was determined to fix the problems of the underclass. One of the first things he did was introduce Forced Adoption. The UK would be the only country in Europe where children could be forcibly adopted against the will of the parents. Of course it was presented as; "we have all these children languishing in "care" who deserve a permanent home". Not surprisingly the exact same argument was used in Ireland during the Children's Referendum. However, in the UK it was not the children in "Care" who were adopted, only 6% of those adopted, were adopted from "Care", the other 94% were made up of children who were taken so councils could hit their targets and receive millions in bonuses.

One such case was Fran Lyon, a young university student who had an unplanned, but not unwanted pregnancy. Fran was shocked to receive a letter put through her mailbox from a social worker that she had never met, stating that when her baby was born, it would be taken for forced adoption. Fran wisely contacted columnist Sue Reid and John Hemming MP. Her story was put all over the news but the council did not back down. Her middle-class parents offered to raise their grandchild, but no, the child would be adopted against the family's wishes. The mother was never accused of any crime and as she was a first time parent, had no record as a bad parent, there was no evidence against her except a doctor whom she had never met, was of the opinion the baby might be "at risk". The system has operated in this way ever since. Fran fled to Ireland and worked with the HSE and advocates under the glare of the international media. Wisely, the HSE had no justification to intervene and Fran settled in Ireland with her child where she has lived ever since.

Since the Fran Lyon case, hundreds of pregnant women have fled to Ireland and France, Spain and Belgium. In the last 5 years especially, the HSE had a policy of hiring social workers from the UK. Many were snapped up even though they were unqualified to work in the UK. It was only in 2012 that the Government set up a registry of social workers, but at the time of writing in 2014, they still don't have a fitness to practice committee and to my knowledge, no social worker has ever been struck off in Ireland. In the UK about 50 a year are struck off.

In the last 5 years, the policies of the UK and Ireland have become more aggressive and the UK will pursue pregnant women fleeing UK social services to countries all over the world. For the last 5 years I have noticed an inordinate number of UK social workers and managers working for the HSE but many have worked there for longer. The HSE became more like the UK in terms of aggressively chasing clients around the world and I have seen the HSE pursue cases as far away as Saudi Arabia. The HSE also started taking children on more spurious grounds like the UK. It is not uncommon for the CFA (HSE) now to take babies at birth even when the parent is having their first baby, simply on the basis that the UK social services had "concerns", even though there has been no assessment of the parent's mental health or ability to parent their child.

In essence we have become the UK system where judges will allow the law to be abused in this way. In one case I was involved in the UK local authority applied to have the baby returned to the UK and an Irish high court judge agreed to the deportation. The UK LA lied to the Irish court and said they had orders granted for the newborn. Under the law, no such orders could have existed but the baby was deported anyway. In the UK court the "Error" was later corrected by a corrupt judge and the orders made retroactively.

Similar cases have occurred in France and Spain where in one particular case, the baby had lived in Spain for 5 months and the mother, who was not accused of any crime, had already been assessed by Spanish social workers that had no issues with her care of the infant. The mother lived legally in Spain and was supported by her parents and the father of the baby. The father was arrested on spurious charges in the UK by Police and the home of his parents ransacked. He was visited by a social worker on remand and a deal was made for the baby. If he applied for custody and guardianship, the criminal charges would be dropped. He was lead to believe that he and his family would be given his child.

The Guardia Civil arrived at the mother's apartment in Spain and took her 5-month-old daughter. She was lead to believe that Spanish social services would take the baby into "Care" until the case was decided in court. In reality the court had already decided without the mother present that the UK had orders for the baby and a Spanish judge, way over his head in these matters, signed the order.

In a matter of hours, the baby girl was in the UK, a country she had never been to. The parents fought all the way through the UK courts. There was no UK order, but again, this "error" was corrected. The parental rights of the parents were terminated and the baby "Freed for Adoption". At the "Goodbye Meeting", the parents took a photograph of the baby they would never see again. I posted the image along with an image of when she lived in Spain; the difference was night and day. The image survived a few days on Facebook but was removed with a court order, just as many others I posted have been removed. Their daughter's image was later posted on an adoption website as a "doe eyed orphan, desperately in need of parents". I have also in some cases posted documents supporting the forgery and illegality of UK cases, even if removed they were copied by others and seen by many.

In a case in France a similar child kidnapping occurred and the baby taken to the UK. When the French courts realized that they had been lied to by the UK, they rescinded the order and went to the UK and fought the case and won. The UK courts ordered the baby returned the baby to the parents in France. Even though there was an order for the baby to return home to France, the local authority defied the order as long as possible and returned the baby after several months.

In a case in 2013, an Italian tourist visited the UK on a work assignment while she was 6 months pregnant. She was in the UK for 2 weeks on a training course and at the airport on her way home, only an hour from boarding the aircraft. She suffered from Panic Attacks occasionally but these were controlled by medication prescribed by her physician. During her pregnancy she refused to take the medicine for fear that it would harm her unborn baby. She was taken by Police and sanctioned under the Mental Health Act. Even though she was an Italian citizen and had habitually lived in Italy, it was decided by social workers in the UK that when her baby was born, it would be taken for Forced Adoption.

What's interesting about this case from a legal standpoint, is that the UK walk into foreign courts and argue under the Hague Convention and a law known as Brussels II, that the UK can claim authority over a citizen or person who has lived continuously in that country for 6 years. So if a child was born in Spain and lived there all its life, the child could be removed at any point up to its 6th birthday. But in this case they were laying claim to an Italian baby of an Italian mother, if their own rules are to be believed. The UK had 3 months before the due date of the baby to repatriate the woman to Italy, but Italy did not apply to the UK courts. Apparently Italian social workers don't chase people around the world to take babies.

It was decided that the baby would be prematurely delivered by caesarian section regardless of the wishes of the mother and the baby adopted in the UK. It was decided and argued that the woman was "Mentally Ill" but only suffered from Panic Attacks, which are quite common. The case made world headlines, it was fought all the way through the courts but in the end the baby was adopted.

If Fran Lyon arrived in Ireland today, her baby would be returned to the UK. An estimated 80 pregnant women a year flee the UK to prevent their baby being forcibly adopted, I have assisted on many of these cases and we have fought them all the way to the Supreme Court. A judge in Ireland made an announcement that Ireland could not be used as a haven for UK citizens fleeing the UK social services, but actually a prominent member of the Child Abuse Industry in Ireland had already made that decree some time earlier but her comments referred to the cost. Some parents seek the help of Ian Josephs and John Hemming MP in the UK and the parents are put into an "Underground Railroad" network of people who are willing to assist in these cases. There are 3 groups that I know of in Ireland who will assist pregnant women in these cases.

In the cases I have been involved in, we have always encouraged people to work with social services in the countries they have fled to. We advise people to arrive 3 months before the birth and to make themselves known to the CFA. If the social workers have any "concerns", they have ample opportunity to perform mental health or parenting assessments. We encourage parents to deal openly and honestly and provide full disclosure of any previous issues. We ask them to get copies of Police Clearances even though most have never been accused of any crime. In most cases these people could be vetted and allowed to look after children. We don't do substance abuse cases or help "Child Abusers" as some people may assume. We are as concerned that children are protected and spend far more time and resources than the social workers involved in these cases.

Five years ago the HSE would have dealt with these cases more openly and honestly than they have recently. The CFA no longer bother having a case conference before the birth as required to under the Children First Guidelines. As the government has not put Children First (no pun intended) on a statutory basis, social workers are under no obligation to follow their own rules or guidelines. The strategy now is to wait until the baby is born and get the baby back to the UK. Even though this is supposed to be driven by economics, no expense is spared. In 3 documented cases, social workers have instructed teams of Gardaí to follow around heavily pregnant women in case they give birth outside of a hospital. I have seen these women followed 24 hours a day for up to 3 weeks until the birth.

As no government cannot make court orders for a child, who has not been born yet as the child does not exist in law, if the mother decided to slip into Northern Ireland or board a flight, the Gardaí could not intervene. We have social workers operating as spies like James Bond, or in this case Jane Bond, wasting valuable resources even though they have no legal right to do this. The mother is not accused of any crime, there are no court orders to allow these women to be stalked 24/7, quite often by 2 Gardaí, often without uniforms so it may be a reasonable assumption that in some cases they may be armed detectives. There is no provision in law for this to occur and no sane reason for this shocking waste of resources.

I have read many stories of how Gardaí resources are severely restricted. Many small stations have been closed, overtime is gone and some Gardaí are using Food Banks or resorting to crime to pay their mortgages and feed their families. I have seen a number of times where convicted sex offenders are released from prison and Gardaí say they simply cant afford the resources every time Larry Murphy is spotted in Ireland but they seem to have unlimited resources to follow heavily pregnant women around, who probably couldn't run very fast, and report on these women who are not accused of any crime to social workers who have no evidence against the mother?

The Irish system has degenerated in the last few years. The objective is to remove every child at any opportunity for any reason; we have now become the UK system. Irish social workers are taking newborns away on the basis of nothing more than the "concerns" of UK social workers, they wont follow their own guidelines and do their own assessments even though they have ample opportunity. While Spanish, French and other social workers will do their job properly, the CFA have adopted a new strategy. Who make up these strategies? Actually I know the answer to that question but will leave it open.

The CFA as I said earlier have hired many UK managers and social workers. When you check on the past histories of the new UK folks, you often see that they were forced out of their position or left under pressure or scandal.

In the Baby P case, the Paediatrician who last saw Peter alive ended up being struck off by the GMC in the UK. Dr Al Zayat was hired by the HSE and worked in Ireland despite the fact that she was banned from practice in the UK. As she was registered in Ireland she could legally work here. Before she was struck off she was already working for the HSE. She failed to attend her hearing as her lawyer said she was depressed and suicidal, all the same time she was seeing Irish children. I believe personally to some extent that Dr Al Zayyat was scapegoated by the UK and in particular Great Ormond Street Hospital and the media. The social worker had requested that Baby P be seen and there was little communication or follow up. Still, a Paediatrician failing to recognize 18 life-threatening injuries cannot be underestimated.

There is no barrier to Ireland hiring rogue doctors or social workers regardless of their previous histories and at the time of writing, there is no mechanism for a social worker to be struck off in Ireland.

Strategy is guided by Ideology and the ideology is that we can take 1,000 children away if it saves just one. Of course taking 999 children away is illegal but the Irish and UK governments want to legalize taking children for no good reason. Over the last 7 years I have been privy to information and have overheard disturbing conversations on the topic of the laws surrounding child protection. What escaped a lot of people's notice is an off-hand comment made by Justice Minister Alan Shatter. He said that they were seeking to "put the family courts on a constitutional basis". Alan was known as "Mr. Family Law" before becoming a politician and is well versed on the topic having written many books and scholarly articles on the topic.

Many people have said for years that the family courts are unconstitutional and illegal under Human Rights Law. How can it be legal or lawful to be tried for the same crime twice under two different Burdens of Proof, to be punished without even being accused of a crime and to be presumed guilty until you prove yourself innocent? These are questions that the Legal Fraternity have struggled with for years while the Social Work Fraternity struggled with how far they could "bend" the laws to the benefit of the Child Abuse Industry. The Irish Government also noticed this "loophole" and sought ways that children could legally be taken for no reason but the State would not be culpable and have to pay out millions in another Redress Board. Enda Kenny, during the Children's Referendum made another gaffe that few people picked up on, he said, "there would be two Children's Referendums". I don't want to delve into the realms of conspiracy theory and ask people to make a connection where there is none.

Family Law as it stands in Ireland and the UK is contrary to Human Rights Law. It is not just an abuse of the parents, but the child's rights under many sections.

What many people fail to understand is that in Ireland, the Constitution is our highest law. It is written to protect the people from the Government. The rights granted to the people of Ireland are imprescriptible; the government can't make new laws if the new law is in conflict with the constitution. Your rights are inalienable, they cannot be taken away from you and you don't need to fight for rights that you already possess. Whenever the government feels the need to have a referendum, it means that they are either giving us additional rights or they are taking rights away from us, either way, the public and not the government decides.

Of course if people genuinely had rights that are imprescriptible or alienable, we wouldn't need Human Rights Lawyers or a Supreme Court to decide if our rights had been violated.

In the past 15 years, politicians have removed rights away by holding Referenda. Where people opposed the constitutional change, the governments of the time just held another referendum until they got the desired result. In reality, the EU, the IMF and the UN are running the Irish government. They are instructed on how to run the country and then rewarded with jobs when they leave office in Ireland. The Children's Referendum was under the instruction of the UN who have constantly called for the rights of parents to be removed so that the State decides Best Interests for children. The Irish public fell for it hook, line and sinker.

When I use the term "Child Abuse Industry", it's important to realize that a Child Protection System needs an infrastructure to support it. If you ran a restaurant and you were losing money by having too many staff and not enough customers, you would have to lay staff off or bring in new customers. In the Child Abuse Industry in Ireland, I would estimate that there are at least 15,000 people who rely on the Industry for a living. While the Government employ 5,000, there are also thousands of Fosterers, people working in Residential "Care", GAL's who work in private practice of for children's "Charities", Lawyers, Liars, Psychologists, judges, court staff, agencies for fostering, adoption, vetting and about 3 times more staff than we have children in "Care". All of these people need to work to make their living. The Industry feeds of the Taxpayer to the tune of €1 Billion a year. Children grow up and turn 18 and there must to be a constant flow of children to support all these jobs. If we stopped taking children, the economic impact would be devastating to thousands of people.

When the government reduced the fees paid to Private Residential Homes from €11,500 per week per child to a maximum of €5,000 a week, one operator threatened to lay off 230 staff. He also said that for €5,000 per week per child, that "at best, all he could provide was a babysitting service". Funnily enough, the government are paying €21 million a year for empty beds in Residential

"Care" Homes and at the same time, judges are complaining that there are not enough beds available to place children in desperate need of Emergency "Care"? To my knowledge, the planned layoff of 230 staff from one contractor never occurred. The Industry wouldn't benefit if children could not be removed on suspicion, lots of money spent "assessing them", lots of money spent on private "Prosecutors" who stretch out cases and lots of "Experts", whether they lie or not, 100 "Charities" having lots of staff who need to be paid and an adoring Media who believe the system can do no wrong.

It should seem obvious to anyone that to be investigated, charged, prosecuted, convicted and punished in two separate courts and systems would seem an obvious Human Rights abuse. It would also seem obvious that a government would notice such abuse and would take action to protect its citizens. The actions of successive governments and Ministers for Justice and Children, have been to protect the Institution rather than it's Citizens, particularly it's constant failure since the inception of the State to "Cherish all of it's citizens equally". The plot thickens.

CHAPTER 6

SEX, LIES & VIDEOTAPE

In 2009 I became aware of Forced Adoption due to a case I was asked to assist on. I had no concept of adoption at the time of anything other than, "doe eyed orphans in orphanages desperately seeking a Forever Home". For years I had accepted the Hollywood portrayal and didn't give it much thought. I saw Foster Carers and Adopters as heroes who sacrificed and opened their hearts and homes to children in desperate need. I was in for a rude awakening.

I have been fascinated for the last few years at how pet owners have taken the whole concept of owning an animal and turned it around to where animals are really humans wrapped in fur. Animals are now "adopted" and potential pet "parents" are carefully screened. I love animals myself, but my view is that I would never own a pet. I had two dogs as a child and loved them dearly. One died of Distemper and I was touched at his loyalty and how he suffered in his final months. The other dog was identical and even had the same name and lived to a ripe old age. When my younger brother brought home the first dog, my father impressed upon us the importance of giving the animal a good quality of life and that if there was one day that we didn't take the dog out for a long walk that he would give the animal to a new owner.

I had many long walks and talks with Shep as a teenager and can well understand the adoration they receive from some owners or pet "Parents" as some like to be known. I can also understand the appeal of caring for a living being more vulnerable than you and how it satisfies a need in humans. The reason I would not own a pet myself is because pets require constant attention. You only have to drive around a neighborhood and hear dogs barking for no good reason. Their owners are at work and many wont even take the animals in when they come home. You have animals that have an instinct to be pack animals and belong to a pack or a family. Ignoring dogs is abuse and if you haven't got the time to devote, don't own an animal.

The adoration of pets goes so far back in human history that the cave dwellers drew pictures of their pets on the walls of their caves. Today many single people would prefer to have Fur Kids than Human Kids. Neuroscientists have recently found that the areas in the brain that are stimulated when looking at children, are the same areas stimulated when looking at pets and animals. Endorphins are released in the same way whether the viewer is looking at a child or an animal. Our brains are wired to take care of less vulnerable people. Even toddlers are "wired" to be stimulated when looking at a younger baby or young animal. There are many videos on YouTube now of where wild animals killed other animals and later found they had young and their instinct was to care for the young.

It is also interesting that the first recorded incident of a child being saved from abuse was by the Society for the Prevention of Cruelty to Animals (SPCA) in New York in 1874. Mary Ellen Wilson, then 8 years old was being severely abused by her Foster Parents and despite repeated reports to the authorities, nothing was done until the SPCA stepped in. Animals clearly had more rights than children at the time and the case was taken all the way to the Supreme Court and received much attention. This led to the formation of the NSPCC, laws governing the protection of child and the birth of Child Protection, or as I have come to call it; "the Child Abuse Industry".

Although many go into Child Protection with the best intentions, the best intentions and best interests don't translate into best practice or best outcomes for vulnerable children, and this is the crux of the issue; **does Child Protection actually benefit children?** The evidence shows that it doesn't. Nobody disputes that children should be protected, nobody. The issue is whether the current system is capable of protecting children.

I have met some lovely people who are foster carers and in every sense, they exemplify ordinary decent people who are doing their best for these children. I have equally met and heard about monsters that shouldn't be allowed near children, vulnerable or otherwise. I investigated a case recently where a young girl was being given "specially prepared meals" from food bought from a "Cheap" supermarket. The girl herself claimed that the refrigerator was off limits and the meals she received were of a lesser quality and quantity than the children of the foster "Carer".

I attempted to report this to "authorities" but was dismissed. I couldn't personally take the case to court due to the In Camera Rule and probably would have been arrested for my efforts. I did manage to get the child a solicitor of her own who agreed to take the case on. In court, the authorities argued that the child didn't need her own solicitor as she had been "represented" by a Guardian ad Litem who spoke for the child, apparently rather than speaking TO the child. The case was dismissed and the child moved to another foster home, many miles away from where she had lived for the past few years. I have heard horror stories from "Care" including rapes and have been almost powerless to intervene. For my intervention in one case a corrupt HSE lawyer went "Shopping for Judges" and was refused by the first judge. Eventually they found a judge who ordered a Committal Hearing but the case was thrown out in the Circuit Court.

The first documented case of Child Abuse was by Foster Carers, not that foster carers are any more likely to abuse, but in the original case, it had to be fought at a very high level before action was taken. It seems the situation hasn't changed much in 150 years, as today there is still no mechanism for children of "Care" to complain about their treatment. You can't complain to police., they are not allowed by law (In Camera Rule) to protect children in "Care".

In one case a father walked into a police station and had photographs of severe physical abuse his child had received in "Care". He took a great risk taking the photographs as the Contact sessions are closely monitored for the slightest infraction. When he refused to delete the photographs he was thrown out and his contact terminated as he had "Emotionally Harmed" his child by asking about the abuse. I have heard similar stories of a child showing up with a fractured jaw and the parent was warned; "Don't Ask!" I am sent photographs on a regular basis of severe injuries that if any of them had occurred in the care of their parents, the child would be removed under an Emergency Care Order until it could be proven who had perpetrated the injury and whether it was accidental or not. By default, Doctors have taken the position that if parents cannot explain injuries or medical conditions that it must be the parent's fault and the case becomes a Child Protection issue. But when children are harmed in "Care", it's an anomaly. I know of a baby taken into "Care" on the basis of a single small bruise, that in the end proved to be a Mongolian Blue Spot found in 40% of Asian babies. When the baby received an actual bruise in the hospital that could not be explained by the staff, the Doctor and social workers dismissed it as a "Red Herring".

In the case of the father, he visited his local police station and was fortunate enough to get an experienced Detective who had dealt with similar cases before and understood the law. He showed the photographs and had written verbatim what the child had said. The detective, a father himself, was very disturbed by the evidence. He explained the situation to the father. "Look, I've been here before. If I accept your complaint, I must go to the social worker and ask her for her version of the story, it's only fair right? The problem is, that as soon as I talk to the social worker, you my friend have broken the In Camera Rule and will likely be arrested and jailed." Naturally the father didn't proceed with the case. What happened next was that the child was placed in a different foster home, of course many miles away and the social workers cut contact with the father despite being under the orders of the court that the child see his father every week for a specified time period. I have witnessed this and heard many others tell the same story.

What I have since advised parents to do at contact is to dial 999 and call Police to investigate and remove the child when necessary as they are obligated to do under Section 12 of the Child Care Act. The likely outcome in every case is that the child will be punished for being abused by having the foster placement changed and visits with their parents restricted. The child will always be the loser in these cases and judges will go along with any dictate of the social worker. I still strongly advise parents to do this, as occasionally you will get a judge who is not prepared to accept Child Abuse and Neglect.

In one case that I am still dealing with, a 4 year old boy with Downs Syndrome who died in "Care" in the UK, the father last saw his son alive 4 days before he died. The haunting image of how this child looked before his death was widely distributed on the social media and yet not one Media Outlet would post the image. As the case is still ongoing until we finally receive some form of justice and inquiry into his death, I must refrain from giving further details unless such information is already in the public domain.

The father was so disturbed that he demanded that his son be taken immediately to a doctor. This was ignored and the child died four days later. The father says it is to his lasting regret that he didn't phone the Police and an Ambulance, as his son would have survived. The cover-up by authorities in this case is shocking beyond belief. The lies given to the media are clearly disputed by documents held by the parents and the advocates with the family to get justice. The entire case would probably, by itself make an excellent novel.

While the In Camera Rule is intended to protect children, it clearly doesn't. It is used by incompetent people to cover up their mistakes and protect the system from any scrutiny. In the UK when the question was asked in Parliament, how many people are jailed each year under the In Camera Rule? Even the Justice Secretary Harriet Harmon was surprised to find the figure at 200 a year. In more recent years the figure is estimated at 400 a year in the UK and at least 40 cases a year in Ireland. Those statistics may not be accurate but I make no apology, as the government will not publish accurate figures, the truth is they don't know. In one case in Ireland a father was jailed in secret for telling his mother that his children had been taken into "Care".

The In Camera Rule is used in a secret court where no media or public are present. This defies the principle of Justice that Justice must be seen to be done. When one such committal was done in the UK, the case was immediately appealed to the High Court in the form of a Writ of Habeas Corpus, which incidentally was held in secret. What occurred was that the President of the Court instructed judges to open up the court for the sentencing so that at least the public could not claim that people were jailed in secret, in secret courts. The trial is held in secret but then the judge opens the doors and allows people to enter as he/she imposes the sentence. The public or media hear the offender is jailed for up to two years but they are not entitled to know what the crime was. What a perfectly corrupt system. Incidentally, Justice Minister Alan Shatter extended the fines and term of imprisonment for people who violate the In Camera Rule in Ireland and no such rule that justice must be seen to be done was instructed to Irish judges.

I mentioned earlier that "opening up" of family courts in the UK had no effect. Journalists wont report the right cases and spend days in court and then being instructed that they are not allowed to report "anything to anyone". When the high profile cases make the news, it's usually because of an advocate tipping off a journalist. In these proceedings in the High Court, the In Camera Rule still applies and journalists are restricted on what they can report. No such restrictions apply in criminal cases and when children are involved as witnesses or victims, the media always respect revealing the identity of the child. In one case in Ireland where 4 newspapers were fined, they had not identified the child but locals knew the family involved. The locals would have known anyway because social workers often go door-to-door to "dig up dirt" on parents and break the In Camera Rule which seemingly doesn't apply to them.

In the original case I wrote about first, the father is seen in his community as a sex offender and the child as a victim of sexual abuse, even though no abuse of the child took place. On one hand social workers can violate the rule with impunity by trying to dig up dirt from neighbors, in courts the media are held to a different standard and cannot report "Anything to Anybody". As I predicted, "opening up" of the courts would have little effect, just as it had no effect in the UK. And again I have to ask the question; "how does this benefit children?" If the rule prevents crimes being reported that occur in "Care", it clearly doesn't benefit them.

CHAPTER 7

THE SÉANCE

"Let's all hold hands and contact the truth"

I couldn't but help get the feeling when I left a family courtroom one time that I had just attended a Séance. A social worker and a GAL went into a trance and began channeling the spirits of "What If" and "Maybe" and "Risk" and "Best Interests" and "Attachment Theory" and "Enmeshed", I couldn't help but feel I saw the ghost of Sigmund Freud crossing the room by the time the Psychologist gave testimony. It was a surreal experience even though I have spent time in Criminal Courts observing and on jury duty.

I like attending meetings; I have always thought that they are a practical alternative to work. However in meetings I have two choices, sleep or take control over the meeting myself as I hate having my time wasted. I have often wondered if judges felt the same. I've worked in very high productive manufacturing places for a large part of my working life. I've seen morning meetings where the leader sits in a room with a few others and many people will pop their head in, and in 30 seconds they are gone rather than sitting for 30 minutes where there was no value added to your attendance. I have seen an hourly meeting every day, 5 days a week with 18 attending which was costing the company 90 man/hours a week without adding any value to the company. I tend to notice things like that having worked in manufacturing and many other areas.

Sleeping in court is not an option neither is speaking out-of-turn. The "meeting" tends to be long if they are not just "Mentions" or simple cases that are largely decided by the lawyers beforehand and only needs to be rubber-stamped by the judge. But you can be lulled into a false sense of security and the stakes are extremely high, especially for the child. Myself and other advocates have always advised parents not to use Legal Aid lawyers, as you are not going to get proper representation. As Ian Josephs, himself a trained lawyer says, they are known as "Legal Aid Losers" in the trade. Sometimes however you can get a regular solicitor who because you live outside a large city, will take on your case and get paid by the Legal Aid Board.

Ian Josephs says that most will give very bad advice, "don't fight, the judge wont like it when you defend yourself" or "Trust me, you don't even need to go inside the courtroom". The Legal Aid loser then comes out and says "sorry, you lost your children". I witnessed this myself one time in southern Ireland when a Legal Aid solicitor told her client; "the HSE are there to protect your child" the mother just looked at me and never saw that solicitor again. After we had left the office the solicitor was on the phone to the HSE manager. In Ireland, the Justice Minister raised the application fee for legal aid. In the UK they eliminated legal aid altogether for family law cases. It has been widely noted that there has been a large increase in Litigants In Person and McKenzie Friends assisting parents, much to the displeasure of the Law Industry. In my own view, the adversarial nature of Family Court needs to be scrapped. The Government needs to eliminate lawyers from all Family Law cases. Let the social worker argue against the parents and let the parents speak in court, many are not even given that opportunity. There would be no "Stretching of Cases" that the current private law firms do and the cost to the Child Abuse Industry would be devastating. Of course the cost to children would be immense, as not many children would be removed on spurious grounds. This wouldn't satisfy the egos of the Crusaders and many children's NGO's would be forced to lay off staff and close their doors.

Your children are too important to leave anything to chance. Ian Josephs advises to represent yourself if you are capable, at least that way the judge will get to hear you speak. In many cases children are removed and the parents never get to speak.

As McKenzie Friends we spend a great deal of time on cases and go to court fully prepared, as do the parents we help. In many cases we also help solicitors and barristers with case law and especially in medical cases. Lawyers are not Doctors and don't know the correct questions to ask. Even when you give them a list of questions, when the expert answers, the lawyer doesn't know if their answer is correct or not. Lawyers do not have the luxury of doing investigations and research. Many Trial Lawyers are prepped on the case 15 minutes before court. Medical cases are especially difficult and can take months to do all the research. In a surprising number of medical cases we have handled, they have often been based on the misdiagnosis of doctors practicing outside of their training and experience. Again, I put this down to corrupt judges who wont insist on a second medical opinion and allow "Experts" who have delusions of adequacy.

One such fictitious condition that parents are often accused of is Shaken Baby Syndrome. In a decade in Ireland there were a reported 21 cases, only one case actually made it to a criminal court, the other 20 cases made it to family court on suspicion of causing an injury that has been proven scientifically impossible. Shaken Baby Syndrome is a junk science with no scientific basis. I'm sure that in the passing of time that SBS will be relegated to the dustbin of history but for now, it still exists in the minds of physicians and prosecutors who have not kept up with medical science.

The legend goes that if you shake a baby, the biomechanical effect is that the brain flops back and forth, which causes shearing of the Bridging Veins in the Dura Mater of the brain. Apparently the violent shaking back and forth does not cause a neck injury and no classic "thumb imprints" on the anterior chest from holding the baby firmly enough to violently shake an infant with such force that the brain is injured. The effect on the brain and eyes is believed to be such that it is the equivalent of a 30' fall or a fall from a 3-story building. The symptoms of SBS are known as the Triad of injuries and include, Subdural Bleeding, Retinal Bleeding and Axonal Injury. In some prosecutions only 2 of the 3 were present and children as old as 4 were supposedly shaken. In one case in Ireland, his father supposedly shook a baby while the baby was strapped into a car seat in the back of the car while the father was seated in the drivers seat. Investigating many of these cases doesn't require any more than common sense to see that these cases are witch-hunts in every sense of the word.

But, the Science doesn't support any of the Theories. Some important facts about SBS that you need to know;

•   Nobody has ever witnessed a baby being shaken and then that baby demonstrating even **one** of the Triad of injuries.

•   In the history of every single prosecution nobody has been caught "Red Handed" and every case was prosecuted solely on the fact that the accused was alone with the infant even for one minute.

•   In hundreds of cases where babysitters were caught "red handed" violently shaking infants on "Nanny-cams", not one single shaken baby has ever demonstrated a single symptom of the Triad, ever.

•   In cases where the accused admitted guilt, they admitted to resuscitative shaking only and never shook the baby while conscious. Shaking is a normal response even for Paramedics to determine Level of Consciousness. As a Basic Life Support Instructor I used to teach "Shake & Shout" for infant and adult resuscitation as per the Heart Foundation curriculum.

•   In the only case in Ireland that was prosecuted, the father admitted, "slamming" the baby. The baby had other horrific injuries but they chose to prosecute this case as an SBS case. It was clearly not a case of SBS.

•   Biomechanical studies conducted to the Gold Standard have proven that short falls from a bed or a couch onto a non-Newtonian Surface will generate the forces believed necessary to cause the Triad of injuries. A fall onto a concrete floor will generate the necessary force even if the floor is carpeted.

With the correct type of underlay much of the force will be absorbed.

• Biomechanical studies performed to the Gold Standard have proven that violent shaking of a Biofedelic Mannequin by a team of athletic men could not generate the type or amount of force that an infant shaking himself in a Fisher Price Jumperoo could generate.

• The Doctor who wrote the original paper wishes, "he had never written the darned thing". Dr Norman Gutkelch has for years testified for the defense.

Prosecutors love SBS, you don't need a smoking gun, a witness, an admission of guilt, a single bruise, a neck injury or other forensics, you just need to prove that someone was alone with the baby for as little as a minute, a doctor to say that the Triad is present and anything else is unimportant. Any expert who testifies on behalf of the defense is likely to be targeted by police and prosecutors. Prosecutors have tried to eliminate Biomechanical studies from being used because the Biofedelic Mannequin does not represent a human child. The infant crash test dummy used in studies by the US Department of Transportation Safety (DTS) to improve safety standards such as vehicles, infant car seats, crash helmets and many other things that may have an impact on the safety of children, is apparently not sufficiently representative of a human infant but is more than sufficient to certify the safety of Baby Seats, Helmets and Air Bags.

The only way that shaking could be proven to the satisfaction of some people is if a human infant was given MRI scans and then violently shaken. However such evidence exists even on YouTube of babies being violently shaken, were examined and this evidence is ignored.

SBS has become an industry, like many things in the Child Abuse Industry. There are instructors teaching course on "Purple Crying" and not shaking babies, there are plastic dolls that are available that have no scientific basis that are being sold to hospitals and social workers, there are experts testifying on both sides of the courts, all making money from the SBS theory. A theory that was based on a 1940's experiment by the DOT where monkeys were strapped into chairs and shuttled back and forth until they died. At no point did human adults shake infant monkeys and the autopsies did not consider the Triad. The "Science" grew over the years and the first case prosecuted was the Louise Woodward trial in Boston.

Having read many post mortem reports and expert reports, I could write volumes on SBS but I am not a physician. What I can do however is translate and explain the "Science" involved for lawyers so they can ask the right questions and know what the correct responses should be.

SBS is losing a lot of ground scientifically with so many cases now being overturned in the USA and other countries. The beauty of learning about SBS is that you only have to spend a few hours on YouTube and watch babies being shaken, or shaking themselves in JollyJumpers, BabyBouncers or see Yoga instructors, bad babysitters and other violently shaking infants and none of these babies suffer the Triad?

In a case of Rickets in Ireland, a Paediatrician was asked how a baby sustained 21 "fractures" and he speculated the baby had been shaken, had received fractures but no bruises and not a single symptom of the Triad?

Which begs a question of Medical Science, how can doctors claim that a baby was shaken when that baby doesn't have a single bruise, when no neck injury is present, when retinal Hemorrhage is not present on the initial MRI but later shows up as the Intracranial Pressure increases? The fact is that they have no interest in keeping up with medical science and there are no consequences for doctors when they misdiagnose a baby and the baby later dies because they were treating the wrong signs and symptoms.

The original Biomechanical Studies were performed by Dr John Lloyd are posted on YouTube. The fact is that shaking cannot cause SBS; it's caused by short falls in many of the cases although many other conditions must be ruled out. Doctors are told that short falls cannot cause the Triad and don't bother keeping up with the science. When babies present to hospitals after falling from a couch or a bed, it is often dismissed. If an MRI were taken shortly after the fall, the baby would typically be asymptomatic. The bleeding occurs over days and builds up intracranial pressure. As the brain gives very few clues as to its damage the symptoms are typically nothing more than the baby is cranky. The signs and symptoms don't become apparent until the baby dies.

You would think that prosecutors and doctors would err on the side of caution and screaming from the rooftops that parents should never place even a non-mobile baby on a couch or bed unsecured. You would think that given the new scientific studies that are showing short falls can generate far higher amounts of force than shaking that perhaps one Paediatrician somewhere would do some further study and publish a scholarly article and the debate can begin, but no, Medicine has unfortunately degenerated into a Religion based on a proposition of Faith and anyone brave enough to stick their heads above the parapet and ask that question, will be branded a heretic. I know of many physicians who do ask the tough questions in the interest of Science and many have been warned by Medical Boards and hospitals that if they go against the grain of popular belief, they are likely to be struck off.

Science shouldn't need defending. A mathematical formula doesn't care what you or I believe and doesn't feel the need to defend itself, in fact it doesn't feel at all, it just exists. Science has always relied on questions there are no absolutes. Even the theory that water boils at 100*C at atmospheric pressure is a theory, and it can be challenged at any time. It's also an experiment that can be replicated at any time by anyone. By constantly challenging a scientific theory, the questions either support or negate the theory. The theory comes out stronger or is called into question. In science there are no stupid questions and anyone can ask a question. By eliminating the ability of anyone to ask a question, we water down the entire field of science. Where other fields of science are making great leaps and bounds, medicine it seems has taken a retrograde path into the Dark Ages. Psychology has weakened the practice of Medicine by presenting itself as a science.

SBS is only one of many theories where science has become a position of faith. Far too many cases of Rickets have been misdiagnosed for far too long. Many of the cases have been very disturbing; babies have died because the signs and symptoms have been missed. I have also assisted in many Rickets cases around the world. In one case at a very early stage, the Paediatrician believed that he clearly had a severe case of child abuse. We gathered as many medical details and history as we could, put the information together and send it off to world-renowned experts on the topic of Vitamin Deficiency Disorders, among them Hematologists, Forensic Pathologists and Radiologists. All our experts said this was such a classic case of Rickets that the Paediatrician involved should be reported to the Medical Council. We presented the Paediatrician with a list of medical tests that our experts needed performed and a factsheet of the latest research and studies. We even offered the Paediatrician the opportunity to contact our experts to discuss the case but no, this was child abuse pure and simple and he was saving a baby's life by having the baby removed from it's parents. When the doctor was presented with this, he said that; "Rickets was something that only occurred many years ago in deepest, darkest Africa" even though we provided scholarly articles from reputable sources to show that Rickets is at epidemic proportions for the last decade.

The baby supposedly had 21 "Fractures" confirmed by a Radiologist. I sent the scans to our experts and they said that this was a classic Rickets presentation. Radiology is not a reliable method of screening for Rickets or Vitamin Deficiency Conditions, the only reliable way is microscopic examination and even then by an expert in the field of Rickets. While an x ray can show a broken bone it is not reliable enough to tell how the bone became broken. The Doctor dismissed relevant questions such as; "how do you break the longest, strongest bone in the body without leaving so much as a bruise?" In the case of this infant, he was sick since birth and had been seen by GP's, Nurses and Hospitals almost every week and never had a single bruise in his life. How can an abused baby have 21 "fractures" and never had a bruise? Surprisingly, the baby with 21 "fractures" but no cast was released from hospital and placed in Foster "Care", not given any treatment or medication. It was becoming beyond a joke.

But even more disturbing, one of our experts expressed concerns for the life of the baby. Because he had obviously been misdiagnosed, there was a grave danger that the Paediatrician had missed a more serious condition and the baby could die or his condition worse and he would suffer life-long consequences. The doctor had already arrived at a diagnosis of child abuse and he needed to look no further or give any further treatment. It was a very disturbing development and we needed to get before the judge immediately and get a second opinion, the baby's life could depend on it.

The social workers, so determined to prove a case of child abuse, saw it as a ploy by the parents to weaken the case they were building up against the parents. Fortunately the baby survived the social workers and did recover in "Care", primarily because he was no longer being breastfed. It was found that the mother suffered from genetic condition, that the baby was never tested for and was breastfeeding. The baby's problems started in the womb and the "Fractures" were likely the result of the trauma of being born. He eventually recovered and is doing well today.

It is clear from this case that the Witch Hunting techniques used by the doctors and social workers, never put the baby at the heart of the issue. If the baby had died because of misdiagnosis, the judge wouldn't be stepping forward to accept responsibility for his role in denying a second opinion. The doctors wouldn't accept any responsibility either and the social workers would get off on one excuse or another. No lessons would have been learned and it would have been just another death in "Care" of another nameless child and the public would have know nothing about it as the system operates in complete secrecy. If Child Protection was actually about protecting children, the social workers or judge should have been the first people to suggest a second medical opinion. If the system saw this case for the epic failure that it was, they would develop strategies to deal with such cases and rule out other possibilities. Simply by implementing a rule that doctors must obtain a second opinion from a qualified expert, would save the lives of many children and prevent them being removed because of medical misdiagnosis.

While the Criminal Justice System uses Forensic Medicine, in family court it takes nothing more than suspicion or the misdiagnosis or an arrogant and incompetent doctor to destroy a child's life by getting caught up in the Witch Hunting for child abusers. This case is far from unusual, similar cases have occurred for years and yet doctors still cant seem to get it through their heads that Rickets is at epidemic proportions. Perhaps the lack of sunlight in recent years in the Northern Hemisphere, the bad advice of slapping on Factor 50 sunscreen on children to prevent sun damage, or the poor quality of food today or that children spend far too much time indoors has led us to the point of an epidemic. As sunlight is a necessity for human life, why are doctors telling us to stay out of the sun for the recommended 1 hour a day as they are doing in other countries such as Norway?

In the case of Louise Mason she had a similar misdiagnosis and it took years to sort out. She wrote a book on her experience and appeared on Irish TV3.

The case of Baby Jayden Wray was another spectacular failure by doctors and unfortunately Jayden died. His grieving parents were wrongly accused of murder but fortunately this was a criminal case and the parents were able to prove their innocence. Again, Great Ormond Street Hospital for Children was implicated as they have been many times in cases such as Baby P.

I have also been involved in cases in the USA that beggar belief. Over and over you see social workers destroying lives of children based on nothing more than suspicion. If doctors and social workers were competent to begin with, such cases would never happen and babies would not die. These cases don't happen in other European countries because social workers are seen as carers of children and not prosecutors of parents. You can't be an advocate and a prosecutor at the same time the roles are incompatible. In other countries only Police and judges have the power to investigate.

Perhaps the worst case that ever came to light was the case of Mark & Nicky Webster. The couple took their sick child to a hospital, which unleashed a nightmare that the family has lived with to this day. They were accused of child abuse, their 3 children taken into "Care" and were arrested. What followed was 2 separate investigations by 2 separate bodies under 2 different Burdens of Proof. The Criminal trial took a long time to come to court where the family law case was decided rather quickly, they would lose their 3 children to Forced Adoption even though they were not convicted of any crime.

At the end of the Criminal Trial they were found not guilty and the "injuries" to the child was in fact a serious case of Rickets. At an early stage of this child's life the baby was constantly sick and didn't take too well to breastfeeding. The doctor advised them that the baby was lactose intolerant and the best alternative was Soy Milk based baby formula. What they were not told is that Soy doesn't have Vitamin D and even though they followed the medical advise, the baby was becoming sicker as time wore on. This is an identical story to the Louise Mason case up to this point in the story.

While they were waiting for the Criminal proceeding to find them not guilty, their 3 children were Forcibly Adopted. When they were vindicated they went to appeal and what followed was in my opinion, one of the worst decisions ever by a judge and in the opinion on many others, a serious miscarriage of justice.

They were told that adoptions were permanent and there was no hope of having their children returned. In the judgment the judge stated that return the children to the Webster's would cause great distress to the adoptive "parents". What I have always wondered is how could the children's new "parents" reconcile the fact that they had essentially stolen these children from the Webster's. The story received very broad media attention and the Webster's appeared on TV many times, often accompanied by John Hemming MP who had been actively involved in the case.

The sad story of the Webster's doesn't end there, as they were seen as child abusers in the family court system, when Nicky became pregnant again, social workers said they were going to take their baby at birth to be Forcibly Adopted.

The couple fled to Ireland under a media storm, and the HSE who fear being seen in a bad light, didn't take the baby at birth. Eventually the council backed down as long as the parents made certain concessions and they were "allowed" to keep their 4th child. However, to this day they are still registered as child abusers, which prevents Mark from being vetted and holding jobs such as taxi driver. The Webster's never received any compensation or even an apology. If they happen to see one of their 3 children who were forcibly adopted, they could be jailed for any contact with them. The doctor who misdiagnosed the baby was never punished.

You may see some patterns emerging in the ideology of these witch-hunts at this point.

John Waters in my view is one of the best journalists and writers of our generation. You either love John or you hate him, but even the haters will read every word he writes, if only to find some little flaw in his thinking. He comes off appearing as a human being and not an automaton, which some love and others hate. This is the kind of journalism I enjoy because it's thought provoking, it's human. There are no sacred cows that John won't attack or sacrifice in the interest of debate. John has written for many years about Child Protection and Fathers rights, he is the only journalist in Ireland brave enough to utter harsh words about our dysfunctional system of Child "Protection" and the Industry that has sprung up around it.

John wrote an excellent piece on the topic of Witch Hunts and made some valuable points that we should bear in mind when discussing the topic. He pointed out that the Witch Hunters of Salem were good, God-fearing people. Their belief in the Devil equalled their belief in God. Because they could only explain the world around them in the context of religion, they killed many of their own innocent citizens. What had actually occurred in Salem is that a fungus on the corn crop produced a similar effect to LSD, a mind-altering drug.

I visited 3 times and did the tourist thing in the village of Salem. I have always tried to reconcile how such atrocities occurred but the final pieces of the puzzle didn't emerge until I had read John's piece. What happened in Salem is that people under the influence of LSD would see someone sweeping their front porch with a corn broom but in their minds, the sweepers were floating through the air riding the broom. These were deeply religious people who never drank alcohol and had no concept whatsoever of being under the influence of anything other than God, or in this case, Devils and Witches.

What happened is now termed a "Moral Panic" or "Folk Devil". Such moral panics have repeated themselves many times over the years. In Germany in the 1930's a madman managed to convince an entire population that a small minority race was responsible for all the ills of society. In 1929 of course there was a global meltdown of the financial system that started with the Wall Street crash and every country was suffering "Austerity". By dehumanizing Jews and

Gypsies they could be reduced to vermin in the minds of the public and eliminated.

The typical strategy by the government was; "Problem, Reaction, Solution". It is amazing how often we see this being used if we look close enough. The government shows us a problem and asks for solutions, by over-stating the extent of the problem the public become worried and cry "something must be done"; the government then implements the solution to an adoring public. If the government just passed the law to begin with there would be outcry but when the public is recruited unwittingly, they will actually demand the solution.

By over-stating the extent of child abuse and neglect over the years, the adoring public cries out for the solution without any resistance. Their faith in the system is based on a position of belief and not evidence. Even when you present them with the evidence, they still wont accept anything that doesn't fit into their beliefs.

If I were to say that child abuse is rare, people simply wouldn't believe me. No amount of showing graphs and statistics would have any impact when people base their decisions on a position of faith and belief. I could show crime statistics to show that the crimes of child abuse and neglect haven't changed much in decades and yet, the size of the Child Abuse Industry in certain countries has doubled in a decade and not in other countries.

For the past year I have been noticing a drip-feed of information that would lead people to believe that there is a severe shortage of social workers in Ireland. Today's headline is that 10,000 Irish children have not been assigned a social worker. It's only a matter of time before someone shouts out "let's add another 260 and see what happens". What these people forget that is during the last "shortage of social workers" we added 260 more and the result was that Ireland took 3.7 times more children into "care" in 2011 as a direct result. So if we add another 260, isn't the likely outcome that they will take more children into "Care" and the problem will repeat itself over and over? Wouldn't the logical solution be to reduce the workforce by 260 and take fewer children?

One of the more dramatic Moral Panics took place in California was known as the McMartin Daycare Scandal. It was the result of another Moral Panic about Satanic Ritual Abuse (SRA). If I were to tell people that SRA did not exist before 1979, few people would believe me. SRA is a Folk Devil that spread even to Ireland and the UK in the 1980's. Celebrities were appearing on talk shows and disclosing the most outrageous stories, many of them quite impossible.

The origin of Satanic Ritual Abuse was from a book entitled "Michelle Remembers" in 1979, before this date there is no records anywhere of organized SRA. In history there have been stories and cases such as Vlad the Impaler but most other folk legend comes from art and illustrations of devils. It's reputed that in Ireland, that St Patrick didn't drive the snakes out of Ireland but the evidence seems to suggest that he banished a cult of serpent worshipers from Ireland.

SRA is a myth that is popular with conspiracy theorists. They have made tenuous connections to secretive organizations such as the Freemasons, the Illuminati, the Rothschild's, the British Royal Family and many more. By 1980 the panic was spreading and people were starting to "remember" fragmented memories of incidents, which became the stuff of Hollywood legend and talk shows. One of the other myths put out by the book Michelle Remembers was the theory of Fragmented or Recovered Memory Syndrome; it is still in wide use today.

"Michelle Remembers" was a book written about Michelle Smith by her therapist. A convention of Psychologists became very interested in the concept of recovering memory fragments and the entire theory of Fractured and Recovered Memory Syndrome was born. Pre 1979, Michelle Smith was the only

documented case, after the release of the book thousands of people came out to say they had been placed on sacrificial altars by mysterious people dressed as devils, pentagrams figured heavily in their "recollections". Therapists everywhere were seizing, and cashing in, on this new "discovery" and it gave birth to Past Life Regression and numerous cases of people remembering being "beamed up" into UFO's and being anally probed. The myth of Fractured Memory was spread to the UK by 2 social workers and rapidly gained currency. It was after all an accepted Psychological Theory by now and Police forces, prosecutors were all caught up in this Moral Panic. In Ireland, Gardai dug up graves and other sites and continues to this day but have never found any evidence to support "Ritual Abuse". Every major Police force in the world has investigated alleged cases of SRA and not a single bone fragment has been found anywhere in the world.

In the McMartin Pre-school trial, allegations started to surface from infants who attended. The claims grew more outrageous by the day and most were based on SRA. The trial ran from 1987 to 1990. After six years of criminal trials, no convictions were obtained, and all charges were dropped in 1990. When the trial ended in 1990 it had been the longest and most expensive criminal trial in American history and also the most extensive Witch Hunt ever conducted.

In the UK, The Cleveland Inquiry and the Rochdale Scandal of 1990 were also heavily featuring SRA based on the evidence of social workers. SRA and Fragmented and Recovered Memory Syndrome were widely taught in social work schools from the 1980's on. The book Michelle Remembers was widely discredited and Police failed to prove any of the allegations, nevertheless, social work and psychology had two new theories whether discredited or not.

Even though the Fractured Memory was discredited it is still used today, even in Irish courts, there was one prosecuted and a conviction made in 2014 on the basis of testimony of a "Therapist" who still practices this.

The worst miscarriage of justice in Ireland was the case of Nora Wall and Pablo McCabe. The trial was presided over by Mr. Justice Carney who still deals with most rape cases in Ireland. It was alleged that Nora Wall, a nun at the infamous Kilkenny orphanage, had held down a 10-year-old girl while McCabe raped her. I wont go into all of the details of the case, as it is available on Wikipedia as are other cases I mentioned here. The basis of the case was on "Repressed memory" in which the accuser alleged she had flashbacks of the rape at age 12.

Nora Wall became the first person in Ireland to be convicted on the basis of Fractured or Recovered Memory, she was the first woman to be convicted of rape and she was convicted along with Pablo Wall and received a life sentence. She was released from jail four days into her sentence when it was found that the DPP had withheld vital evidence from the defense. Eventually her accuser recanted her story and it was found that the Gardai had done a very poor job of investigating the case. She was a few years later exonerated in the High Court. Despite being exonerated, she has never received any compensation from the State for her ordeal. A very small sum was offered however she refused. Her prosecutor later became Director of the DPP. Judge Paul Carney still looks after rape cases.

What is interesting about the Nora Wall case is how she could have been found guilty in a justice system that is supposed to be predicated on the belief that 10 people should go free before 1 innocent person is convicted. Also interesting is that even before she convicted, numerous people were condemning her. When it comes to cases of sexual abuse of children no limits seem to exist to the vile diatribe that will be leveled against the accused, not the convicted, but those merely accused. When the sentence was handed down, it was the most severe possible under sentencing guidelines. At the time the scandal of the abuse in religious institutions was at fever pitch. It seems that even the judge was swayed to give the maximum sentence based on public opinion at the time. These are exactly the conditions that exist in a climate of Moral Panic.

The media whipped up the frenzy and the dregs of the newspaper industry gave huge attention to the story. The "Sunday World" did an "exclusive" front page spread and "Journalist" Paul Williams made tenuous connections that Wall had supplied victims to convicted paedophile priest Brendan Smyth, based on a counselor who allegedly worked with victims. Having worked with victims of sexual assault myself, I could not imagine any counselor, therapist or volunteer disclosing such information. However, the Sunday World went ahead with the story and later lost a libel case against Nora Wall and were forced to pay €175,000 in compensation to Wall. Despite the large award, little coverage was given in any media of the compensation. The only journalist who called the story correctly and gave a balanced account was Kevin Myers.

Extract from the judgement of the Court of Criminal Appeal on 16 December 2005 "It seems to this court that the applicant was further prejudiced during the course of her trial by evidence of which the defence had no prior notification, namely, that Regina Walsh recalled the alleged episodes of rape by reference to 'flashbacks and/or retrieved memory'. There was no scientific evidence of any sort adduced to explain the phenomenon of 'flashbacks' and/or 'retrieved memory', nor was the applicant in any position to meet such a case in the absence of prior notification thereof."

My final analysis of this case is that the case would never have come to trial if Gardaí had conducted a competent investigation to begin with. The DPP should never have prosecuted the case without first ensuring that Gardaí had investigated the source of the allegations and if there was any doubt, not prosecuted the case without a reasonable hope of success. The judge should not have been influenced in any way in judgment or sentencing. The newspapers should have reported fairly what happened without resorting to Gutter Press tactics and saved themselves a lot of money. If a climate of a Moral Panic had not existed at the time, the case would never have come to trial. If Fractured or Recovered Memory were barred from being used as evidence the entire case would not have got past the DPP.

If we don't learn the lessons of history, we are doomed to repeat it. Rather than governments allowing and rewarding social workers and psychologists to create Moral Panics and Witch Hunts, the governments should be trying to prevent such a climate to occur.

I haven't even scratched the surface of the miscarriages of justice that have occurred yet but for the sake of brevity I will just cover a few more.

The case of Eddie Hernon and Dr Moira Woods is another fine testament to how Moral Panics, social services and the Irish justice system, when put together can create miscarriages of justice and destroy the lives of children and their parents.

Eddie is a personal hero of mine and to many. If his case were examined closely it would prove to be a damning indictment to everything that is wrong with Child Protection and Justice. The case spans over many years but took 16 years to get some form of justice.

Eddie had to leave Ireland to find work as many fathers in Ireland did for decades. He left his wife and daughter in Ireland and went to work in London. On a visit to see him in London, his daughter experienced a spot of blood on her underwear. Her mother took her to a series of doctors as the "nothing to worry about". The mother's cousin began to circulate rumors that she believed Eddie had sexually assaulted the child. After the visit to London the mother and daughter returned to Dublin and again saw a consultant, nothing abnormal had been detected; the mother sought to quell the rumors and was advised to take the child to the Rotunda Hospital to eliminate any suspicion.

At this time in the 1980's the concept of Sexual Assault and Rape being treated differently from other crimes was beginning to gain currency. The Rotunda had set up SATU; the Sexual Assault Treatment Unit had recently been set up and was being run by Dr Moira Woods. Woods had been a controversial figure even outside of Medicine and was known as an activist and was involved in many "feminist" activities. She also married Cathal Goulding a controversial IRA figure at the time.

When Moira Woods examined the daughter and suspected sexual assault even though 2 other physicians had not suspected this. A Consultant Gynecologist at the Adelaide Hospital in Dublin had previously examined the child and the consultant wrote a letter stating; I have reassured (mother) that everything is in order. I could detect no evidence of trauma". The original diagnosis made the day after the blood spot was found was a "small graze, probably the result of the child's own manipulation. The mother does not feel there is any possibility of sexual abuse". However, Eddie was kept away from his daughter for the next 3 ½ years.

Eddie tried reporting the case to Gardai and the courts but the mother was warned by social workers that if she sought to have the files released to the court, that her daughter would be taken into "Care".

As a side note to this story, I mentioned earlier that the HSE claimed in 2011 that there were 541 "confirmed" cases of sexual assault of children and yet there were not 541 Garda investigation or 541 DPP prosecutions. It's also interesting to note that in the Dail, it was mentioned that there appears to be a "Turf War" between the HSE and Gardai when it comes to sexual assault of children. I would also like to mention that I have pointed this anomaly out to politicians and to the Irish Media but there seems to little interest in anyone getting to the bottom of whether the HSE (CFA) are letting off about 500 paedophiles a year or whether the CFA are "confirming" sexual assault of children and removing these children from homes when they have not in fact been sexually assaulted. It is very disturbing that Gardai are not investigating the sexual assault of children. In my own case, trying to report the rape of an underage girl in "Care" resulted in corrupt HSE lawyers trying to jail others and myself for reporting a crime.

Eddie's story did not end when he won his case against the Eastern Health Board and was allowed unrestricted access to his daughter. Many other fathers had contacted him and claimed that, Woods and SATU too wrongly accused them. Eddie had filed a complaint to the Irish Medical Council, however it took 10 years for the case to be heard as the Fitness to Practice Hearing was strongly contested by Woods and others with legal wrangling. Eventually Woods was found guilty of Professional Misconduct although she was not struck off the Medical Register. Woods sold her considerable Property Portfolio and moved to Tuscany where she "practices" as a Bed & Breakfast Owner. Neither Eddie nor others ever received any apology. A more in-depth version of the story is available on a website entitled IrishSalem.com along with many other horror stories.

Eddie went on hunger strike when camped outside the Dail. In the process he suffered a heart attack. A form of vindication came for Eddie and his family when they won their case against the State in 2011, however in the article in the Irish Times, Eddie, the man who had brought down Moira Woods, was not even mentioned by name.

You tend to see a pattern of Radical Feminism that emerges from many of these horror stories. Men are evil beasts and apparently the world would be better off if women ran it. Given that the practice of Social Work is heavily weighed with women and a few Radical Male Feminists, I shudder to think of what other fields of endeavor like politics would be like without a gender balance. I have been a Feminist most of my life, but I have never been "Radical" in any of my endeavors. As a male, I recognize that for many years that there has been an imbalance and that women have come off worse and are under-represented in many areas. I also feel that to a large extent that, "We've come a long way baby" in redressing many, but not all, areas. I have also always believed that inequality will never be totally eliminated not just for women, but also for persons of different races or religions, there will always be some hint of racism and prejudice that is inherent in all human beings. I'm reading an opinion piece in the newspaper today where Frances Fitzgerald feels that "We need more female leaders, it's just good business practice", it seem though that having inequality in Parenting is just fine. Thousands of fathers are written out of their children's lives, often by courts and social workers and the fact that these children will likely have poorer outcomes in life is lost on the Minister, herself a social worker by trade.

I can remember visiting India in small towns and villages where children had never seen a Caucasian. I had children who ran away from me and others more brave who wanted to touch my skin to see if I was "real". I remember as a young child in the 1960's in Henry Street, Dublin when a black man walked down the street. Everybody stopped to see him and a few old ladies made a "sign of the Cross" as he passed. This is not racism; it is simply an instinctive reaction present when we see "Strangers". I have also noticed a phenomenon in the last decade where Irish men see beautiful Polish and Russian women in Ireland and their reaction I believe is a different instinct coming into play. Diversity has been a very good thing generally, if only to enlarge the Irish Gene Pool. Our xenophobia is improving slightly, but it doesn't explain why an inordinate number of foreign national children have ended up in Irish State "Care".

My first experience with Radical Feminism was when I was asked to be the only male volunteer at a Women's Crisis Centre. It should have clicked at the time that this was a form of discrimination against me. They were looking for a "man around the house" to do "male things" such as fixing and heavy lifting that women seem to be incapable of. I was carefully screened, Police checks, interviews and endless training. It was engrained in me that some men are inherently evil beings with a great capacity for domestic violence.

I knew nothing about the topic of "Battered Women" as it was known at the time and it had only been 2 years since Erin Pizzey had opened the first Women's Shelter in the world in the UK. The concept of Domestic Violence was only beginning to emerge at the time and a Radical Feminist Agenda drove much of the ideology, however, nobody could claim that Erin Pizzey was radical in any way. Perhaps described as a strong voice to help others and a role model to all, but never a radical. While Erin identified a need in society and chose to do something about it, her ideas we coopted by militants and radicals who wanted a fight rather than lend a helping hand. Women's Shelters were springing up in every major city and Rape was top of their agenda. Erin now is a campaigner for Men's and Father's Rights.

At the time I was also taking some university courses in Psychology mostly out of interest rather than applying towards a degree. The Women's Shelter became my laboratory and as I was also steeped in the philosophy of "Self Help" that had become a fashion at the time. Over a year I was accepted by all the staff and had met many of the clients over and over again. I had to take the counseling training but I was not allowed to give any counseling or advise to any of the women. After a few months I was asked to play with the children and show them that not all men are like daddy, there are men out there who are not violent and controlling and I was held up as a role model to the children.

One day I noticed a boy of about 8 controlling older children who were twice his size and could have sent him screaming to mammy with one push. But the girls were accepting and allowing his control. He had watched mammy and daddy and come to the conclusion that a man had to control everything. "We will eat at what time I say we eat, you will only do the laundry when I allow you to. I want to know what you did today, who you talked to and what was said." These are characteristic of Domestic Violence. Children grow up in a controlled environment and learn all about relationships from their parents. I also learned from the children that the girls seem to trigger the control. I tried to teach the boy that it was not his job to control others and the more you try to control people, the more they rebel and the less in control you feel.

I spoke to the Director and the president one day about what I had found. I was taught that Domestic Violence is the man's entire fault. If he would just leave her alone then everything would be normal. This answer didn't make any sense to me because I had also noticed that many of the clients had gone from one abusive, controlling man to the next. I also found that in every case I saw, that every woman had been raised in a home where their parents were abusive to each other and the classic Control featured heavily in their life.

I asked the question; "If these women are 'Normal', then why is it they keep repeating the same patterns and picking abusive men?" I was told that I was crazy but it would was only years later that I discovered the Erin Pizzey had made the same observations. My services at the shelter became less and less wanted over time and I drifted away. Before I left the shelter, I answered a call from a man who was a "Batterer" as they were known then and met him for coffee. I was about 25 at the time and he appeared in all respects to have the outward appearance of a "normal" man. At the same time I had read a small article in a newspaper about a Treatment Program for men being offered in a far away university. I contacted them and they suggested that this "Batterer" should lead the group and that for a small cost that they would provide us with the class materials and help and advice over the phone. I would have nothing to do with the group and not attend but I arranged a room, a messaging service and got the group started. It only cost a relatively small amount to set up. At this point I was told I was not welcome at the shelter and politely asked to leave. I was given a small parting gift but the staff and counselors were not happy with this, I was to have a party and be given a scroll signed by all the staff that I kept for many years after.

A few months later I moved away and followed my dream of owning a business. One day I met a Professor of Psychology from the local university as a client and the topic of Battered Women came up. After talking to her for 5 minutes she had set up a lecture for me to talk to her colleagues, mostly faculty at the university. Being adept at public speaking from instructing First Aid and Emergency Medical classes, I gave a 50-minute talk about what I had observed and worked in my brief Psychology training into the lecture. At the end I asked for questions but there were none. I summarized by saying that if you believe that if the cause of domestic violence is only the men, you couldn't be more wrong. It is a learned behavior that can equally be unlearned even in a self-help support group. The feedback we received from many of the men was that it was like a huge weight of responsibility being lifted from their shoulders. Afterwards many of the men left their partners because they could no longer identify with them. They didn't want a partner "pushing their buttons" and many didn't want a partner at all because they recognized that they might be trading one abusive partner for another. When I walked off the stage I was met with a "round of indifference" with only a few people clapping dispassionately. What could have been an opportunity to wipe out Domestic Violence in one generation was missed. I wasn't repeating the dogma of victimhood and offered a solution that at the very least was worthy of debate but my efforts fell on deaf ears and closed minds.

32 years later, not much has changed with domestic violence except of course the exaggerations of the Domestic Violence Industry who now claim that 1 in 5 women are victims. Very few self-help groups or treatment programs have sprung up to help men, none whatsoever for women. The radical feminist agenda is that men are evil and women are victims. I'm happy to see today that the younger generation of women has no interest in Feminism whatsoever.

They recognize that men and women are different and will always be different. These young women have no interest in being Victims or Survivors; they simply wont tolerate any lesser role than being a strong, independent woman. They are not prepared to see men as superior to them and give them power by virtue of their manhood. They recognize that men are not the enemy and you don't need to be subservient to a man and that in finding the right man, that the Macho Man was a non-starter. Most of these strong young women had a father in their life and learned that men are not just "sperm donors" or "weekend dads" and that men and women need to bond as a family and work together as Nature intended. They are not frightened of men as the radical feminists are. By having a good father they learn to relate and understand men better and use them to their advantage. I shudder to think of female children being raised without a father or grandfather and uncles. It's not always possible for a child to have a father but if Sociology and Psychology were doing the job that they purport to do, they would call for all children to have full access to both sides of their family tree.

Unfortunately this movement of women rejecting feminism is only small at this point and the Radical Feminists have worked their way into positions of power. People haven't yet valued the contribution that single mothers make towards society, or single fathers for that matter. It seems that the radical feminists even oppose single mothers. They have also tried to "normalize" the view that biology counts for nothing and adoption is a practical alternative to the outdated concept of family and motherhood. You don't have to ruin your figure, you can always adopt from a Gestation Carrier.

The lessons of Nature, that children are our future, and not a burden on society is one that many people have not yet learned. We have built a giant pyramid scheme as our economy and need continual growth and a fresh supply of children to support the rich at the top in the hope that the riches will trickle down. Not every marriage will last and women will end up getting the short end of the stick sometimes. I will discuss Fathers Rights in further detail later.

My point being that even if you do not have children yourself, children will grow up to be taxpayers and support you later in life when you cant support yourself. Raising children to be happy and well-adjusted taxpayers in the future is critical to our survival. At the present time of writing, 30% of all Irish children are living in consistent poverty and 700 are homeless in emergency accommodation. Hardly "Cherishing all of the children of Ireland equally" that the great architects of our Constitution envisioned. The tax breaks given to Corporation and the rich are enormous when compared to the little trickling down at the bottom of the pyramid. Ireland tolerates tax cheats and tax exiles. I realize that the Government isn't a bottomless pit of money and that people need to take responsibility for their own action. It's not sustainable for a government or a family to spend more than they earn but governments have done a poor job of managing and setting priorities, which is also not sustainable.

Even at the height of the Moira Woods fiasco, 25 years ago, a civil servant blew the whistle and was ignored. Joe Robins in the Dept. of Health wrote a memo to the Department Secretary. He said; "There have been far too many exaggerated comments and statistics put out by persons such as Moira Woods, Ann O'Donnell and Clodagh Corcoran who are turning child sexual abuse, in particular, into an industry".

Mr. Robins was obviously a visionary. He could have also, if people had listened to him, prevented the formation of the entire Child Abuse Industry that has sprung up around the Child Protection System, a billion a year industry.

I am not the first person to mention this discrepancy between reports, prosecutions and "confirmed" cases; in 1997 Eddie Hernon wrote a letter to the Editor of the Cork Examiner. The letter was in response to Deputy Alan Shatters "Protection for Persons Reporting Child Abuse Bill". Three years previously in 1994 Deputy Shatter had met with Eddie and 3 other fathers who had been wrongly accused. At the meeting the members of Accused Parents Aid Group stated their concerns over the high number of false allegations. In 20 years there were over 50,000 reported cases of alleged or suspected child abuse and neglect made to Health Boards (social services). 50% of these reports were investigated and confirmed but less than 5% were prosecuted and less than 3% resulted in a conviction.

In 2013 and 2014, there are over 30,000 reports per year and the number has increased year on year. Out of 30,000, there are 1,500 "Confirmed" cases of abuse and neglect. Almost none of these cases are "confirmed" by Gardai or the DPP. Again, I refer to 541 "confirmed" cases of sexual abuse of children but most of the 39 prosecutions by the DPP were mostly "historic" cases where the victims were adults.

What Eddie pointed out in 1994 was that 95% of all child abuse allegations were false. Moira Woods was not prosecuted even though she was found guilty of Professional Misconduct in 11 cases.

In my own experience in one case where we were helping a mother, the child's grandmother was determined to remove her son from the mother's care. The grandmother recruited a former friend of the mother and urged her to make a false complaint of child abuse. The grandmother also used a relative who was a member of An Garda Síochána to "check out" a colleague and myself on the Garda PULSE Crime Computer System. When we found out, we reported the Garda member to the Garda Ombudsman who took prompt action. The Garda member was demoted and given a reprimanded but no prosecution was possible as there was not sufficient evidence. No action was taken against the grandmother for perverting the course of justice.

The HSE opened an investigation and saw that we were involved in helping the mother, who incidentally had grown up in "care", and had no concerns. By the time the Ombudsman had completed their role, the HSE had already closed the case. We contacted the social worker again and demanded that the grandmother be prosecuted, the evidence was irrefutable and the Garda Ombudsman could have testified in the prosecution. The HSE refused to prosecute under the Act even though there is a provision to prosecute false and malicious complaints.

To my knowledge, nobody in Ireland has ever been prosecuted for making false and malicious complaints. Every year the numbers of reports increase and "calling social services" has become the weapon of choice, not only for malicious grannies, but also Doctors to prevent parents getting a second opinion, teachers and other people coming in contact with children. By contrast in the UK there are regular prosecutions and about 50 social workers are struck off the register for falsifying reports, in Ireland, these social workers get promoted. Many UK social workers, managers and directors who have been fired or forced to leave, come to Ireland and work for the CFA or HSE.

It's also interesting to note that many people claim that 1 in 4 girls and 1 in 5 boys have been sexually assaulted. Again the crime statistics cannot support these claims. 32 years ago in the Women's Crisis Center they claimed that 1 in 19 women were 'Battered", a scientific poll found the statistics were 1 in 139 were assaulted, however very few of them were assaulted on a regular basis so were unlikely to be "Battered Women". Now the claim is that 1 in 5 women are victims of domestic violence. Think of 5 women you know, your mother, sister, aunt, one of them is a victim of domestic violence? Of course the usual "these crimes are under-reported" is used a lot. So you have a situation where rape of children is over-reported and "confirmed" but rape of adults is under-reported? I will address the topic of child sexual assault in a later chapter.

If your income depended on a lie or an exaggeration and creating a doubt and fear in the minds of your customers, wouldn't it be likely that you would play on the fears of those customers to increase your income? Insurance is one thing that comes to mind for me, I am forever being over-sold insurance for everything but now I never bother insuring anything unless I am legally required to.

We have an industry built on lies, 95% of reports are false, at least. People are exaggerating an over-stating the extent of child abuse and neglect. This does nothing for actual victims; it creates more victims by wrongly accusing innocent people. In the case of Domestic Violence, most women who are murdered, are killed by their partners, in a decade in Ireland, 89 were murdered by their partners, so statistically 1 in a million women a year will be murdered by their partner.

Actual cases are very serious and in my experience, are inter generational and a learned behavior. By over-stating the extent of the problem, we run the risk of ignoring actual cases. I have seen cases where DV was suspected even though in one case the mother had not had any relationships with any man for

10 years, and yet her 2 children were removed. She had even fled her home country to get away and had little contact with her family, in case her abuser, who only attacked her once, found out where she was. Social workers are exaggerating cases of DV, in the first case I wrote about they got the woman to leave her husband and go to a shelter even though she had never been abused. They lied to the judge that she needed to be in the shelter and lied to the mother that she would get her children back if she went to the shelter.

The system is totally out of control when such injustice is allowed to occur. You have social workers practicing as amateur detectives and psychologists. Many I have met are typical of the "Rogue Cops" you see on TV shows, they are going to save children even if they have to lie cheat and steal to do it. They don't care about the law or what the judge says, Protecting Children trumps the law and their professors at school told them they could do this. It's no great surprise that many of them leave the first year if they are lucky and smart enough to get a job elsewhere for the same money.

Judges are so afraid of protecting their own reputations that they will get "Experts" to lie for money and then claim that on the available evidence, they decided the only way possible, keep the child and then if they child dies in "Care" they can "wash their hands" as if they played no part. Nobody is the captain of this great ship, as they are not allowed by law to know what happens on the lower decks. When the numbers start slipping the managers issue edicts and fatwas and press releases to an adoring media who will happily cut & paste any fatwas and add their name to the article. And the victims are gagged and you never hear of most of the 8,000 cases a year in Family Courts.

In reality, the private Law Firms acting as Prosecutors have far more control than even the social workers. They ask social workers to "Sex Up" and exaggerate cases and they have a financial incentive to stretch-out cases as long as possible.

CHAPTER 8

"CARE"

Louise ended up in "Care" as a baby, her mother suffered from Post Partum Depression. I can still visualize the stories of how her foster carers didn't allow her to play outside "in case she got hurt". When her mother came to see her she would carefully screen for any injuries, even tiny cuts and scrapes and there would be hell to pay if Louise had a scratch on her.

When Louise tells the story of when her mother would come for visits, she would wait at the window, afraid to blink in case she missed the moment that her mother would round the corner and break into a smile at seeing her little girl. When she tells this story, she smiles and appears sad at the same time. She didn't understand why she couldn't live with mammy, and frankly after hearing the story, neither can I. I have never heard of a case of Post Partum Depression lasting 18 years.

Sometimes mammy didn't show up, but unlike some other foster carers I have heard of, she wasn't told, "your mammy doesn't love you any more". The reason her mother couldn't make it to every visit was because of a combination of factors. Sometimes she wasn't allowed to by social workers, sometimes the foster carers were not available or busy, and sometimes she simply hadn't the bus fare for the long journey. She had fought the system for her daughter until she could fight no more. When you are up against the might of the State it's almost an impossible battle. The system of using private law firms to prosecute parents is incentivized to stretch out cases as long as possible to make as much money as possible. Against a budget of €10 million, the CFA lawyers have consistently stretched it out to €30 million for the last few years. Because the upper management of the CFA and the Department of Children and Youth Affairs has no legal entitlement to know what is happening in any case, there are no controls in place. These law firms seem to have been around for years and don't appear to have to bid on the government contract annually as you would expect.

In one case I mentioned earlier, the HSE had brought in a "Hired Gun" Barrister on a number of cases at €3,000 per day plus expenses. It was reported in the news that he had made €1.3 million for 11 months work. He wasn't actually needed in many cases as the same CFA lawyers had been involved in these cases from the start, it was only when they started to lose these cases that they would bring in the hired guns, and surprisingly, judges allowed this. In 2 cases that my colleagues and myself were involved in, the same barrister was brought in. My colleagues and I often find us stacked against a team from the State against one McKenzie Friend. It's not uncommon to see 7 solicitors and barristers from the State against 1 person. In every case they try to delay and delay, which of course is in their financial interest. In our case, we don't get paid anything and it's in our interest to conclude the case as soon as possible. I have seen one case stretched out to 5 years and the amount of compensation requested by the 1 Litigant in Person is less than 1% of the sum the State has paid out to lawyers in that 5 years. Because the case is In Camera, no Minister, senior manager or anyone outside the courtroom would be entitled to know what happened inside. The Mafia, the Stasi, the KGB would be envious. The In Camera Justice System is a scam perpetrated on taxpayers. Even though this barrister was fired under the orders of the Minister for Children, he has recently reappeared still representing the CFA, no doubt at €3,000/day.

In cases that I have assisted on where we could not find a McKenzie Friend to help, parents had to use solicitors at €500/day and also barristers at €1,500 a day. In these cases my colleagues and I did all the research, the case law and investigation. We have even written out all the questions for the experts and got affidavits from our own experts when we couldn't afford to have them appear in person. The objective of the State is and has always been to abuse the parent with Legal Abuse Syndrome; they will spend millions to prevent paying out thousands.

You can understand why Louise's mother lost her daughter forever. Louise doesn't understand why her mother couldn't fight for her and her mother has become so damaged by the entire process that she had no fight left in her. In other cases I have seen where mothers with Post Partum Depression recovered in a few weeks with some assistance from GP's, Mental Health Professionals, Medication and Home Help for a few hours every day. A case of Post Partum Depression lasting 18 years is something that probably should be written up in Medical Journals, but in the Alternate Universe of these secret courts, anything is possible.

I met Louise's foster carers, they are very nice people. Louise has a very good relationship today with them and their children. Louise calls her foster mum "mum" and has no relationship with her birth mother. In her time in "care", Louise was sexually assaulted; she wasn't believed by her social worker. She ran away and walked into a solicitor's office and demanded to talk to the judge. Even as a child, Louise was very intelligent and wise beyond her years. This is not uncommon of children in "care". Many children in "care" say they never had a childhood. They were not allowed to play outside, sometimes they were given hand-me-down clothing, fed differently from the foster carers children and I find in many cases today, are not allowed phones, computers or access to the internet in case they talk to their parents and families. For many, "Care" is a prison for children. They are often systematically isolated from their parents by social workers.

"Your mother doesn't love you any more, she can't be bothered to come and see you, and she is mentally ill and not capable of looking after you". Quite often the truth is, that against the judge's orders, the social workers prevented the parent visiting. In one case a young girl was forced by the Foster "carer" to attend a sport that she had no interest in. When the mother came to see her daughter she was covered in bruises, I have the photos. When the mother complained, her access was cut altogether. When we intervened the children were moved to another home and the mother still has no access. By taking photos, social workers argued that the mother was causing emotional harm to the child. When you see your child, it's under the scrutiny of a social worker with a clipboard who writes down every little detail. You would think that audio and video would be a far superior method, but apparently not.

Louise turned out ok but it took years of work by her friends and new "family" to help her, the government gave no support. Louise is an excellent mother; I can say that because her children are excellent. They are intelligent, well behaved and much loved.

Louise has a support system that is denied most "care" leavers. She has had challenges in her life that no child should have to suffer, it has left it's mark, but still she persists and has grown enormously in the last few years. Louise has always loved children and from an early age wanted to care for children. After leaving school she took training in Childcare and went to work caring for children. Her career was short lived when a social worker found out that she had been in "care" and had been sexually assaulted. Social workers deem "Care" Recipients to be such a high risk to children, that girls who spent any time in "Care" are 66 times more likely to lose their children to "Care".

Let me repeat that so that you understand this clearly. If you were in "Care" for any amount of time, you are considered "Damaged Goods" by social workers and are 66 times more likely to lose your children to "Care".

It doesn't take a genius to figure out that this in fact Einstein's very definition of Insanity; "to repeat the same experiment over and over and expect different results every time". You may recall that earlier I mentioned judges seeing "Inter-Generation Recidivism". The offspring of children those judges placed in "Care" many years ago, are now appearing before the same judges.

Are our judges Insane? Apparently so, if they keep repeating the same mistake. They have created a self-generating system that grows and grows and shows no sign of stopping. Few judges have the courage to stand up to this system and have become "Rubber Stamps" for the insanity of social services. I have seen more than a few of them who probably get the adrenalin rush that the Crusader's of Children's Rights get when they break up families, often breaking the law in order to do so.

I am blaming the judges here for creating this system and allowing the corruption to take place. The proverbial "Buck" has to stop somewhere and there has to be checks and balances built into the system. I also blame the judges for the children who have died, were raped, disappeared and suffered poor outcomes in life. Someone has to stand up and take responsibility or to apportion blame when nobody else is willing to.

The view that most people have of Foster "Care" is that selfless parents feel they have space in their hearts and homes to care for vulnerable children. I don't doubt for one minute that Foster Carers are anything other that good people who have the best intentions, not unlike the Salem Pilgrims who were equally good people. I'm sure you know and admire a foster carer who is a nice person and maybe even some children being "cared for". But my question is; "Why don't these children have far better outcomes in life?"

Few people realize that fostered children are "Emancipated" at age 18. This is of course a sanitized term used by social work which means they will be dumped on the streets on their 18th birthday, many times before they have finished school or even during their exams.

One such "cared for" young man I met was John. He came home from school one day to find all his possessions wrapped in a bin bag and a social worker with a letter saying he had been "emancipated". He was 2 months from his Leaving Cert exams and wanted to go to Trinity College. He ended up in emergency accommodation many miles from school and didn't even have the money for bus fare. As a parent, can you imagine throwing your child on the street on their 18th birthday?

My parenting instinct wanted to bring John home with me and be the father he never had. I wanted him to be an 18 year old and not have to worry about accommodation, food, clothing or any of those things that 18's have no concept of. I couldn't do anything for John or the thousands of other "Johns" who have "Aged Out" of the system over the years. My resources are better spent by preventing the "John's and Louise's" from ever entering the system to begin with.

You could reasonably expect, that if one of your neighbors dumped their child on the street at age 18, that they would be shunned in their community. But when the State IS the parent, somehow this is acceptable? I know that many foster carers keep children past their 18th birthday. I know of one case where the "child" is 45 years old and is now the carer for the only parents he ever knew and has never left home.

And when you consider the cost to the taxpayer, we are paying an average of €334 per week per child, sometimes from age 0 to 18. The actual cost has actually increased over the years because the CFA or HSE cannot find Foster Carers themselves, they rely on Fostering Agencies who take their cut. In Ireland every year we are paying about €120 million a year for foster "care" which is mostly a "cottage industry". The fees are tax-free and expenses are paid over and above the weekly fee. About 90% of children live in foster homes. Many of the fostering agencies are run by social workers and one such business sold in the UK for £18 million a few years ago.

The other type of "Care" is Residential Care. For this, taxpayers are paying a whopping €5,000 per week per child. One of the operators of residential homes said a few years ago, that for €5,000 per week per child, that the best he could offer was a "Babysitting Service" and threatened to lay off hundreds of staff. This was in reaction to the government "Austerity" which had cut the fees from €8,500 per week per child to a "mere" €5,000. That's over a quarter of a million per child, per year, for a babysitting service.

Despite a supposed cap of €5,000 a week, a story appeared in the Irish Times on 22 April 2014 which stated that some operators were charging €13,000 per week per child and that the taxpayer was paying €20 million a year for empty beds. I know of cases where the HSE have spent over a million a year on some children who were sent to the UK or USA for special treatment programs. If you take for example the children from the Roscommon House of Horrors, nobody could reasonably argue that these children deserve and need special assistance. Very few are sent to these facilities and I'm sure a lot of justification would be needed.

So on one hand you have kids of 18 being dumped on the streets and many of them will have poor outcomes in life, on the other you have empty beds at between €5,000 and €13,000 per week not being used at a cost to the taxpayer of €20 million a year. A question I have wondered is whether a deal was struck with these Private "Care" Operators to fiddle the books and make up for the shortfall? I have equally read stories of judges screaming at social workers in courts because supposedly no beds were available?

And what happens to these children after they turn 18? Many have been systematically isolated from the family so going "home" is not an option. Many are very angry with their parents for not fighting harder to get them home or coming to see them every week. It's not until these kids become parents themselves, which many do far too early, that they find themselves staring down the barrel of a social worker, that they begin to understand what their own parents suffered.

What actually happens is this,

- 50% of the prostitutes on the streets came through the "Care" system
- 80% of "Big Issue" sellers were in "Care"
- 80% will have poor outcomes in life
- 80% of "Care" leavers are unemployed after 2 years
- 13% of "Care" leavers in the UK have 5 GCSE's compared to 58% of all others
- 9% of "Care" leavers go to University compared 46% of all others
- 50% of inmates in Young Offenders Institutions have been in "Care"
- 26% of adult inmates in prison were in "Care" as a child
- 25% of girls in "Care" have been pregnant by the time they leave
- 50% of the girls in "Care" are single mothers within 2 years of leaving
- 7% of under 18's in "Care" have a criminal conviction, against 2% of all others

The statistics I have used above are from the UK and there would only be slight differences between Ireland and UK Outcomes. In the past I have been accused of making up these and other statistics, which is not true. The fact of the matter is that the DCYA, the HSE and CFA won't release proper statistics. A few days her appointment as Minister for Children, I wrote to Frances Fitzgerald and asked for these statistics, I didn't get a response. Before the Children's Referendum I asked again and the response I got was that they don't keep statistics on many of the questions I had asked. In hindsight I should have pursued it further but simply didn't have the time.

I eventually got some questions answered through independent TD Mattie McGrath who kindly pursued the matter on my behalf. One of the most disputed statistics I gave was that a child in Irish State "Care" is statistically 6 times more likely to die than children in the general population. I had passed these statistics to the people who campaigned against the Children's Referendum and Kathy Sinnott bore the brunt of the criticism. Health Minister Leo Varadkar (who would become Taoiseach in 2017) accused us of making up the statistics and published some statistics of his own on the Fine Gael website.

The fact is that in the UK, a child is 3 times more likely to die in "Care", in Texas the likelihood is 10 times and everywhere you find government statistics you find that children are more likely to die in State "Care" than in the care of their parents. By playing a numbers game and disputing whether the number is 1, 2, 3 or 6, people are completely missing the point; "isn't a child in "Care" supposed to be safer than children in the general population?" If they are not, and the evidence seems to prove that "Care" is anything but a place of safety, then what's the point of placing children in "care"?

I am not a Statistician but I came up with these figures as diligently as I could and they were made in good faith. As the Child Abuse Industry doesn't seem to publish anything that makes the system appear in a bad light, as other countries and their media do, I still stand by the figure I had come up with. Rather than cherry picked data from a good year, I expect the government to show data from the last 2 decades so that an accurate picture could be drawn up. While the government can criticize an individual such as myself, bear in mind that I don't get paid, I don't have the resources, I have been denied access to actual data and also that I have no "agenda" and have never been personally harmed by the system. If anyone disputes these statistics the feel free to make the data available to the public and explain the methodology used in compiling the data.

The largest study of Outcomes of children in "Care" was by Professor Joseph Doyle at MIT. Doyle is a Business professor and because he is not a "Social Scientist", his study, the largest of it's kind ever with 15,000 subjects over a period of 12 years is also widely ignored even though his study was conducted to the double-blind "Gold Standard".

Doyle took all the variables into account and his main goal was to discover if children actually benefited from "care", mostly from an economic perspective. The results were dismal. 80% had extremely poor outcomes. When the State steps in and decides that a parent has failed in their duty, it is not an unreasonable expectation that the child will be better off for the intervention. In fact, the whole objective of removing the child is presumably to place the child in a more beneficial placement and the only practical method of measuring this benefit for the child is that the child should have a far better outcome in life.

Outcomes for children are supposed to be the objective of intervening in the first instance. If the child is with a dysfunctional mother and has no father or relatives, if the mother doesn't clean and bathe, feed and nurture the baby it will surely die and placing the baby with a trained foster carer who has the resources and the money, should guarantee that child a far better outcome.

The problem is however, when you compare the natural parent to the corporate parent, the natural parent wins hands down almost every time. When social workers go into court and lie and exaggerate the case, they rule out any hope that the judge could see an opportunity to help the parent or forces social services to help the family rather than split them up. The justice system is stacked against the parent, any judge can verify what I have seen on most occasions, a huge number of "experts" with unlimited budgets on one side of the room and a lone parent with a Legal Aid Loser on the other side who wont even put up a defense. It's no wonder that parents lose most of the time and it's no surprise that my colleagues win so much of the time. By leveling the playing field and picking cases that we know we can win, it's not hard to understand our success. We come prepared for court, we do the research and are not intimidated by €3,000 a day Hired Guns. And we are paid nothing.

When a story appeared in the newspapers about the HSE going over-budget on legal services, it was followed soon after by a press release by the Minister for Children looking into the possibility of giving social workers some legal training. She seemed to forget that her predecessor had set aside €3 Million for the child protection to set up their own legal department. Either idea was a non-starter to begin with as the legal fraternity would never be satisfied giving up a "cushy number" where you don't need to compete, nobody can tell you what to do and you can exceed your budget and triple your profits. The reason I feel confident in making this statement is that I have an audio tape and two witnesses of an HSE solicitor threatening a family's solicitor that they should not fight and "stretch out" the case as long as possible. The HSE solicitor can clearly be heard to say that "you have kids too", who presumably could suddenly come to the attention of social workers.

What the minister and some people who work for the DCYA in Mespil Road believed that by following our model of using McKenzie Friends that they could bring down the cost to within budget of €10 million. Our website and Facebook page were scoured every day by the DCYA and I have kept the screenshots to show the IP Addresses taken from our website. Even though our website was later hacked, I had kept a close watch on who was accessing our website and had backups of the data that was hacked. Because anyone outside of these secret courts has no clue as to what happens inside, it became necessary to obtain the information "elsewhere".

When I describe the Child Protection System as a massive ship without a Captain, I am not exaggerating in the least. The law has been perverted to protect the system to such an extent that even "the system" doesn't know what's going on. If any Minister for Children tries to speak with any authority on the system, they are either lying to you or breaking the law. The law is clear, you cannot say "anything to anybody" and it would be a further injustice for any sitting Minister to intervene in any case before the courts. Enda Kenny put his foot in it once by intervening in a case of a constituent but was put in his place by Alan Shatter. More recently ex TD Mary Kenny fell afoul of the secrecy by speaking to a judge. It is not an exaggeration to say that I know more about what happens in the courts than any Politician or people working in Government Departments. I find it absurd that the people at the top of the organization have no idea and no control over the system.

Of course in writing this book, I am falling afoul of the law by openly discussing cases. Even though I have not identified a single child or their parents I could be hauled into court (again) by a corrupt CFA lawyer and a corrupt judge. The problem however is that because I have had cases in many countries and often had similar cases more than once, the onus would be the "prosecutors" to prove which case that I wrote about. Not only that, as I would not accept any less that a full public trial with the media present, the CFA would be less likely to prosecute. But the real "kicker" with the in camera rule is the fact that the prosecutors themselves could not, by law, disclose "anything to anybody", even a judge, without breaking the in camera rule themselves. Perhaps "Absurd" is not strong enough a word to describe it. The In Camera Rule is not about protecting children; it's about protecting a System.

In 2009, I protested with the aunts of Danny Talbot outside the Dail to bring attention to the "Deaths in Care" scandal. Sandra Lamb and her sisters and family, the McAnaspie family and a group of up to 30 of us protested outside the Dail, the HSE head office and the Garden of Remembrance. Danny had spent most of his life in "Care" as his mother was incapable of looking after him. Danny was fortunate in one respect that he had an extended family outside "Care" who loved him deeply. Danny had a hard life in "Care" that no child should have to suffer. His aunts were in regular contact with him but Danny needed professional help that he was not being given. When Danny started "going off the rails", his aunts were on the phone several times a day to the HSE to get help for him but their pleas fell on deaf ears. Eventually Danny died. The aunts could have at that point, just left it at that, Danny was dead and there was nothing more they could have done for him, but they were so concerned at what they had learned about the system that they didn't want Danny's death to be in vain, they wanted to bring attention to the problems within the system to hopefully save other children. The protests were held on Wednesdays for almost a year before anyone took notice.

Quite often with protesting outside the Dail, you hope that some opportunistic politician will jump on your bandwagon and then the media will take notice. After a while Deputy Alan Shatter took notice as his portfolio was Family Law and indeed he was known in the trade as "Mr. Family Law" before his foray in politics. Alan invited the Lamb Sisters and others in and all of a sudden became a vociferous voice for children in "Care". At the time, Children's minister Barry Andrews was also taking notice and asked the HSE for a report on how many children had died in "Care" in a decade. He was told by the HSE that it was none of his business. He took a case to court and lost, the old "anything to anybody" and a "sitting minister" cant become involved in these cases was rolled out. Eventually Barry had to enact special legislation even to find out how many children had died. Personally I would have argued in court that you cant protect someone who is dead just as the family of Daniel McAnaspie did in court to get copies of Daniels HSE records.

At first, 23 children had died in "care", that would be about in line with the national average. Then it was 29 and eventually went all the way up to 260, although the numbers were eventually whittled down to 196 in a decade. What people don't realize is that even within the HSE or CFA, one area doesn't talk to the other, they don't say "anything to anybody" outside their area and the upper management doesn't even have a right to know. Nothing has really changed substantially since the re-branding except maybe they keep better records on deaths.

Deputy Alan Shatter set up a website LetInTheLight.ie that has since gone but I have screenshots of it. Another death that came to light was the death of a young mother of 2 babies. Tracy Fay was known to one of the protesters and this information was passed on to Barry and Alan. The interim report on the horrible death of Tracy Fay was circulated to the TD's, but was not for publication. Alan Shatter used his Parliamentary privilege to release the report on her death and I salute his bravery in doing so he was heavily criticized by his own party for doing so. Tracy was found in a coalbunker and died of a heroin overdose. Many other children or young adults who escaped from "Care" or aged-out, also died under similar circumstances. In a few of these cases the children who died were being "babysat" in private residential homes at €5,000 a week (or in reality €13,000/week).

Tracy was abandoned by her mother and dumped in "Care" but her mother never suffered any consequences for her failure. This is one indication of where the system is failing, if child abuse and neglect is a crime, which I believe it is, Police should investigate it. You would think the system would have kicked in and given Tracy the care and psychological help she needed but the fact is that very few children in "Care" who have suffered a trauma, or are in need of Mental Health Services, receive it. We are paying civil servants and governments to look after these children but they are clearly not looking after the "Tracy's, Danny's, Louise's and Johns". While the CFA seem to have unlimited budgets to prosecute parents and bringing in experts and psychologists who they know will lie for them, they have no money to provide mental health services.

I am working on a number of cases where social workers fabricated stories of sexual abuse. In all of these cases I have spoken the children, all of whom deny any sexual assault, and none of them have received any psychological help. It would appear that the social workers don't believe their own lies because the children have not received any therapy after being sexually assaulted.

I have also seen Foster Carers fight for their children, usually against social workers, to get treatments or therapy for the children they care for, as any good parent would. It would be wrong to see Foster Carers as the "Enemy"; many are as frustrated as anyone else. But as long as the Foster "Care" Industry refuses to accept that "Cared For" children have very poor outcomes in life and nobody is willing to even recognize this fact, I have no issue with "tarring all foster carers with the same brush". If this is really about what is best for children then everyone should be working together to improve the system.

The Foster "Care" Industry has firmly planted its roots on the side of the Child Abuse Industry and not on the side of children. If Fosterers are just as frustrated at being lied to by social workers as parents are, then let them stand up publicly and say so. But of course if a fosterer does stand up, they will likely lose the children they are trying to protect and not get any more children to look after. So you see, even fosterers are just as frustrated and just as gagged as the parents or anyone else. They don't even appear in court and nobody asks their opinion. Instead of a judge asking the person who is with the child 24/7, they bring in a Guardian who purports to speak for the child. When that child is raped or dies, the GAL is nowhere to be found and never held responsible or accountable in any way.

The scandal of the deaths in "care" was not exposed by any Children's "Charity", social worker, politician, expert or anyone working within the system. The only reason the story came out was because of the Lamb Sisters, the McAnaspie Family and others who I wont mention by name, protested for almost a year before anyone took notice. You would assume that NGO's are at the coalface of children protection and would actually know what's going on in the system but they don't. You would assume that at least **one** of the 4,000 social workers on the front line would have blown the whistle but no, there are no Irish whistleblowers, their Unions wouldn't tolerate it.

You would also assume that with 196 deaths of children, that the "independent" panel of experts, who investigated these deaths, would have found even 1 social worker responsible? Even on the Balance of Probabilities, people are human and make mistakes, surely the social workers that ignored the phone calls and please of Sandra and Debbie Lamb would be held accountable in some way for the death of Danny Talbot? Not in Ireland even though social workers are struck off regularly in the UK. The "Independent" panel was made up of a team of people whom I have often referred to as the "Usual Suspects". These are people who make their living in some way in the Child Abuse Industry and none of them have ever uttered a harsh word about the system. In the strongest condemnation I have ever heard from any of these people, they said the system "**was not fit for purpose**". All the usual rhetoric, "lessons will be learned, blah blah, we have instituted measures, blah blah, this will never happen again" etc., etc. was rolled out and by the time the Children's Referendum was rolled out, it seemed that no child had ever died as a result of being "protected". Everything that was ever wrong with the system could be fixed by giving children a magical set of rights.

In the final analysis, "Care" does not benefit most children, 80% have dismal outcomes in life. This is not a topic that the social work fraternity want to discuss because they don't want the Benefit to children being "Demonstrated and Measured", or in this case, the lack of benefit. The social work blogs are replete with "Damned if we do, damned if we don't", "poor social workers" and how they are doing an impossible job. The truth is that they **are** doing an impossible job.

I wrote earlier that one court case I attended had all the hallmarks of a Séance, this was not an exaggeration by any means, and case conferences are not much different. I believe that asking anyone to use the Crystal Ball Method that Psychology and Sociology has become, to look into the future and be able to predict future events with a degree of absolute certainty, is the very definition of "an impossible task". As 70% of all cases are now based on the premise of; "Risk of Future Emotional Abuse" it is clear that Crystal Balls are being used and that the description given by John Hemming MP of the; "Thought Police approach to Child Protection", is more than apt.

To go back to the case of Fran Lyon, Fran had never been a mother so there was never a "Baseline" or history there to do a proper assessment. It turned out Irish social workers later disagreed with the UK, but I wonder if Fran had not had the good sense to contact John Hemming MP and Columnist Sue Reed and drew international media attention to her plight, if the Irish social workers would have channeled the same spirits as their colleagues in the UK? Strange those Irish social workers also disagreed with their counterparts in well-publicized cases such as the Webster's and the mother who was too stupid to parent a child? At the same time many cases where the parents didn't generate any publicity, in every instance the Irish social workers rubber-stamped their UK colleagues decisions.

We don't ask Police to detect Future Crime or Doctors to predict Future Illness, so why do we expect social workers to determine future crime and future mental illness in children? We do it because they tell us that they are capable of doing it.

Sociology and Psychology are products, which are over-sold; they cannot deliver on their promises as historically they have never delivered on their promise. In fact, nobody has measured or demonstrated the benefits of many treatments. There are no Lab Tests or X Rays that prove the existence of a mental illness so no scientific method of proving the efficacy of a treatment. For over 50 years of Social "Science" being used by governments to engineer society, the result has been a massive failure. Of course not a spectacular failure as most of this happens in Secret Courts. Even when we pervert Justice and allowed the 1,000 children to be wrongly taken into "Care" to "prevent that one child swinging in the wind", the system has only increased in size and more children are dying.

"Professionals" in the Baby P case visited Baby Peter 60 times and never saw the threshold to removing Peter being met. 18 of those visits were by social workers. If you ask a Plumber to do brain surgery, the operation could still be a success even if the patient dies as long as the Success Criteria is met. By the same token if you ask a Brain Surgeon to do Plumbing and don't give them the proper tools and knowledge, the operation can be a complete failure or a complete success depending on what Success Criteria you apply. With a vaporous term as Best Interests, and no clear definition of what Best Interest even means, the system is working as it should and social workers don't understand why they are being vilified.

The social workers and manager in the Baby P case didn't understand why there was so much public outcry. After all, they did their job properly according to the success criteria of "Best Interests of the Child". They were not struck off by the HRC or suffered any legal sanctions. They did what they were supposed to do and even their sacking was unfair and the Manager Sharon Shoesmith was reinstated. The publics outcry was about a 17-month-old baby who lived a miserable existence, he was tortured for his entire life. There is not one person reading this, who if they knew Peter was in danger who would not have intervened. In Ireland we have Section 12 of the Childcare Act, which allows a Garda to intervene and remove any child from anywhere, despite the lies we were told during the Children's Referendum, the law in Ireland has never been a barrier to protecting a child. Similar laws exist in most countries and I could not see any Police Officer in any country being reprimanded for acting in Good Faith to rescue a child.

Police could have saved Baby Peter at any time but were not given the opportunity. If Police had investigated they would have found the nutcase upstairs living with 2 Rottweiler dogs had previously been investigated for abusing a toddler. It would have set off alarm bells for any rookie investigator, but social workers are not detectives and don't do Investigation, they do vague and vaporous Assessments.

The problem with social work is that they are taking the wrong children for no reason and not taking children who are in actual need of care. We are sending inexperienced and untrained people into homes to do a job that they will never be capable of doing. The reason that social workers will not take the risk with any parent and remove every child they can has little to do with Baby P. When you send a detective to do an investigation, the only issue is whether a crime was committed or not and whether charges can be laid, police officers are not social workers. When you send a social worker out to detect the crimes of child abuse or neglect they must decide if they can "fix" the family or prosecute them. The two roles are incompatible; you can't be an advocate and a prosecutor at the same time.

This is why the Child Protection System in Ireland and the UK is a failure. What happens in other European countries is that social workers have no power to remove children and would never be allowed to "bend" or pervert the law. Even the judges in most countries have, and use their investigative powers and the judge and Police could have walked into Baby Peters house at any time.

What is extremely disturbing is that in Ireland, the CFA and HSE have about 1,500 crimes of child abuse and neglect being "confirmed" every year, but how many of those cases are being investigated by Gardai? Almost none. Also disturbing that there are 541 "confirmed" cases of sexual abuse of children, but not 541 corresponding Garda investigation or DPP prosecutions. How is this even possible that sex crimes against children are not investigated and punished? I hope dear readers that you will get to the bottom of this "sex scandal" because when I raised the issue at a press conference, no Irish journalist was interested.

In Ireland, we don't need the Baby P case as evidence that social work and family law are clearly not working as we have a case in Roscommon that spanned 11 years. Again, any Garda could have stopped the misery of these children, but as Gardai apparently have no duty to Serve & Protect children, having abrogated this duty to social workers, the children of Ireland are only "protected" during office hours, by people who have no training or experience in Crime.

The system is in every respect a recipe for disaster and all we can expect in the future is more Baby P's and more Houses of Horror. Unless there is a fundamental shift in the whole thinking of Child Protection and throwing out the Lobbyists and Experts whose only contribution is to proffer the failed "solutions" of the worst possible model of Child "Protection" used in the UK, more children will die, go "missing", be raped and continue to have dismal outcomes in life after the intervention. Unless we employ a more scientific Success Criteria and have every judge in Ireland reject the vaporous slogan "Best Interests of the Child", we are going to repeat Einstein's "insanity" and continue to the results of the failed Social Experiment for generations to come. We need to follow far better models that are used in other countries and have social workers as advocates and only allow Police to investigate crime. Hundreds of millions could be wiped from the child protection budget that is now spent on "professionals" that could be used for the direct benefit of children. How much economic sense does it make to spend €100,000 on breaking up a family when "fixing" the problem by spending a fraction of that sum on helping the family has been proven more beneficial?

In my 7 years of research, I came to certain conclusions and I came to those conclusions independently of others. Every once in a while I talk to other people who have reached their conclusion independently and find that they have reached the same consensus. It's especially nice when the observer is a person who has never been personally affected and has no motive or agenda to criticize the system. While many have different ideas and solutions we all mutually agree on the problem. The intervention is worse than the alleged problem to begin with. I have heard people use terms like "heavy handed" and "using a sledgehammer to crack a nut". The majority of people agree that "Care" is not the panacea that we believe it to be, it is actually more harmful as is evidenced by the "Care" Alumni themselves, who can attest.

Friends and clients regularly send me articles and videos from around the world. Earlier this year I received a video link on YouTube of a TedTalks given in Baltimore given by Molly McGrath who was then the Director of social services or "Child Welfare" as they are known locally. It is called "Rethinking Foster Care". I was reduced to tears and still am every time I watch the video. Molly, herself a social worker recognizes that social work in its current form of child protection is not working and doing more harm that good. She also recognized that this is an Industry that serves the interests of the industry but does not benefit the children. As she says, "Foster Care is the problem" and "the error IS the intervention".

She also mentions the egos of the people involved in saving children, something that has not escaped my notice either. It's not uncommon to see social workers and CFA lawyers giving "High Fives" to each other outside courthouses when they have performed a "Parent-ectomy" as some of them refer to it. I have seen for myself social workers sneering at parents and condescending remarks being made. But I have also seen the other side of it where suicidal parents who have lost their children forever and suicidal children have lost their parents forever. A UCD study into suicide in 2012 found that children in "Care" are 10 times more likely to die from suicide than children in the general population. This statistic alone should have set off alarm bells for the media and the public into an urgent inquiry on why this is occurring. I did mention it at a press conference and was met with blank stares. Shouldn't a child in "Care" be 10 times **less** likely to attempt suicide? If not, then what's the point of removing them from home?

In a report by Focus Ireland in 1996, an extensive investigation was done on youth homelessness in Ireland. It was found that children were being dumped by the State, in other words their parents, on the street. Since 1996 nothing has changed significantly since. If we think of Foster "Care" as a large factory designed to take a blank canvas at the input and then turn that canvas into a rag in 80% of cases at the output stage, I really couldn't put a better analogy forward than that. I intensely dislike seeing Foster Kids being seen as "damaged goods", they are human beings who have been given a bad break in life, but this is how the social work fraternity views "care" Alumni themselves. If a girl spent time in "care", she is deemed such a risk that she is 66 times more likely to have her child removed and the cycle will repeat itself forever. We need to break this cycle. Shouldn't Care Alumni have far better outcomes and be widely sought after given the time and money invested in their "Care"?

As the "Batterer" struggles continuously for control, social work blusters from one failed theory to the next. The more control you apply, the more out of control you will become and likely it will end in failure. Like the men who were taught to control have learned in self-help groups, that the solution is actually to have less controls. Rather than continuously adding more social workers and more laws and increasing the industry, maybe the solution is to do the complete opposite? Rather than adding 260 social workers and seeing more children being taken into "care", maybe the solution is to cut 260 social workers? Rather than spending a Billion a year on professionals "protecting" children, let's spend the billion directly on children themselves?

A friend of mine has 4 children, one with special needs. On a salary of less that €60.000 a year, he and his wife are able to give their children a good quality of life. If somebody paid me €5,000 per week to care for a child until they were 18, I would probably be able to afford to send them to the best schools in the world and afterwards have enough money them to Oxford or Harvard and still have enough money to pay for their marriage and first house. So how is it that a private firm getting €5,000 a week for the same child will turn that child into the next homeless person, prostitute, drug addict, convicted criminal or in the morgue? This is absolute insanity to be taking children from good homes and paying ridiculous sums of money to "professionals" and "Charities" to destroy the lives of these children.

Perhaps now you understand why I have this annoying habit of using quotation marks around the word "Care".

When you blog or debate the topic of Foster Care, you will find that the public perception is that Foster Carers are Angels and Heroes, in my own view they are for the most part. I have met many carers and they are good people. They do their best and I don't envy them. Foster Care is a road paved with good intentions. I could equally say that the majority of people working in Child Protection are very good people who do their best. Any fosterer who has been at it long enough will tell you that the system is abusive to children. They will tell you that social workers lie and exaggerate and generally are not very helpful. The reason that many continue to do what they do is for the children.

Despite what many believe about Guardians ad Litem, they are even worse in the majority or cases and don't represent the views or wishes of the child. If you asked the vast majority of children in "Care" what they want, they want to go home. How much economic sense does it make to pay some GAL's €300,000 a year and then pay their solicitors and barristers a similar amount to represent a child when a foster carer could do a better job? I have seen the shameless promotion by people who make their (very good) living from GAL services complaining that not all children in "care" have a GAL as every child should. They say a GAL speaks for the child, but I have seen so many cases where the child is saying they want to go home when the GAL is lying that they are happy in "Care". I have come to the conclusion that a GAL is just another social worker working against the family and the child and it would be an exceedingly rare case for a GAL to go against the social worker. I have also seen many cases where children were raped or died because GAL's didn't heed parents or foster carers. To that end I have come to the conclusion that GAL's are more harmful to children than helpful. Where social workers are subjected to some scrutiny, GAL's are unaccountable and there is no regulation whatsoever, they are not even required to be vetted in this unregulated industry.

Don't blame children in "Care" for the position they find themselves in. As one man said during the Ryan Report, "I was just a kid". These children grow up too soon learning that adults can't be trusted and in order to survive, they learn to look after themselves. If you grew up without knowing the love, belongingness and safety that a family brings, your outcome on life, and in life, might also be very poor.

CHAPTER 9

THE IDEOLOGY:
NO CONSPIRACY REQUIRED

After World War two, most of Europe lay in ruins. Millions were dead, millions of children were orphaned, millions of wives widowed. People who had enough of war got together and were determined that this was never going to happen again. America sent retired business executives to Japan and Germany to rebuild the countries and poured in millions in aid. Many people think the concept of Japanese workers doing calisthenics at work and much of the culture and work ethic is rooted in Japanese culture but much of the culture that Japan adopted after WWII was American. In the 1920's in the USA the workers at International Business Machines (IBM) used to do calisthenics before work. The USA also installed military bases throughout the world at the time that still exists today.

The United Nations was born out of a need to learn from history and not repeat the mistakes of the past. Towns and cities were devastated and economies ruined. The UN was set up as One World Government and many of the laws and regulations that we live under today are a result of the UN. The UN also made Human Rights law and got every country on board, there were minimum standards that civilized people lived under and oppression by governments or dictators would no longer be tolerated. If the people of a country lived under tyranny, the UN would decide to intervene as the Worlds Government. It was an ambitious plan and it was developed for the most altruistic of reasons.

In 1946 United Nations International Children's Emergency Fund (UNICEF) was set up by a unanimous declaration by all members and lead my a man by the name of Maurice Pate. UNICEF had only ever intended to provide emergency aid after WWII but evolved, as any organization has a tendency for growth, evolved to broaden it's scope beyond an emergency relief agency. By 1980 when James P. Grant took leadership, the concept of specific Human Rights for Children was taking shape and the Declaration on the Rights of the Child, a beautiful document in my opinion, was rolled out. The Declaration was of course not a law as such, it was merely declaring that children deserved the right to housing, food, clean water and education which surprisingly enough needed to be taught to governments. As an aspiration document it is a thing of beauty, as human rights law, it is a disaster.

In his tenure from 1980 until he died in 1995, Grant had expanded the organization to more countries. In 2008 it was said by Nicolas Kristov of Grant, "a little-known American aid worker," had "probably saved more lives than were destroyed by Hitler, Mao and Stalin combined".

Grant had a different concept than many aid organizations, best described by the concept of teaching a man to fish rather than giving him a fish for a day. Instead of just feeding starving children, he realized that it takes a community to raise a child. It seemed pointless to just feed children if their parents were starving and a long term solution was to help the community and the children would be looked after in that way. UNICEF was present in many of these communities and not just in war or famine zones. His initiatives and programs were so successful that they became a model for other organization.

When Grant died, a new ideology was taking hold. Where we once talked about children 'in need", it shifted to "at risk", the theory that something may, or equally may not, happen at some point in the future. The term "Rights of the Child" gained currency and replaced "Needs of the Child". Also rather than putting the needs of children and helping children in actual need, UNICEF focused on putting the Rights of Children at the fore, which has proven to be a disaster.

Rather than their primary focus being on helping children in need in communities, they focused instead on a bureaucratic exercise of getting governments to sign up to the Convention on the Rights of the Child. Every country in the world has signed up to the UNCRC with the exception of the United States.

Even though almost every child in the world is entitled to a set of Children's Rights, **the UNCRC does not protect a single child in the world**; it merely gives them the "**right**" to be protected. Possessing a right and exercising it are entirely different things. Under the US Constitution, the Supreme Court decided that nobody had a right to be happy; the constitution only guaranteed a right to the **pursuit** of happiness. In the world today the Human Rights Industry is a massive juggernaut. If your rights are being denied you have to exhaust all local remedies, which includes the Supreme Court, before you can even apply to the European Court of Human Rights (ECtHR) or the International Court of Justice (ICJ). In Ireland the Supreme Court is backed up 10 years and the ECtHR, 3 years. If you take a case before the ECtHR for a Family Law injustice, it's likely that the child will be an adult before the case is heard. I know this as I have completed 3 applications.

In the world today, millions of children die of starvation and lack of clean drinking water. There are child soldiers, child marriage, child prostitutes, child slaves, Female Genital Mutilation, the death penalty for children and many other horrific punishments against children, all in countries where their governments have not only signed up to, but ratified into law these rights. Many countries have even signed up to Optional Protocols such as the prevention of Female Genital Mutilation (FMG).

In theory, every child is supposedly "protected" by Rights, in practice, when countries fail to deliver on these laws; at best all the UN can do is utter a strong condemnation. When a child dies of Hunger, FMG, Torture, Prostitution or Slavery, there are no consequences for failure or non-compliance, but at least the child died with their "Rights" intact. This is why having Rights is not working.

Effectively, the most endorsed Human Rights Treaty in the world is nothing more than a bureaucratic exercise. In general, the UN has become a fat, bloated policeman, who at best can only utter a strong condemnation when whole populations are being denied human rights. Even when they decide to give a bad report to a country or utter a condemnation, larger countries have the power of veto. We have seen many conflicts over the decades and we have seen the inaction of the UN who has failed 100% of the time in every conflict and in many cases the USA has stepped in as the "Worlds Policeman" to remove dictators or intervene where they are not needed as the case may be.

The fact is that the UN no longer serves its intended purpose. We have a fat policeman with no teeth and no jail to keep prisoners. The problem with having a fat, lazy dog minding the chickens is that the chickens may feel protected when they are not. The old dog also prevents us putting in a younger, more aggressive dog as we can only afford to feed and house one dog at a time.

The UN has strayed from its original mandate. They have grown into other areas such as Global Warming/Climate Change and have been a dramatic failure. Their departure from Science to using flawed models have lead to a lack of consensus even though the Climate "Scientists" are quick to point out that they have consensus when in fact so many reputable scientists disagree. Regardless of your views on Manmade Anthropogenic Climate Change, you would have to admit that the management of the entire debate has been a fiasco. Many will not agree with me but the simple fact is that Science in general, has been reduced to a position of Faith and Belief. Climate Change is a religion, you either believe or you are a Denier. There's no room for healthy skepticism or debate, you are either with us or against this. And if you are against us you are a heretic and deserve to be discredited. You may see some parallels here with the Salem Witch Trials, Paediatric Medicine and the Child Protection System in general. This is not how Science works you need questions and debate. It is however how Conspiracy Theory works, it is also how "Soft Science" works, you need to take a leap of faith and base your belief on a Theorist rather than a Theory.

Because the UN has pursued it's mandate of becoming One World Government, it has grown as organizations have a tendency to, when left unchecked. When Jim Grant died he left an efficient mechanism that exceeded everyone's expectation. His focus was the Needs of Children and preventing children from being in need in the first place. It's cheaper to bring seeds and water pumps to a community than it is to enter that community in a time of war or famine and deliver food and medicine. It's easier to prevent a fire than put one out. The shift from Needs to Rights Based Protection of children has not benefitted children.

Grants successor Carol Bellamy took over after his death and was forced to leave before the end of her second term. A new regime and ideology that included Radical Feminism and Psychology and Sociology took firm root. The concepts we are seeing now are based on an ideology that a child is not just a separate entity from its parents, their concept is that the child is Autonomous and can decide for themself. If they are too young to decide, the State will step in and decide for the child.

The Ideology is based on the Best Interest of the Child Principle; the BIP is the driving force and the only Quality Criteria behind UNICEF and the UNCRC. In reality BIP is a big stick used to beat parents with but has no Legal, Scientific or Moral Value. When you apply the BIP, UNICEF Operation is a great success even though the "patients" are dying. By the higher and more scientific principle suggested by Charles Pragnell, "To the Demonstrable and Measurable Benefit of the Child", UNICEF is a failure. Granting children "Rights" has not benefitted any child.

Even in Ireland and the UK we waffle on about the rights of the child but completely ignore children in actual need. With 30% of all Irish children living in consistent poverty, with 130,000 affected and now 700 children homeless and placed in emergency accommodation and with special needs children being denied an education, all of which are expressly forbidden by the UNCRC, has ratifying the UNCRC actually benefitted Irish children?

People are judged on the actions and not by their words. While Grant was a man of action and a visionary, Bellamy was a bureaucrat. During her tenure as Director, Carol Bellamy shifted the whole focus and ideology and allowed more Sociology to get a foothold. Sociology is also of the opinion that Biology counts for nothing, that "Family is an outdated concept rooted in Tribal Tradition". This is right out of the social work textbooks.

Sociology makes it possible to devalue motherhood and fatherhood because the belief is that the biological parent counts for nothing. You can take a child and in their best interests supplant that child in a stranger's house with no consequences to that child. The child can have 2 mommies, 2 daddies or a single "Parent". This works well with the BIP. However in practice it has never worked well, not just in terms of Outcomes for these children but by another measure largely ignored and unknown to the public at large.

With new medical advances Surrogacy has become an industry, Motherhood has been devalued and term such as "Gestational Carrier" has now become commonplace to replace "Mother". For many people, these sanitized terms do not fit well. For many of the people whose job it is to rip a newborn from the breast of its mother I'm sure that the sanitization helps them de-humanize their victims. Most humans don't have the capacity to harm another human being except in anger. When they have dehumanized their victim, the person becomes an object devoid of feelings.

In her controversial tenure, she was determined to shake up the organization even though Grant had left a well-oiled machine. Her reforms didn't sit well with many of the staff and some resigned or threatened to resign amid the controversy of UNICEF becoming more political rather than the non-partisan approach it had from its inception. Bellamy had formed alliances with large corporations such as an Infant Formula manufacturer. At the same time, infant mortality rates were spiraling in countries like Iraq and children were dying in the hundreds of thousands under sanctions imposed by the UN after Saddam Hussein had invaded Kuwait. Her position was becoming untenable, where Grant could have marched an army of Emergency Aid workers into Iraq with Saddam's blessing, Bellamy was resorting to her training and experience as a politician. She also began stockpiling and carrying a large inventory of goods, foods and medicines which are sold to many countries. She was forced to resign half way through her second term. In her defense, the UN General Council did not help her in any way. The children of Iraq had been used by both sides as political pawns and 500,000 infants died as a result of UN policy.

We only have to look to Syria to see how the UN no longer serves its intended purpose. Far from its lofty goal of becoming "One World Government" and being a policeman, it has degenerated into a bloated bureaucracy that if it were a business, would have gone bankrupt many years ago.

I have to laugh sometimes at the conspiracy theorists making tenuous connections to Bilderberg's, Illuminati, Freemasons and talking about the New World Order and a massive conspiracy of secret bodies bent on world domination. The fact is that the UN was formed in 1946 as a New World Order with the goal of having One World Government and no conspiracy, no leaps of faith and no secret societies are needed. The New World Order **is** the UN and all of this is well documented. There are no evil masterminds, only good, God fearing people with the most altruistic of intentions and their goal is World Peace and not domination. But as the UN has proven to be a massive failure, I don't think we have anything to fear. Perhaps when WWIII is finished and people have had enough of slaughtering others, we can sit down again and unite all the nations to form a New World Order where war will be a thing of the past?

The Adoption Panacea

In her groundbreaking work, Nancy Verrier introduced us to the "Primal Wound". She was of course talking about adoption but actually Foster "Care" is worse in terms of causing this damage to children. I spoke briefly about Adoption earlier and I would like to expand on the topic in this chapter. Talking about Ideology is a good place for talking about Adoption.

I have come to the conclusion, that Adoption is one of the worst forms of child abuse ever devised. Going back to my first case I told you about a toddler who would wake up screaming from his afternoon nap or in the middle of the night, mumbling about his "2 mammies" and women taking him away from his brother and father. I would not have believed that a baby between the age of 6 and 14 months could have suffered from Post Traumatic Stress Disorder but having witnessed it for myself, I am a convert to the concept of the Primal Wound that Nancy Verrier wrote about.

My view of adoption used to be fairly mainstream. My concept was of doe-eyed orphans languishing in orphanages and foster homes and big hearted couples fighting an impossible battle and opening their hearts and homes to a child who was in need of a "Forever Home". I lapped up the hype along with everyone else until I saw the Adoption Industry for what it really was. The demand for children has always existed. After WWII, over 60,000 British children were shipped off to Australia for "Oranges & Sunshine". What later emerged was that many of these children, who had been evacuated from London and large cities, did in fact have at least one parent or extended family capable of caring for them. Instead, a bureaucratic decision was made to ship all the children to Australia and some to Canada. The vast majority of these children ended up as slaves working on farms for no reward. A few years ago the Prime Minister of Australia apologized, however many of the slaves had already died years before in the many years it took to get recognition that they were in fact trafficked.

In Ireland, a similar tale of over 60,000 "bastard children" who had the audacity to be born outside of marriage contrary to Catholic Dogma, sometimes these children being the product of rape. Their mothers were sinners and penitents, many of them children themselves and their babies stolen and sold to the highest bidder for the "sin" of being raped. We hear often of the Magdalen Laundries but no children were actually adopted from there. The Magdalen Order of Nuns ran advertisements calling themselves the Magdalen Asylum.

For the sum of £100 pounds they would "take care of the problem" and the girl wouldn't have to pay penitence by working 3 years in slavery in the Magdalen Laundries. It has always been illegal in the Irish State to sell human beings so the Magdalen Charity would gratefully accept "donations". In their newspaper advertisements soliciting donations, they stated that they begged funds for 130 "Poor Penitents" within their walls.

When a couple expressed an interest in a child, they would be asked for donations to feed and clothe the child while they were being screened. Let me state at this point that I believe that the nuns and clergy did their best. It was a world "long ago and far away". The State did little in the way of protecting children and someone had to step into the "breech" as it were to protect children. Again we see a case of good people with the best intentions doing the best they could under very difficult circumstances. Best Intentions don't always translate well and when they operate under the filter of religious dogma, that it was a sin to have sex or a child out of wedlock, the results could only be predictable. If the dogma allowed for these children to remain with their parents and the "problem" of unmarried mothers, who have existed all through history, the Church would have been praised for their efforts rather than demonized.

The infant mortality rate in Ireland during "The Emergency" as WWII was known, hit as high as 50% and was as bad in these mother & baby units as it was elsewhere. When a baby who was unfortunate enough to be born out of wedlock and died, the Catholic dogma was that they were not allowed to be buried on consecrated ground. Many were buried at night on the margins of the cemetery. In Galway in 2014, the bodies of 800 children who died over the years were discovered in a compartment that was formerly a septic tank. Babies didn't have the right to enter Heaven and had committed no sin so were supposedly sent to Limbo as the prevailing dogma was at the time. Such was the contempt for these unfortunate infants that they were not allowed to be raised by their mothers, were "sold" to the highest bidders and if they died, they died in "Original Sin". Let us not forget, this was the face of Child "Protection" in Ireland and also to some extent in the UK. I have an aunt who successfully raised her child quite successfully with the help of her family, which shows me at least that if catholic dogma was left out of the equation, that children would always do better when raised by family.

The current dogma of the Catholic Church has significantly changed in recent years. Limbo no longer exists and stillborn children can now be buried to rest in peace. To me the idea of any religion setting themselves up as the Moral Guardian of Society has never sat well with me. I have no issue with churches dictating to their congregation but they don't speak for me or other religions. Religion should never be the Guardian of Morals, as it has no exclusive right to speak for people outside its congregation. Historically all religions are extremely flawed and religion has never benefitted any population when serving as a form of government. We can see today the effect of Sharia

Law in many countries; Sharia Courts even exist in many Western Countries. Religion must be separate from Government, but it must also be separate from Justice.

In my own view, Religion is a form of Entertainment but I respect the right of anyone to believe anything they wish as long as they don't hurt anyone in the process and have no more influence over Justice or Governments than anyone else. Because the fields of Science, Medicine, Psychology, Sociology and the whole spectrum of Child Protection have degenerated in a "Religion", where our beliefs about the system are based on a proposition of Faith rather than evidence, we do a great disservice to children in believing that Child "Protection" actually benefits children. I have given many examples here of how the system is clearly not working.

We are taking 184 children on the off chance that 1 has been abused and causing far more harm by the intervention. I base this number on my own estimations that for every "Care" order of the court, that only 1 person will be charged with Child Abuse or Neglect in relation to the Order. Let's not become fixated on this number and focus on the children instead. There is obviously a serious problem when the HSE can claim 541 "confirmed" cases of sexual abuse of children but there are very few criminal prosecutions to match. When Dr Phil says he would rather see 1,000 children taken to prevent 1 child "swinging in the wind", he is normalizing Witch Hunting tactics and Phil, like most in the field, seems to forget or denies that "Protection" is far more harmful in most cases than the alleged abuse or neglect. The shift from the Needs of Children to the Rights of Children has been an unmitigated disaster. Because of normalizing Witch Hunting as an acceptable form of "protecting" children, we are harming far more children, we are also ignoring the Rights of children in the process, the 183 or 999 children wrongfully removed end up having their Human Rights abused under Article 8 of the Human Rights Act, the Right to a Family Life.

I have met and debated with many people whose views are so entrenched in the Gospel of Child "Protection", that even when you present them with the evidence, they wont accept any new information that goes against their beliefs. Psychologists call this "Cognitive Dissonance" but I prefer to call it as I see it, a "Religion of Child Protection". Many of the proponents of this Religion have only heard one side of the story. They have not met the children, talked to them, inspected their homes, interviewed their parents or attended court. They accept the dogma after hearing one side of the story just as people will accept the Bible, Koran or Torah and anyone who says otherwise is dismissed as Heretic or a Conspiracy Theorist.

I believe in the years to come that we will see proponents of Shaken Baby Syndrome as killers of babies because they deny that babies can die of short falls even though there is ample evidence that these short falls and not shaking, are what produce the Triad of symptoms known as SBS.

I believe that Doctors, in hindsight, will see that Rickets was at epidemic proportions since the 1990's and that they wrongly engaged in Witch Hunts of innocent parents.

I believe that if the United Nations and the Children's "Rights" Mafia threw out the Best Interests of the Child Principle and recognized that Sociology and Psychology are not robust enough tools to use to destroy innocent families, and replaced BIP with; "To the Demonstrable and Measurable Benefit of the Child", that we would have a far higher standard of protecting children.

I firmly believe that if Ireland followed far better models of Child Protection rather than blindly following the UK, that Ireland could have a World-Class Child Protection System.

I also believe that if the In Camera Rule was abandoned tomorrow, that it would restore Justice to an "Alternate Universe" that has become our Family Courts. As people would have a better understanding of how children end up in "Care" and people would realize that the Intervention and "Care" is indeed the problem, we could set about to restore justice and eliminate the spending a Billion a year on children rather than spending it on an Industry that does not benefit children. I read that last week in the UK, The Children's Tsar has stated that opening up Family Courts would result in the deaths of more children in "Care" by suicide. When asked how she knew this she pointed out that she was a social worker, "I Know".

As Ian Josephs has continually pointed out since the 1960's, "There should be No Punishment Without Crime", this is one of the basic principles of Human Rights Law. If child abuse and neglect is indeed a crime, then we need to let Police handle crime. We can't have social workers trying to predict "Future Crime" and operating as the "Thought Police" as John Hemming MP has pointed out. We also can't have social workers in the dual-role of being Advocates and Prosecutors of families at the same time. We can't have an alternate Justice System where you are innocent in one court and guilty in another, the whole concept of Family Courts is completely contrary to Human Rights Law.

If 50 years of Social Work has taught us anything, it should have taught us that when Governments try interfering in Nature, it has always resulted in failure. Nature teaches us that Biology is everything; social work pretends that Biology is a vestige of our Tribal Roots and that Biology means nothing. Because the Social "Sciences" are based on a position of Faith rather than hard Science, it has become a Product that has been over-sold and like any other organization has had a tendency to grow, unfortunately into a monster which harms far more children than it helps.

At the same time, Psychology and Sociology have proven to be wonderful tools when applied in the form of Advocacy, it has proven to be a failure in controlling Society as it is not robust enough in being used as anything more than Subjective Opinion. If "Care" is supposed to protect children, then why don't these children have far better outcomes in life and why is the suicide rate of "Cared For" children 10 times higher than children in the general population? These are the uncomfortable questions that nobody wants to ask. While social workers are playing the victim, their victims are dying at an alarming rate. If as many social workers died as did children in their "Care", I would be concerned.

CHAPTER 10

EPIDEMIC OF FAT

The field of Child Protection takes some pretty strange turns sometimes and issues that you wouldn't think are protection issues cropping up. I have heard social workers saying that a foster carer holding a child's too tight while crossing the road was child abuse. When a man got drunk and relieved himself in a back alley at 3 in the morning and was caught by police, he ended up on the Sex Offender Register and next he knew his children were being removed on the basis he was a convicted sex offender. Lately the discussion has been around feeding children and strangely enough, feeding family pets. Social workers are now being told in one area to examine the dog's food dish and water bowl, as this might be a child protection issue. Apparently if they can't look after their pets they shouldn't be looking after children. They have broadened the definition so far to include the most pedantic reasons for taking children into "Care".

As a friend once said to a social worker, "who the hell gave you the right to come into my home and tell me how to parent my children?" a very interesting question. I completely understand and accept that children need to be protected. But who "owns" your children, you or the State? Obviously when I say "own" I am not advocating slavery or the sale of children but children need to be protected from themselves. Despite the rhetoric of Children's Rights Mafia, children are not autonomous and need constant supervision, they need adult guardians to make decisions for them and to do otherwise would be neglect and a failure in the duty of a parent. But when we say "Protecting Children", do we mean protecting them at all costs or to the detriment of other things? Who sets the boundaries for when intervention by the State is necessary? What guidelines are there for the Threshold to Intervention being met? This is not a question to be taken lightly.

Is it justified to remove children who are obese? Would it be justifiable to remove a child from a mother who is deaf? A mother who is blind? A mother who is temporarily incapacitated because of sudden and temporary illness? Is it justified to remove children who are Home Schooled? If a mother decides to have a Home Birth with a Doula instead of a Midwife, is this considered abuse? In all of the examples I gave above, children have been removed for those very reasons. Many of the situations are so easily fixable but there is no incentive to fix minor problems. Social workers don't get their egos satisfied and the Industry doesn't make any money if the child stays at home.

Ian Josephs uses one argument of Punishment Without Crime. This is in fact a Human Rights issue for the child as much as the parent. To expand on Ian's argument, when a child is removed, shouldn't there be a parallel Police investigation? How is it possible to remove a child from parents who have committed no crime? In Ireland how is it possible that 186 children are removed or the subject of Supervision Orders, but only 1 person will be charged with a crime? In the vast majority of cases I have seen, there were no police investigations, I have seen this in Ireland, the UK, Canada and the USA.

But getting back to the Threshold to Intervention, when is it ok for the State to intervene? When a crime is committed and the child is dead? This of course would be an extreme case but has happened. When there is a report from a vindictive neighbor or mother-in-law? This would make up the bulk of interventions, cases are screened and the children visited at the investigation stage. On one hand if we wait until the child is dead, it would be pointless for social workers to intervene. On the other hand, social workers can visit a house 60 times as in the case of Baby Peter, or over a period of 11 years as in the Roscommon House of Horrors. Even though the system is stacked in favor of the State against the parent, you will still get false negatives and false positives. The wrong children will the removed and children like Baby P and the Roscommon kids are left to suffer.

When you look at the guidelines for intervention and the Threshold being met you only have very vaporous guidelines, it's not hard to see why social workers get it wrong most of the time. Would Police do a better job? If you were asking Police to predict future crime and future outcomes, Police could do no better. The job of Police is to Serve & Protect, supposedly the citizens. Police only investigate after a crime has been committed so most of the time they are concerned about what happened in the past. In the very rare cases of actual child abuse and neglect, the Police take control of crime scenes and hand the children over to social workers who have no role, experience or even training in investigating crime. If a baby were picked up at a heroin den or crack house, it would be done by Police and not social workers.

The roles of Police and Child Protection are very different. As Police in the UK, Ireland, Canada and the USA have abrogated their role in protecting children to social workers, crimes against children, even the sexual assault of children, are not investigated by Police or punished by Prosecutors. When those crimes happen to children in "Care", there is no mechanism to report to Gardaí who would be breaking the In Camera Rule by investigating. Consequently, children are not protected to the same standard as adults. You need no more proof of this than the fact that the HSE claimed 541 "Confirmed" cases of sexual assault of children and the DPP only had 3 prosecutions the same year, mostly of historic cases. Essentially, children in Ireland do not receive the same protection as adults because Gardaí are not investigating every case. The Irish Constitution makes no distinction between the rights of children and adults, in most articles the words "Person" is used and applies equally. I believe that if only Gardaí investigated the crime of sexual abuse of children, there would not be 541 confirmed cases a year and the guilty parties would be punished. By allowing social workers to investigate crimes against children, we are doing a great disservice to them. We are allowing children to be harmed by being taken away from innocent families and allowing crimes against children, especially the children in "Care" to go unpunished.

We also have a situation that would never occur if Police, and only Police, had the role of investigating child abuse and neglect, Police wouldn't be taking the wrong children on nothing more than suspicion. Police usually have very compelling evidence before making an arrest but even the get it wrong far too often. Social workers on the other hand appear to live in a different world to you and I, unlike Police they do not operate on a system of Evidence Based. They see allegations as being sufficient to abuse the human rights of a child in order to protect them. They don't do investigation, they do assessments after the child has been taken, and when they fail to prove one theory they will move on to another. The reasons keep changing all the time form one order to the next. Of course this is not Justice, at least not Justice, as we believe it exists.

When you examine what went wrong in the Baby P and Roscommon cases, Police could have stepped in at any time and removed the children. Even if they were wrong in removing the children, nobody would have blamed them, they acted on good faith and have the right to err on the side of caution. In the cases of the Moral Panic of the blue eyed and blond Roma children removed on suspicion that they had been abducted, Gardaí used their powers of S12. The public reaction was mostly that they over-reacted in both cases. In one case the parent had a Birth Certificate and sufficient documentation. The children were removed for a few days until DNA evidence proved the parents innocent. Arresting a child, which essentially this was has dire consequences for the children. The girl who was abducted now dies her hair; such is her terror that she will be removed again. If she's like other children I have met, she probably has nightmares and is suffering from PTSD. It seemed clear to me that the Gardaí had misused S12 in both of these cases. The law says that the children must be at serious risk of harm or in imminent danger, and that Gardaí must establish the danger, which I don't see the threshold being met.

But regardless of the merits of the case, it was an eye-opener for many in the Child Abuse Industry to see how easily a child can be removed without evidence. We were lied to during the Children's Referendum that it is almost impossible to remove children unless there is very compelling evidence, people believed the hype they were told that a parent can "literally have their hands around the neck of a child and throttle that child to an inch of their life before the State can intervene" or that "taking a child into Care is an absolute last resort that only takes place after all possibilities have been eliminated". My colleagues and I have been saying for years that children are removed with no evidence, on nothing more than suspicion, and that the vast majority of children in "Care" don't need to be there and the system has degenerated in State Sponsored Kidnapping of Children for the benefit of the Child Abuse Industry.

We don't hear all the stories because people are gagged. People have tried to gag my colleagues and me and maliciously prosecute us for reporting the abuse of children in "Care". The parents are gagged again that if they breathe a word to anyone, that the relationship with their child will be severed. This is a system in crisis protecting itself. When you are backed into a corner its fight or die. Any scrutiny of the system is opposed. You have corrupt CFA Lawyers breaking the law to maximize their profits. You have "Experts" and Lobbyists who really have no clue as to what happens to children in "Care". You have judges protecting their reputations, damaging children by taking them away from their parents and then not accepting responsibility when a child that they placed in "Care" dies or is harmed.

In the Roma cases the Garda investigations were incompetent, heavy handed and harmed the children involved, which presumably wasn't their intention. I was actually quite surprised that the story became public, similar abductions occur every day in Ireland and the parents and media are gagged so that the public would never know. We have a situation in Ireland where social workers who have no legal right to invoke a S12 using it daily, in hospitals for example to remove newborns, but they get away with this because judges pervert the course of justice on a regular basis. The only legal way a newborn could be removed from a hospital is if the hospital was on fire and a Garda felt the need to remove that child.

I have seen in 3 cases personally where teams of Gardaí have round-the-clock surveillance on heavily pregnant women at the behest of the CFA or HSE without any legal right or obligation to do so. My colleagues have witnessed this also and it would seem quite likely that at least 80 times per year, Gardaí are spending millions watching heavily pregnant women for weeks at a time even though the Garda Management claim they don't have the budget to follow Larry Murphy and predators who have been released from prison. I see no reason that in the Roma cases, they could have used this mechanism rather than harming the children involved.

The Roma cases were the tip of an iceberg that the Irish Public no nothing about. The Irish Public know nothing about the wrong child being removed for months, they know nothing about what I witnessed in court one day where 3 children were removed in the space of less than a minute without the parents being present and without any evidence being heard. The "Experts", Lobbyists and Child Abuse Industry no nothing about what happens in secret family courts, they pretend they know but they have only heard one side of the story. For me to even disclose these cases is against the law of saying "Anything to Anybody".

However I could not successfully be prosecuted in an open court because it would be illegal for the prosecutor to say "Anything to Anybody" of what occurred. Additionally, the onus would be on the prosecution to prove in which court the case occurred. Because the folks in Cavan have no access to or legal right to know what happens in Cork or Waterford, they would be unable to prove which court or case I am disclosing and I am involved in cases all over the world. At least in the UK Sir Justice Munby has decreed that cases are recorded and written judgments handed down or published, so effectively, Ireland has the most draconian and Secret Courts in the Free World.

Let me be clear on this, the In Camera Rule is supposed to protect children and not the system. I have given good examples here of how the rule works against the children in "Care". It is absurd and ridiculous that Police cannot investigate crimes committed "In Camera". It is equally absurd that a system is allowed to operate beyond scrutiny, Justice doesn't happen in Secret. Accountability is not possible in a secret court if Justice cannot be seen to be done. Children cannot be protected if nobody is allowed to know what happens or if judges cover up wrongdoings. There is no mechanism for Gardaí to investigate crimes against children in "Care", and this, beyond any other point I have made, should be extremely disturbing to anyone who cares about children.

The system is built on negatives, we "Protect" children from harm and the system is very adversarial, there are no positives. Social workers are doing an impossible job because nobody can predict future crime or outcomes, they especially can't do it with the crystal balls or Psychology and Sociology. We have all the evidence before us that almost everything we believe we know about Child Protection is a lie. There are no happy endings from an intervention in families, social workers are not advocates, they are there to take away and damage your child and every parent lives in fear of them. Parents are afraid to take their child to doctors and hospitals for fear that a very minor injury will unleash an inquisition. This is the same climate that existed in Salem 300 years ago. And it's not evil people with evil intent, with the possible exception of the private law firms working for the CFA, this is about good people, so in fear of a child being in danger that on the least little injury, that they are prepared to unleash an inquisition on the child, and in the process, harm that child in the belief they are protecting them. If a child is born addicted to Heroin or Crack or Alcohol, I say take that child at birth and if the family are not capable of raising them, then as a last resort let the child be raised by strangers. But when a child is taken, it should only be based on Evidence and not on the basis of Good Intentions or the vaporous slogan of Best Interests. The Child Protection Systems in Ireland, the UK, Canada and the USA are not in the Best Interests of anyone other than an industry, an industry that does not love any child.

The negatives are born of anger; child abuse and neglect make us angry and rightly so. I have witnessed many self-righteous social workers on the witness stand and at conferences; they can't look the parents in the eye. Ask the right questions and see them getting angry, question them and you are a heretic, you must be a child abuser yourself if you don't agree with them. When you point out their failings the anger comes out. When you see Police and Forensic Experts testifying, they are not there to bolster one side against the other even if they are hired by the Defense or Prosecution. Of course in Family Courts the "Experts" would only be paid if they presented a damning report and 70% are unqualified. But in Criminal Cases, the police and forensics have no interest in innocence or guilt, they are there to assist the court and are impartial. Child Protection on the other hand is angry people who cannot see any positives in parents which makes them lie and exaggerate because they take child protection very personally and if they don't accomplish a "Parent-ectomy" they believe they have failed personally. This is not how justice is supposed to be done, but because you haven't witnessed it for yourself, you can't see what is being done in your name. I often wonder if in later life if the accusers, prosecutors and judges in Salem ever felt guilty for what they had done. I know quite a few older social workers who have lasting regrets.

Do we have an epidemic of Obesity? Is it due to processed foods? Is it due to lack of cooking skills? Is it really a child protection issue? Politicians and others have waded into the debate in recent years and personally I believe that "you are what you eat" so yes, it is very much a child protection issue. It's also interesting to compare what we feel about food to how we feel about other areas of protecting children. I believe that food is of critical importance to growing children and for those children to be healthy and happy.

While governments see the solution as taxing "fattening food" what they should be doing is limiting the crap that food manufacturers are selling as "food", especially to children. Recent research has proven that more natural, unrefined and unprocessed food can reverse certain types of Diabetes and reduce Body Mass Index rapidly. Even "farm fresh vegetables" you buy at a farmers market is likely to contain pesticides and poisons. Cooking of food is absolutely critical to kill off the bacteria and simply washing vegetables before using them improves food safety. It is virtually impossible these days to buy fruits and vegetables that do not contain some poisons. We eat meat that contains antibiotics, hormones and other medicines that were given to sick animals; this has helped produce immunity to antibiotics. We are now seeing evolving bacteria that has become immune to antibiotics.

If I started a company tomorrow to sell a food product that was dangerous, it would never get to market. However if I made a "food like" product that had absolutely no nutritional value or a high sugar or fructose content, I would have no issues. Documentaries such as "Supersize Me" and many other similar stories have shown us that food suppliers are indeed selling us dangerous foods, that if this was all we ate, our health would suffer or we would die. Worse yet, if you read the labels on infant formula, you would understand why paediatricians are seeing an epidemic of obesity in 6-month-old infants. While it is beyond the culinary skills of most people to make simple meals like soups that taste as good as you can get from a can, the prospect of making infant formula would be far beyond most people. So why does the government not regulate and place more tax on the bad foods and eliminate all taxes on healthy foods?

What I have never understood is how companies are allowed to market products specifically targeted at children. Children don't have any purchasing power other than sweets and soft drinks. Would any parent serve their child nothing but "Happy Meals" every day until adulthood? Chronic obesity starts out in childhood and leads to more health problems later in life. As the taxpayer will pay the price for these health problems, would it not make more sense to apply an ounce of prevention earlier in life?

Would it not be more beneficial to teach children about food and cooking from a young age in schools? On TV this morning I was watching a survey, which claimed that 85% of all food sold in supermarkets contains added sugar. For years we were told to eat Low Fat and now we are being advised to eat Low Sugar. Many manufacturers don't actually add Sugar in the form of sugar you would buy in a shop, but in the form of Fructose which is far more "fattening". They can get away with false advertising by being "creative" with the labeling and the truth. For years we were told by the Tobacco Industry that cigarettes are "safe" and recommended by doctors.

Governments are afraid of large corporations, politicians rely on them to get elected and re-elected. When you drink Cola's and carbonated drinks, you are drinking about 40% "Sugar", or worse yet, Fructose. A friend of mine worked as a checkout person in a supermarket and remarked that that by looking at any person, she could almost guarantee what products their shopping basket would contain. Personally I would put more stock into what she believes about the Food Industry than most Dieticians and Nutritionists. I will be forever grateful to her for teaching me to read and understand the labels of everything I consume.

Chefs mostly work from raw foods and can make tasty and nutritious meals from scratch, however it takes many years of practice and study to become a good chef. It seems that "Food Science" has become as un-scientific as any other science. Whenever I have seen parents serving "fizzy drinks" to children, I must admit that I have often "stuck my oar" in. Children given large amounts of sugar will predictably become obese and have more health problems.

While governments strictly regulate many aspects of out lives, there is very little regulation of the Food Industry itself, at least in terms of making manufacturers produce healthy foods for children and also allowing them to market to children. Giving toddlers 6 tablespoons of sugar would be considered abuse. Giving the same child a fizzy drink with 6 tablespoons of sugar or fructose is acceptable. We don't sell alcohol to minors, so why do we allow sales of sugar added foods to toddlers? As sugar has a similar effect in the brain to cocaine for young children, why is it not as strictly regulated as alcohol?

I have tried eating "healthy" myself and bought fresh fruits and vegetables from Farmers Markets but I found the cost was far more than what I could buy a tin of soup in a supermarket. I could never replicate the taste of the commercial products and didn't feel any better for eating "healthy" for weeks at a time. You also have to consider the high cost of cooking food in Ireland and the UK; we pay far more than any of our neighbors for electricity and gas. It also takes a very considerable time cooking than it does reheating a commercially prepared product. The simple fact of the matter is that obesity is here to stay and governments can only blame themselves for their lack on governance. For too long we have let large corporations dictate and now we are seeing the effects. Perhaps a greater danger we face is allowing these corporations to control the world's food supply and our water.

As I write this, there are protests all over Ireland over the privatization of Irelands water supply. Possibly 100,000 people marched in the streets over the installation of water meters. The numbers differ depending on whether you are getting your information from RTE or other sources. Initially, RTE had barely mentioned the topic and there has been scant reporting in the Irish Times and Independent. On Facebook and Twitter, a large percentage of the reports are by citizen journalists with "expensive smart phones" as Minister Joan Burton was quick to remark. It's interesting that a TD would make such a remark when the TD's allowance is €750 every two years to buy a phone. It seems we have a media that is asleep at the wheel and doesn't consider the revolution happening on social media or chooses to ignore it. "The revolution will not be televised".

I have a friend who is a lobbyist in Washington DC and she would tell you that many of the laws that are passed are written by corporations and that the only motive of any corporation is profit. You see connections where corporate lawyers end up being appointed judges and given positions of power as a reward for loyal service. Lobbying is not illegal and likely will never be. Politicians depend on political contributions to get elected and those contributions were not made out of the goodness of a corporation's heart. And they were not made without the understanding that the favor would be repaid at some point in the future or a sense of loyalty that a similar contribution would be made at the next election. You only have to follow the careers in Ireland to see the influence of corporations and political parties and who is a member of what board or CEO of a "Charity".

For anyone to believe that such lobbying doesn't exist in Ireland and the UK would be incorrect. Having stood outside the Dail during protests, you see the staff and the TD's coming and going but you also see a lot of others, not just in the Dail itself but at the restaurants and bars frequented by the TD's. It used to be that if you wanted something done in Ireland that you needed to pass around a few "brown envelopes" to influence the decision. Politics is and has always been corrupt in any country in the world. I have followed the careers of some people over the years and seen people appointed as directors to boards of companies and how many controversial people just seem to rise and rise over the years. While politics may not be well paid, it would seem that once a politician serves a term or two, they will never want for anything, this is especially true of the Party Faithfull and not so much for the Independents.

Although many people go into politics for the most altruistic or reasons and wish to represent their constituents, they come home to their constituencies representing the government to us. While the politicians change over time, there are many in the background who are permanent fixtures. When you look at CEO's of "Charities", Directors of large Corporations and NGO's and you follow their careers back they have long affiliations to political parties. Even voters and party supporters have long affiliations and if you need something done, you need some of these people to make it happen. Nepotism is rife with the Ruling Class handing down to the next generation.

While we have come a long way in stamping out the corruption that was rife during the Haughey years and after, we still have a long way to go before we reach true democracies that exist in other European countries. Every system in Ireland is affected or infected by corruption and the Child Abuse Industry is no exception. Every time a new law is introduced, it creates a new quango or industry somewhere. As Ireland has been modeling itself on the UK system you can see 5 years in advance what is going to happen in Ireland.

There are indeed Irish lobbyists for the Child Abuse Industry. For an industry that is a billion a year and growing, a lot of jobs are at stake and a lot of private interests to be protected. I mentioned a few earlier with the Legal and the "Care" Industries. A tendency we have seen in Ireland and the UK is towards privatization of services and resources. In the USA and UK, many jobs that were once performed by civil servants have been privatized with large corporations taking over government services for profit. Ireland has seen less of this, as our civil service unions are far more powerful than their counterparts in the UK.

In the UK in the area of child protection, we have seen a massive shift in handing over jobs to private companies. The main advantage being it costs less to produce the same services and you don't pay for what you don't use. If turnover slows down you don't lay off civil servants or need to hire them. If you need a foster carer you make one phone call to an agency. Obviously you don't even need to worry about standards and nobody is regulating the agencies. Many of the agencies are owned and operated by social workers and psychologists.

To a large extent in Ireland, a very large proportion of the Child "Protection" System is already in private hands. Most of the "Care" system, the Experts and Contact Centers, the Guardians ad Litem and the ever-present lawyers who act as Prosecutors in Private Practice. The Government have 4,500 people working in the CFA, mostly social workers and there is at least double that number of private citizens or companies working for profit. With any Industry, there are jobs at stake and the system requires a steady flow of children into the system to make up for the children ageing out and dying. Managers play a constant numbers game and the decision to take a child into "care" falls on the manager. The managers often make their decisions based on the numbers of foster carers that are available and sometimes refuse children if there are no placements. I didn't know that occurred until a social worker told me one day that the manager was "screaming for kids" as the numbers were dropping. It has since been confirmed by other social workers in Ireland, the UK and the USA.

Having worked in manufacturing for many years and having engineered production lines, I am very aware of input and output and how both can affect production and ultimately, profit. We often think of "Charities" as being a not-for-profit organization and don't often consider the infrastructure and management behind it. For example, Barnardos Ireland is a €21 million a year "industry" that has many employees that need to be paid, they have properties and shops that they must pay the rent, utilities and taxes on whether the shop is profitable of not. Barnardos also run the largest Guardian ad Litem company in Ireland and in 2011, their balance sheet shows they made €16 million from the government by selling "Services". They offer a broad range of services to parents and government. In turn they also employ a law firm who provide solicitors at €215/hr. for their GAL's who charge I believe about €125/hr.

While we tend to think that Child "Protection" is largely civil servants, in truth far more people in private industry support the CFA and their jobs depend on input and output. It's interesting to see the political connections of the 100 or so Children's "Charities" in Ireland. No System could exist without the infrastructure to support it, or without people holding out their hand expecting to be paid. The system relies on growth and a continuous supply of children.

Fortunately for the industry but not so fortunate for children or the taxpayer, the Child Abuse Industry has seen unprecedented growth in the last decade. Even in tough economic times, the lawyers manage to triple their profits, the demand for foster carers and agencies has doubled and the Psychologists, Experts and "Charities" have all made profits. What has also increased is the number of children dying, being raped and abused and being dumped on the streets at 18.

There are over 8,000 family court hearings a year and the length of time to deal with a case has increased dramatically. There has also been an increase in High Court applications, mostly to deal with the mistakes and human rights abuses by the judges in the District Courts. More people are now forced to defend themselves as the cost of Legal Aid has increased. While we are told that Ireland actually has the most generous Legal Aid budget in Europe but the application fee has increased to €170 which is the most expensive in Europe. The generosity of the government benefits the lawyers far more than the clients. Still, we should be grateful because the UK have all but eliminated Legal Aid altogether for family law cases. In the UK you can lose your child forever to Forced Adoption and you are not entitled to help to defend yourself. The UK used to have the most expensive Legal Aid however; Legal Aid in Family Law in the UK is almost non-existent having been removed in Family Law cases. The UK and Ireland have the most expensive legal system due to its adversarial nature.

When you look at some of the statistics that are actually published, especially from the Courts Service, you see a picture of where judges will grant Orders in 100% percent of cases and others less likely to grant orders without first hearing the evidence. I mentioned earlier a case where a judge granted an Emergency Care Order in the space of less than a minute, without hearing any evidence and without the parents being heard or even being represented in court. No judge should have the power to order such a draconian measure without hearing evidence and without hearing both sides of the story. This power should especially not be placed in the hands of less experienced judges in District Courts. In most European jurisdictions judges do not have arbitrary power to impose such a punishment without first investigating for themselves. In fact they have a duty to investigate and have the power to walk into a home and decide for themselves.

Irish Law is based on English Law and many of our statutes were actually written when Ireland was part of the British Empire. For example, Ireland has a law which has since been repealed called the Illegitimate Children Act of 1930. As ominous as the title of the act was, its intentions were honorable in that it made a statutory law that fathers of "Illegitimate" children are bound by law to pay for child support and funeral expenses of their offspring who died. What is interesting about the Act is the fact that the words In Camera are not mentioned. Also the fact that 84 years after the act was published, that a proper mechanism for child support doesn't exist today and fathers have very little "Rights" when it comes to their children.

Most of Europe uses a type of law known as Napoleonic Law or *Code Napoléon*. What is interesting is that in countries where English Law is used, is that in these countries, the child protection and family law systems tend to be more problematic and controversial. I am not an expert in law but simply making an observation that the countries with fewer problems seem to have a better Justice System. Also in the Napoleonic Code System is the provision for Inquisitorial Proceedings compared to out Adversarial System. Social workers in Spain and France don't need to build a case after they have removed a child, it is simply not their decision to remove any child, and it is the job of the Police and the Courts. What frequently happens in many European countries is that the judge has a "Meeting" between the parents and social worker without any lawyers present. This can be done without removing the child, it can be done at very short notice and the judge is obligated to investigate rather than being fed "evidence".

The Inquisitorial System's main objective is to get to the absolute truth of the issue. Parents don't find themselves with one Legal Aid solicitor they met for the first time 30 minutes ago, fighting for their children against a barrage of "Experts" and lawyers in a court where they are deemed guilty until they prove themselves innocent. They also don't find themselves bankrupt as the system is not incentivised as the Irish and UK system is, to stretch out cases as long as possible to increase profits for CFA and GAL Lawyers, their Hired Gun Barristers, GAL's, Experts and Hired Gun Experts who lie for money. Cases can be dealt with in hours rather than months and the 999 children of innocent parents are not removed to begin with. Of course this wouldn't suit the billion a year Child Abuse Industry in Ireland and Irish taxpayers have deep pockets to keep throwing money at a problem that will never go away.

Believe it or not, the Inquisitorial System was suggested in Ireland by Kieran McGrath who is a trained Lawyer as well as a trained Social Worker about 20 years ago but has not gained any support. Politicians in Ireland have always been swayed more by the lobbyists of the Child Abuse Industry rather than listening to people in the system. I also mentioned Joe Robbins earlier who warned the ministers and Dept. of Health that the lies an exaggerations of the extent of Child Sexual Abuse was being over-stated by Moira Woods who was later to resign in disgrace from SATU in the Eddie Hernon case.

Today, no lessons have been learned, we have the HSE claiming 541 "confirmed" cases of sexual abuse a year but nowhere near that number of prosecutions. It's a safe bet that 541 children were removed from at least one parent based on these confirmations, or to put it another way, at least 500 children are denied a relationship with one of their parents even though they are not accused of any crime. It's not hard to see how the rest of Europe looks at Ireland and the UK in utter shock at the Human Rights abuses of children under the guise of Child "Protection". John Hemming MP called a meeting with other countries over their concerns of UK Child "Protection" and was shocked that almost every country in the world responded. At one point at least 2 countries were considering taking the UK to the ECtHR over human rights abuses of their citizens. We don't have a "John Hemming" in Ireland but I can disclose that 3 countries that I know of have expressed similar concerns in Ireland and sent their ambassadors to meet Irish Ministers.

Conspiracy Theory.
When Madelyn McCann went missing, her parents didn't wait around as
victims for news, they took a more pro-active approach to find her. They went
public and attracted as much attention as they could. They circulated pictures
in the media very quickly so that if Madelyn had been spotted, a vigilant public
would report to police. Kate would appear on TV with her hair brushed,
speaking in a defiant and purposeful voice and appearing to be a victim. Gerry
always appeared articulate and sensible despite the obvious pressure they were
under. Besieged by journalists, surrounded by police, they never once let their
guard slip, the topic was getting Maddie home and the world was gripped and
vigilant. Every child on the street of every city was scanned looking for that
distinctive birth defect in Maddie's right eye.

In my mind, they had done everything right, even leaving their children
sleeping. If someone really wanted to abduct the child, it would have made no
difference whether the parents were sleeping in the next room or not. They got
publicity, which would have made it near impossible for someone to hide the
child or freely walk down the street with her. The children were being checked
on regularly and only someone who would have known that the children were
in a particular room could have kidnapped her. It's also possible she woke up
and strayed off but her parents were close-by.

It didn't take long for the conspiracy theorists to spew their vile hatred. They
thought that Kate was a bit too calm and collected, that Gerry, simply being
male, must have sexually assaulted her and killed her. The McCann's are
educated, middle-class, articulate people. They are both Physicians and used to
working in high stress situations. They don't fit a Hollywood "ideal" that you
see on TV. Kate wasn't crying and pleading with the kidnapper; Gerry wasn't
threatening to kill the kidnapper. They were very purposeful, "this is what
Maddie looks like, look at her eye. Call the police if you see anything".

It emerged later that the police involved were inept, Maddie could have
crossed several borders but no attempt to "Lock down" the area was made
immediately. Even the police resorted to conspiracy. It was clear that Kate and
Gerry had a good alibi and no motive, but when conspiracy takes hold, all logic
goes out the window. The police not wanting to appear inept or admit that they
had made very serious mistakes, turned their attention to the parents, but
couldn't even do this competently.

Once the McCann's were under suspicion, the conspiracy theorists took
over. Nothing is ever simple with a conspiracy theorist. I wouldn't be surprised
someday if a Psychologist says that Conspiracy is a mild form of Schizophre-
nia, or other form of mental condition. The allegations against the McCann's
were vile and continue to this day, even from Portuguese Police. People
connect dots, take leaps of faith and delve into realms of fantasy. The way
people look, how the speak, how they dress and every little inflection is picked
upon. It is the very modus operandi by which many social workers operate.

What many of the conspiracy theorists forget, is that this is not just about the McCann's, it's about a little girl who is terrified without her parents and family. The have made the whole story about the parents and seem to have forgotten Maddie. Regardless of their feelings about the parents, doesn't a little girl deserve to go home to her parents? Wouldn't you think that if the conspiracy theorists really cared about Maddie, that they would put the child first and leave out the parents?

It seems clear in many of these conspiracies that it's not about doing the right thing for the right reasons. It's about our own prejudices such as working-class versus middle-class. It's about watching crime shows and thinking that this qualifies you as a Criminologist or a Detective. It's about judging people by your standards and beliefs or mistaking intuition for fact. In the real world detectives need to identify with the perpetrator to see if it their actions would be reasonable and practical. It's not sufficient to latch onto a theory and try to prove that theory only; you must also eliminate and exhaust every other possibility. Most of these theories fall flat in the first few minutes under questioning. If a father supposedly "beats his child", why doesn't he beat his other children? And wouldn't the other children know that their sibling had been beaten? People become so linear in their thinking that when it comes to problem solving, that they arrive at a solution first and then try to make a case to fit that solution.

In my approach to solving problems, other than following a scientific approach, I don't consider solutions until I have all the information to form an opinion. It's as simple as; "you cant solve a problem until you know the cause" Only by investigating properly and gathering all the information can you arrive at a conclusion. I may have my suspicions and biases but these are cause to investigate further, not jump into a solution immediately. I see this time after time in social work and it's not about the child, it's about painting the parents as abusers or neglecters. Taking leaps of faith and connecting dots and delving into flights of fantasy.

A social worker gave a report after visiting a home and obviously didn't expect to be questioned by someone who had also inspected the home, better yet I took photographs. The house was filthy because the dishes from breakfast were still in the sink. The dogs water and food dish were empty, they obviously can't care for an animal. So I asked, did she check the cupboards and fridge to see that there was adequate food of a good quality? Would you leave dog or cat food out if your toddler played with it and ate it? Did she check the children's bedrooms to see that they had adequate clothing, toys, and safety gates, cupboard locks? I knew she hadn't, but I tend not to ask questions that I don't already know the answer to.

To some of us, the world is a wonderful place; full of new experiences and new adventures, to others the same world we live in is a place of terror. To some there are paedophiles on every corner waiting to abduct children.

Everyone wants to rob or take advantage of you. The world is a terrible place and nobody can be trusted. Everyone has ulterior motives and some people put up a barrier of self-defence and rarely allow anyone inside.

I would hate to live in a world of suspicion. I have worked in some jobs where you had to walk on eggshells and other places where everyone worked together for a common goal. I have also visited countries "where the walls had ears", and many also suspected that the government was reading your thoughts. Today, in truth, the government have access to our emails and social media, our phone calls are stored for future reference and the Thought Police are very real. Under anti-terrorism laws I can be searched, the laws can be perverted to search people for other reasons that have nothing to do with terrorism. Most of us don't care about this, as it hasn't affected our lives. We don't worry about it because we have done nothing wrong, but few people realize how our lives can take a turn for the worst at the whim of a civil servant. I have worked at jobs where failure is not an option, you have very strict protocols to follow and there are no margins for error. If you make a mistake, you need to put your hand up right away and say so. I look at the world of child protection and law and see a very flawed system. People in wigs and costumes deciding the lives of others as if they were deciding on what food to eat and the incompetence, even of judges beggars belief.

People are arrested without charge and can be detained for long periods. The Police are allowed to lie to you but you are not allowed to lie to them, it can be held against you in court. Police no longer Serve and Protect the Public; they have become revenue collectors for the government. I drove from Mullingar to Dublin one night and was stopped 4 times in roadside checks. In every case they checked my road tax and insurance, not once did a Garda check to see if I had been drinking.

Having seen some countries run by dictators, having seen anarchy where police can do nothing, having seen how gangs and criminals have taken over areas, I don't want to live under such conditions. I believe in the rule of law, democracy and justice. I want to be able to go for a walk without carrying weapons and not live in fear that the world is a terrible place. I have grown too old to worry about what others think of me. Believe me when I say that you don't want to live in anarchy or under a dictator. While democracy is not a perfect solution, it is better than most systems. What concerns me now is how democracy has been weakened, I have seriously questioned whether the novel "1984" is being used by governments as a blueprint for society because the parallels are uncanny.

We live in an imperfect world, human beings have not reached such a stage of development yet where justice exists and is perfect. I compare the worlds of Science, where there is no room for error, to the world of government and law where Science has been replaced by Religion of Science. We can commit injustices against each other by dehumanizing others, and all that is required is that we place a label of "Child Abuser", "Conspiracy Theorist" or a Mental Health tag on another human being. Governments can kill entire populations with war and corporations can kill by the Profit Motive. We can't progress as human beings until we move forward and go back to Science as being a basis for this improvement. We need "Evidence Based" Medicine rather than allowing Doctors and governments to call people Heretics for merely asking questions.

I have struggled with the question of whether Conspiracy Theory actually exists. In Science you must continuously ask questions. In the 9/11 debates, many experts came forward to question whether the events unfolded as described by the Investigating Commission. Many pilots said that the aircraft that hit the Pentagon would have been quite impossible. Engineers and Physicists wondered how 2 gigantic engines could have disappeared? To me these seem like perfectly legitimate questions but I do not believe the theory that the CIA or Mossad or governments conspired to kill thousands of their own citizens. Building 7 collapse seems a perfectly plausible situation given that much debris had fallen on it and through it, the fires on 2 floors and the inevitable earthquaking of the Twin Towers which weakened it's structure. What I can't seem to understand is how the BBC could announce the collapse some 20 minutes or so before it actually collapsed. Does this make me a Conspiracy Theorist?

I run into similar situations frequently. I am sent Post Mortem Reports and Medical Lab Results on a regular basis and they don't make a lot of sense sometimes. If I challenge the reports or simply ask questions for further clarification, I'm accused of being a conspiracy theorist or that my opinion counts for nothing as I am not a qualified Pathologist or Physician. On TV and Hollywood movies, there is a dead certainty in these stories, the Pathologists are never wrong and have no motive to lie. In real life they are frequently wrong and fundamentally human. When you have corned a Doctor or Pathologist, they will frequently resort to; "I am only expressing my opinion". In real life you frequently see the human failings and the need to protect oneself when those failings are opposed. You will see where police and prosecutors feel they have an airtight case on their hands but the case starts to unravel when you start to apply the rules of Science. In many cases they have jumped to the Solution first and built the evidence to fit.

My job is easy, I don't need to be a physician to investigate medical cases. I have the gifts of hindsight and second-guessing. It's a lot harder being an investigator in the first instance and being under pressure to come up with a solution. A baby died, someone or something is responsible, time is ticking, and the public are baying for blood. I don't get paid for helping others and I can pick and choose my battles, I have no vested interest in the outcome other than to seek justice. I am not Superman or Batman or a "self-appointed do-gooder", I am simply a person helping others. I don't solicit cases, people ask for my help and I help if I can. To me this is the price that any of us pay to live in a democracy, to help each other and to be an active part of society. If a car breaks down at the side of the road, people will come to help. If someone falls on the ground, most of us would rush over to help. Being human, we put ourselves in the position of the victim and hope that we live in a world where people would help us if we needed help. But in a secret world behind closed doors, we don't see the people fall. In the secret court, the judge can't see the home, meet the children, talk to neighbours and has to rely on the government officials to inform them.

Too many people are disconnected from the outside world because to them it is a scary, terrible place. As a child I believed in monsters and devils because it fit in with my beliefs. If something happened I cold explain it away with a monster being responsible, although I have to admit that this excuse didn't often work on my mother as she often had more scientific explanations. I once ran all the way home because I had "stepped on a crack" and believed I had broken my mothers back. To my surprise when I arrived at my doorstep my mother was polishing it on her knees with that "red stuff" that the women of the time used. I can picture women at the time in a scarf tied around their hair and the ever-present apron, that often smelled of onions and other foul odours.

My belief in devils and monsters waned as the world around me made more sense and there were plausible explanations for strange events. I am however keeping an open mind about ghosts and banshees having witnessed my aunts and mother being "visited" on many occasions.

My belief in God crumbled at around age 12 when I started to think about what had been quite literally beaten into me as a child by Christian Brothers, Teachers and even my parents, who remained devoted Catholics until the day they died. I also learned at that age not to question authority, even if there was no malice in my line of questioning. How could Noah fit all the Marine Animals in the Ark? Why does a God of Love not allow unbaptized babies and children of unmarried mothers into Heaven? The whole concept of religion didn't sit well with me, there were "Mysteries" that nobody ever wanted to answer and I always disliked Pomp and Circumstance, "kneel down, stand up, sit down, endlessly recite prayers". I learned that the matter was not up for discussion, you either believed or you didn't. I didn't.

I came to a conclusion that people base their beliefs on a proposition of Faith. They can't prove that God exists, but equally, equally I cannot disprove it. I intensely dislike being called an Atheist or Agnostic, but there is no name given to those of us who don't care one way or the other and are not obsessed thinking about it. I'm not opposed to Religion as long as it is not extreme, if people want to believe that an imaginary friend that they love exists up there in the sky, as long as it makes them better people for it and as long as it helps them and gives them comfort and joy and they don't harm others, then religion is a good thing. I have no interest in going to Heaven as it might be filled with people whom I wouldn't have any desire to associate with now. To teach children that babies cant go to heaven or that they will be plunged in a pit of eternal fire and poked by devils is a form of child abuse in my opinion. Equally teaching some children that they will have to suffer in life to get a reward in death, perhaps 72 virgins, is equally abusive.

In the Middle Ages people struggled between religion and science. The Pope said the world was flat and any argument to the contrary was heresy. People looked at the moon and planets for millennia, or 2,000 years as the case may be, and wondered why all the heavenly bodies were round and rotated, but the Earth was flat. Science answered a lot of questions and made sense, religion still relied on unexplained mysteries that man was incapable of answering. When people ask me; "if there is no God, where did you come from?" I answer; "If God exists, where did he come from?" I have come to the conclusion that in my lifetime that nobody will ever give a satisfactory answer to existence as our brains are not capable of understanding. Equally, I don't fully understand the behaviour of Electrons and Protons, but having studied Electronics for many years and even used Electron Microscopes, Particle Accelerators, Cryogenics and many "Rocket Science" constructs, I can say you don't need to understand them fully to use them to your benefit. No Scientist fully understands everything or would be capable of assimilating all that information.

What Science has never attempted to do, is control our morals or behaviour, religion has. While you can use an army and sophisticated weapons to control a population for a period of time, you cannot control Thought. You can make a person do your bidding when you point a weapon at them but once you take the weapon away, you no longer have control. With Religion, you control the mind with an invisible weapon and reward and punishment don't even need to be dealt in life, as either will be decided later when the person is dead. Religion has never needed to deal with Morals, people would believe because it would help them make sense of the world around them. But religion has always felt the need for Power. Popes, Bishops, Caliphs have always had armies who enforced morals. When religions learned to control governments there was no longer a need to have armies, they could have all the control they needed.

When religion began to lose its power, governments started to take control. A friend of mine who is a policeman once told me that the job of the Police was "to keep honest people honest". By keeping a visible presence, people thought of the consequences of their actions. When you're driving you see speed limits everywhere and reminders that if you speed you could die, kill someone or lose your driving privileges. And driving is a privilege and not a right. We pay taxes to build the roads and infrastructure and collectively over the years have built an extensive network of roads so that we can quickly and safely get to our destinations. I have driven in countries where bandits could attack at any time and I don't think anyone would want to live in the Middle Ages or the Dark Ages that many of our neighbours are currently living in. We have to work together for the benefit of society. We have to pay taxes to contribute to a better world for our children and to prosper as a society.

There has never been a time in human history where humans didn't go to war against their neighbours. While we idealize some aboriginal peoples or "First Nations", we seem to forget that many of them had wars also and were no less barbaric than their invaders to their own people. In many countries around the world today this barbarity exists, sometimes in the form of a government run by a brutal dictator and sometimes in the form of religion where the dictator is a religion. As much as we would like to think of ourselves as civilized, we still support slavery and heavily rely on it existing in other countries for our own benefit.

While many think that slavery was abolished after the death of Martin Luther King, the truth is we just "Outsourced" it to other countries. We have shut down all low-tech manufacturing in Europe as we could not compete with China and "Developing Economies" elsewhere. Where once in Ireland the UK, many working-class people made reasonably good livings doing repetitive work that was labour intensive in factories. People still bought homes and sent their children to higher education. As a child in the late 1950's and early 60's I can remember our family's entire collection of clothing could fit in one wardrobe, now a baby has more clothes. We can buy a new t-shirt for €1 but to produce the same item in Ireland would cost €28. Virtually everything we produce could be made elsewhere for a fraction of the cost. We go into "Euro Stores" and "Pound Shops" and buy inferior products that wont last.

I'm reminded of a story of an 8-year-old girl going to daddy and saying; "look daddy, I drew a picture for you". Daddy then holds up his smartphone to the girl and says; "sure that's nothing, this phone was made by an 8 year old in China". It would be comical if it were no so true.

The people now manufacturing these products are paid tiny sums of money and expected to work for months at a time without seeing their families. People die making these products because there are no safety standards. Instead of leg irons or a steel collar around their necks, they are chained in bondage by money and an economic system that is becoming unsustainable. The Trickle Down Theory is no longer working, most of what trickles down is taken by the government in taxes. Even in Ireland many people are "Wage Slaves", to some extent we can live in relative poverty as long as we have our families and our TV and Churches for our entertainment. The problem is that the economic system is not working for 80% of us. The economy is a giant Pyramid Scheme that relies on continuous growth and every so often the economy collapses. The rich are getting richer and it's not trickling down after taxes are paid. Should you be worried? If you are relying on a State Pension to support you when you are too old or frail, you should be very concerned.

For our pensions, we rely on younger people coming into the system to support the old, but now the old are living longer. Hospitals no longer supply "Health", they only deal with illness and ill health. The Police no longer Serve & Protect the citizens, they have become tax collectors for the governments who can't keep up with the debt. Law no longer serves Justice but benefits the Law Industry. Social Services cannot "Engineer" Society and crime rates, poverty and social injustice are getting worse. The Media have become entertainers and "News" is driven by profit.

While I paint a bleak picture, I don't believe that our situation is so dire that it can't be fixed. I still go for a walk or cycle and don't forget to smell the roses, smile when I see a baby or feel joy when I see a person doing a good deed. I think it's important to be realistic and look at the bigger picture. If you believe in God, all the better, you are lucky to have the gift of Faith. However, to have faith that Governments will look after us when we need it is pure insanity. Even though you may not be personally affected, all of us are vulnerable and could be inflicted with poor health at any time and our circumstances can change quickly.

The world is not an equal place and we are not entitled to Happiness. We should be entitled however to the "pursuit of happiness", but many do not have the equal opportunity. We are supposedly protected by Human Rights but in reality we have to fight with governments to vindicate those rights. A "Right" by it's very definition is something you possess, in the Irish Constitution those rights are "Imprescriptible" meaning that politicians cannot make laws to over-write those rights which we already possess. Our rights are also "Inalienable" meaning that we don't have to be granted those rights we already possess them. Still, if this were true, we would not needs Human Rights activists, lawyers and judges, nobody could refuse us those rights and we wouldn't need to fight for them. In reality, I see human rights being abused every day in District Courts and these injustices take place by well-meaning people in most cases, many of whom are unfamiliar with human and civil rights and are incompetent. I would include judges in this category and if my statement were not true, we would not need higher courts and experts to vindicate rights, which we already possess.

Most of us would place the blame fairly at politicians and governments. During the boom in Ireland we were being told to get rich by selling houses to each other. Banks were lending at 110% with no money down. I was told I was stupid for not buying a house at the time but I reasoned why should I pay €450,000 for something that's only worth €150,000? And as a mortgage was a 25-year commitment at least, when the economy tanked in 10 years, how would I pay my mortgage? I was told that the good times were here forever, mostly by young people who had never lived through a recession. I was told that buying your own home was a great investment; it could only go up in price. When I pointed that if your home goes up in value by 100%, that so do other homes so any gain you made would be passed on to the seller of your new home. A few lone voices like Eddie Hobbs, David McWilliams and Constantine Gurdgiev were pointing out the fallacy but nobody wanted to believe the economy was about to crash. Bertie Ahern was egging people on and giving bad advice and the Financial Regulator was asleep at the wheel. When the famous Tribunal was held and Bertie had to account for his earnings, he apparently won it at the Bookies. We were told to buy Eircom shares but as someone who has had an interest in the stock market for many years, I was advising people against it.

When you meet politicians, judges and people in authority, you come away thinking that these people are not any smarter than you or I. Politicians are actors and well versed in talking for several minutes but actually saying nothing. I have only seen a few journalists ever in Ireland who are not afraid to ask the tough questions and persist in getting an answer. Vincent Browne is one of the few. I have also seen where journalists who wanted to be the Watchdogs of Society being edged out of their positions. The other media whores who cut & paste news releases are almost irrelevant; in reality they don't need to exist and a computer generated image would suffice in many cases with a fictitious name to add to the bottom of any government propaganda. We place our trust that politicians will work diligently and represent their community.

In reality, when you look back at the last decade in politics, the only good politicians have been Independents. Of course Independents have no real power but they can put forward private members bills and they have the attention of the media and the public. In Party Politics, the Taoiseach is basically a Dictator. TD's are not allowed to vote with their conscience, they must vote what the leader wants. Of course the Opposition is a smaller number and will be drowned out by the party in power. I only know of one politician in the past decade that has worked diligently and honestly for his community. Mattie McGrath was also the only politician who voted against the Children's Referendum. In an unprecedented case, every party and other independent voted in favour of taking away parental rights in the guise of protecting children. Mattie was better informed that most, he had seen for himself the damage caused to families in the guise of protecting children and even today has a keen interest in these issues. Other independents have admirable records and while I might not agree with their views, at least I can say that they are being seen to take a stand one way or the other on issues, and unlike Party Politicians, are not puppets for party policy or the dictates of the Taoiseach. Fine Gael and Fine Fail are two sides of the same coin, there are from dynasties of the Ruling Class where nepotism rules and the same surnames keep cropping up. Sinn Fein have been a major disappointment even to staunch supporters and Labour may not even exist at the next election.

The only way forward for Ireland, after being brought to the edge of a financial precipice by one party, and launched into free-fall by the other party, is to get rid of the Party system forever and have an elected Senate free of any party. Just because you may not have an interest in politics doesn't mean that it won't have an interest in you and affect your life. The only logical choice is to have independents and let them work it out how to run the country and recover. We have a puppet government that is run by the EU, the UN and the IMF and our very survival depends on a radical transformation of how Ireland is governed.

If you spend time around politicians, you will also find that the country is actually ran by Civil Servants and their Unions, and the lobbyists for corporations or Industry.

There is a tendency in any organization or organism to grow. The Child Abuse Industry has seen unprecedented growth in the last decade. Every time there is a catastrophic failure in the system, the government call in their pool of "Experts". In the Child Abuse Industry the same 18 or so people have been involved for many years regardless of who is in government. The Unions, some of whose bosses are paid outrageous salaries, also dictate government policy. But while the Unions can tell social workers how to do their jobs, the Lobbyists have the power to introduce Legislation. As the Industry grows, more failures are inevitable. It's interesting to note that the failures are never brought to the publics attention by any social worker, union, children's NGO, politician or lobbyist for the industry, in every scandal, the news was broken by members of the public.

Whenever an employee fails in their duty, as any good people managers will tell you, the excuse is always the same;

- We don't have enough people
- We don't have enough time
- We don't have enough power
- We don't have enough money

The response of politicians is always predictable. Whenever a system fails, the solution is always to put more laws in place, tougher fines and sentences, more stringent procedures and Zero Tolerance, which of course have never worked. They will give more people, more time, more power and more money and the next failure will be even more spectacular. In the process the organization grows along with their failures. If you double the number of children in "Care" and the suicide rate of children in "Care" is 10 times the national average, doesn't it follow that more children will die from suicide in the name of "protecting" them?

In 2010 we were told there is a "shortage of social workers" as caseloads were increasing even though criminal convictions of child abusers had not increased in decades and 260 positions were added. The direct result was that Ireland took 3.7 times more children into "Care" per capita than the UK the following year. Caseloads didn't drop in number, they actually increased. More children also died in "Care" but the Industry had a bumper year with Lawyers seeing a huge increase, more cases brought before the court and more money for the children's NGO's. Even the Unions benefitted with more union dues. The more failures in the system meant more work for the "Experts", and more dead children.

In governments now for many years, Lobbyists have had an impact on our lives with new laws being made to protect corporations and increase their profits. Corporations and governments now control the basics of life. In many US States, it is illegal to grow your own food, collect your own rainwater, feed the poor, be homeless and you must be connected to the Power Grid. A few years ago I stopped buying Nestle Products as the CEO decreed that Water was a commodity, a resource to be traded and controlled by governments and sold by corporations. Many people have said that Water is not a Human Right. In Spain they have taxed the sun believe it or not, you must pay a tax on power generated by Solar Panels. It has become virtually impossible to buy foods that are not Genetically Modified Organisms (GMO's) in some countries.

When I first heard about GMO's I thought that this was a wonderful science. The Irish Potato "Famine" would never have occurred with GMO potatoes, The Salem Witch Trial would never have occurred and we could produce foods in areas of drought and prevent famine and save millions of lives a year. We could have 2 or 3 crop seasons in less hospitable areas and world hunger and famine would be a thing of the past. We could even produce Bio Fuels to power our houses and run our cars. I still think that GMO's have a wonderful potential for good and could improve the quality of life for everyone. We could turn the Sahara Desert into the Sahara Forest and maybe even grow food in space?

But of course anything that has a potential for good has an equal and opposite potential for bad. Rather than GMO's being given to the poorest of the poor who are starving to death, the seeds are patented to large corporations. But not only have these corporations developed these GMO's for profit, they want to ban Heritage Seeds so that only GMO's are sold. A few years ago driving thousands of kilometres through France and Spain, I couldn't help but notice that corporations owned every field where I saw crops. If the farmer owned the land, the corporations owned the crop.

The danger in this is that the Global Food Supply is no longer in the hands of the public and most of these GMO's and crops are owned by one corporation, Monsanto.

The "Monsanto Protection Act" whose more formal name is Section 735 of the "Consolidated and Further Continuing Appropriations Act, 2013," or H.R. 933, an appropriations bill that President Obama signed into law. It effectively gives Monsanto the power to ignore any court orders. Since the act came into law, Monsanto has never lost a case against any farmer.

This is a perfect example of how Corporations and their Lobbyists can influence politicians and governments and ultimately have serious repercussions for ordinary people. In most countries now, Water is considered a "Resource" like Oil to be privatised and sold as a commodity. The Profit Motive clearly doesn't benefit the public. In the world today millions starve to death every year and die for lack of clean water. Nobody dies as a result of lack of food availability, people die because they cant afford to eat or buy water. If a famine strikes a region, we have the capability to send in armies immediately and resolve the situation.

When we look back at how Grant ran UNICEF, his philosophy was; "It takes a community to raise a child". You couldn't send armies of Aid Workers into a community to only feed the children and ignore their parents; you have to feed the community. In most cases you can prevent famines by "Teaching a man to fish" rather than "Feeding him for a day". Prevention and a proper Global Sustainability Program are far cheaper than putting out fires after they have started.

I have always thought it very odd that in Ireland to see so much money being spent on advertising by the Road Safety Authority in teaching people how to drive. Speaking as former Paramedic who attended many Road Traffic Collisions, I'm not trying to minimise the severity or extent of the problem of road deaths. I have always said that the most dangerous thing you can do every day is getting behind the wheel of a car. What I see as having worked well in Road Safety is the fact that thanks to the EU, Irish roads have improved considerably in the last 15 years. What has also improved considerably is the safety of vehicles on the road. We have far safer cars, anti-lock brakes, airbags, seat belt laws, better child restraints and National Car Testing to remove unsafe cars from the road. We have the "Points System" which we adopted 25 years after many other countries and more enforcement of Road Traffic by Gardai. I find it odd then that the RSA could spend so much on advertising when it was the EU, which had a more significant impact on Road Safety.

Isn't it also quite odd that no money is ever spent teaching parents to better look after their children, except the many millions spent in secret on "Professionals" and NGO's? In 2011, Ireland took 3.7 times more children into "Care" on a per-capita basis than the UK. Did the Irish suddenly become a nation of child abusers? What could possibly justify such a dramatic increase? The crime statistics don't support the taking of so many children; the Garda statistics don't show a dramatic increase of investigations for neglect and child abuse. The HSE at the time were crying out that they had a "shortage of social workers" and many children in "Care" didn't even have an assigned social worker. A prominent member of a Children's NGO told me of a case where a child in "Care" had not seen or been assigned a social worker in 14 years.

The only significant event that occurred was the fact that the HSE had added 260 new social work positions to their already 4,000 staff. I can also say at the time that the HSE were using Agency Staff for supervised visits, many of whom were not qualified social workers. It would be safe to say then that the unprecedented increase in "Care" Orders was a result of putting more social workers in the field. I would estimate the cost of adding 260 new positions to be over €50 million when you add up all the costs. Have the children of Ireland actually benefitted from adding the new positions? In the past few years, the situation has gone from bad to worse, more children are homeless and living in poverty than ever before and the only beneficiaries have been the people working in the Industry.

Why don't we have advertisements teaching parents how to look after their children? Why don't we have social workers assisting families instead of prosecuting them? Why is it that the default method of "protecting" children is to remove them from their homes. In the past few decades parents have become terrified of social workers and bringing their children to hospital. In the USA and Canada for many years, new parents were given a copy of Dr Spock's book on "Child Care". It is possibly the best manual on raising children ever written. Surprisingly few Irish parents have ever heard of it. Social workers are not seen as advocates, they are there to find any excuse to take your child, this is the public perception, and they are not wrong. While social workers in other areas of practice are advocates and do great work in most cases, in the area of "Family Services" as they like to call themselves, they are prosecutors looking for any excuse to take a child. While Baby P is used as an excuse, because parents are sneaky and cover up child abuse, it's "safer" to remove a child into "care" and if the 183 or 999 children are taken to prevent the "one child swinging in the wind", then this is the price that we must pay for protecting children. Or so the legend goes. The "Theory of Collateral Damage" isn't working to the benefit of children and the major beneficiaries are always the "Professionals".

A former Prison Governor who is now the UK's "Tsar on Adoption" has even stated on the public record that the State only gets it wrong in 2% or maybe 4% of cases. Martin Narey is a former CEO of Barnardos UK who now advises the Department for Education. By his reckoning about 160 children a year are wrongly Forcibly Adopted. But this is the prevailing "wisdom" of child "protection" that it is ok to harm some children in order to protect others. Narey is also on the record for saying that more babies should be removed at birth from "failed" parents and forcibly adopted. Of course social workers strongly disagree with the term "Forced Adoption", they prefer more sanitized terms.

Martin Narey, despite his time at Barnardos, has no qualifications whatsoever for Child "Protection". He is not a qualified social worker, but then neither are most of the people who are seen as "Experts" in the field. Most have never even met any of the children they purport to "protect" and accept on blind faith that the system is working as it should even despite the strong evidence to the contrary.

In the UK many of the laws and practices come from the Department for Education (DfE) but it seems that every time they attempt to try to counter the accusations from people such as John Hemming MP or Ian Josephs who coined the phrase "Forced Adoption", they are proven wrong by their own experts. In a recent publication in April 2014 on the topic of Adoption, they were served with a damning report by Julie Selwyn, which has caused shockwaves in the social work community, but has had little impact in the field of Adoption. When the DfE commissioned a report into "Care", again to refute John Hemming and Co., it was another damning indictment. Many of the statistics I quoted earlier on "Care" came from that report. When many of us pointed out that social workers were using Court "Experts" who would lie for the highest bidder in Family Courts. The DfE commissioned another report from Prof Jane Ireland that was another damning indictment of a system gone horribly wrong. Prof Ireland found that 70% of the reports were inadequate. She found that many of the "experts" were not even in current practice and made their living from "reports".

You would think that in the case of Sally Clark where she was wrongly accused of murdering her babies, that "Lessons were Learned" from these miscarriages of justice and that "practices would be put in place" to "prevent further occurrences" but no, the situation has only become worse since.

Sally Clark, a mother and a solicitor lost a baby to Sudden Infant Death Syndrome. When her second baby died of SIDS, it was at a time of another Moral Panic, which was started by a paediatrician by the name of Roy Meadows. Meadows theorized that women were killing children in order to draw attention to themselves. He invented a crazy theory known as Munchausen's Syndrome by Proxy (MSbP). The theory goes that if a mother wants a second opinion for her sick child, that she may secretly be making the child sick to gain attention for herself or may even kill the child.

As with all Psychological Theory, there is no medical test to verify the presence of MSbP, it only requires that the mother wants a second opinion and may take the child to several doctors. Meadows himself was a paediatrician and not a psychologist. He became the darling of the courts and was awarded a Knighthood. He is believed to have testified in 5,000 cases, many of them Family Courts held in secret so there is no way of knowing the exact number. His ex wife has claimed he is a misogynist and he only testified against women. He never even met or examined the women he met and yet accused many of them of murdering their own child. This is the beauty of some of these theories you only need certain conditions to exist and you can diagnose a person you never met, collect large sums of money as an "Expert" and not get your hands dirty or have to look at the face of the person you are accusing of murder.

Sally lost her first baby to SIDS and by this time the Moral Panic of MSbP had social workers, police and prosecutors trawling cases of babies who had died of SIDS. Thousands of people were now prosecuted for cases going back years. Meadows was a hero to many but he never produced any of his supposed research to Peer Review. When her second baby died of SIDS, prosecutors first tried Shaken Baby Syndrome but decided that MSbP would be easier, they didn't even need forensics.

SIDS is not an actual Cause of Death of a baby, it is a term used when the cause was unknown or unidentified. After many years of SIDS research, we are no further ahead today than we were 40 years ago. Many people believe that vaccinations have played a part in SIDS but the fact is that there have been no Gold Standard Studies and no Double-Blind Studies because Doctors believe that it is unethical **not** to vaccinate babies, therefore there are no proper scientific studies for the safety and efficacy of vaccines given to children. I am not opposed to vaccines. Children die of entirely preventable conditions and in history, entire towns and cities have been wiped out by spreadable diseases. My own view is that I would love to believe that there is a Silver Bullet or Magic Pill that can be given to babies to prevent these needless deaths, until I see proper double-blind studies into safety and efficacy I will reserve judgement.

Sally spent 3 years in prison for a crime she did not commit. I cant begin to understand the pain of losing a child even though I help parents whose children have died in "Care". To lose 1 child is unimaginable, to lose a second child and then be accused of their murder, based on a flawed psychological theory such as MSbP is criminal far beyond the witch hunters of Salem. At her appeal, Meadows had stated that the statistical probability of a second child dying of natural causes was 1 in 73 million. He had made this figure up from nowhere. When a member of the London Statistical Society, who had actually done the research, proved that in fact a second child is in fact 68 times more likely to die of SIDS, the case against Sally Clark was in ruins and Meadows reputation shattered. To date, he has never produced any of his research for peer review.

While MSbP fell out of favour after the Sally Clark fiasco, it is still being used today by the CFA and was used in 2013 by the HSE, even though it is not listed as a disorder in the DSM, the "Bible" of Psychologists. The myth of MSbP lives on today as Fabricated or Induced Illness which is still taught to social workers and doctors. It was said of Meadows that in the thousands of miscarriages of justice he caused, that Meadows caused more deaths by suicide than Dr Harold Shipman, the UK's "Doctor death", and yet although Meadows was struck off by the GMC, he was later reinstated on appeal. Sally Clark never recovered; she died by "Misadventure" by drugs and alcohol by the pain of losing 2 babies and being the victim of overzealous witch hunters who were never punished.

When Sally Clark lost her second child to SIDS, another "very dangerous doctor" as the media labelled him, David Southall, called Police, as he had also believed that her second baby had been murdered. Southall was another proponent of MSbP and it later emerged that he had conducted experiments on babies by restricting their breathing to simulate suffocation. He used very controversial methods and was later struck off by the GMC. He was not prosecuted, as there was insufficient evidence. Southall also has never presented any of his research for peer review.

Even today, many paediatricians feel that Meadows and Southall were unfairly treated and that doctors should be allowed to destroy lives and kill patients as long as they have the best intentions. This a philosophy which must stop, most doctors still believe that it's ok to wrongly accuse parents and that children should be taken on mere suspicion. This is what I call the "Theory of Collateral Damage", as Dr Phil says, "I would rather see 1,000 children taken if it saves one swinging in the wind". This has historical precedence, it happened in Salem 300 years ago and is still occurring today in secret courts near you.

For some inexplicable reason, we are no further ahead as to why babies die of Sudden Infant Death than we were 40 years ago. Medicine, or rather Psychology, has taken a foray from the research in the 1940's Department of Transportation study where monkey's were strapped into car-seats and slammed back an forth until they died. For centuries babies have died and nobody knows why. I have asked parents to describe in detail how their children died, this may seem a cruel exercise, but was entirely necessary as the parents had been wrongly accused of killing their babies. When a baby dies, it is a great tragedy even for the community. We look at babies and our hearts melt, we want to cuddle and protect them. When that baby dies we look for reasons, someone to blame, leave no stone unturned, it makes us angry. It makes social workers, doctors, police officers and judges angry, after all, we are all human.

When a baby dies for an unknown reason, we search and theorize reasons, we cannot get "closure" until something or someone is found responsible. We resort to ridiculous theories like Shaken Baby Syndrome even though there is no evidence in existence that it is even possible to shake a baby to death. We resort to MSbP, that the parent must have done it. We convict people on SBS simply on the basis that they admit being alone with a baby for 1 minute or id a child dies of SIDS, then it must be murder and it must be the parent who is responsible. Since the 1940's we have taken these side roads which have no scientific validity and because we are not looking for other causes, we are not doing the research. When a baby dies 10 days after being vaccinated and the baby is in hospital, it's called SIDS. When the same baby dies 10 days after vaccination and the baby is at home, it's called Murder, either by SBS or MSbP.

No doctor wants to believe that vaccinations might be causing the deaths of a small number of babies, they would rather believe that a parent, who loves their child, is responsible. Even though there is irrefutable scientific evidence that short falls cause the Triad known as SBS, the religion and the industry of

SBS continues to deny science. Doctors and the SBS Industry are killing babies by believing that short falls cannot produce the Triad. You would think that they would err on the side of caution and advise parents not to place babies on beds or couches, just in case they might fall off and rupture Bridging Veins in the Dura Mater of the brain. They could still cling to the myth that SBS can cause it, but just to be safe, strongly advise parents to place babies in Crips, Cots, Carriers or even on a blanket on the floor, but never on a couch or bed because even a fall of 18 inches onto a Non-Newtonian surface can be deadly.

You would also think also that by default, that the protocols for any baby that has been slammed against any surface would be that the baby receive an MRI Scan and the parent be strongly advised to monitor the Fontanels and record the Head Circumference daily and follow up every day for at least 2 weeks after a fall? To report on the babies feeding, moods and sleep? No, they would rather follow an unscientific theory that the original theorist no longer supports and wishes he had never written the paper. It's not really about babies, it's about doctors arrogance and not keeping up with current science. It's about satisfying egos and dealing with anger in an unhealthy way. If I were a parent today and were shopping for a Paediatrician, the 3 questions I would ask is,

1. Do you believe in SBS?

2. Do you believe that Rickets is at epidemic proportions

3. Do you believe that in some cases that Vaccines can injure children?

Whenever laws fail, the usual response of politicians is more laws, more stringent laws, zero tolerance, criminalizing more people and the usual guff. Rather than admitting the failures, the emphasis has been to take more children and place them for adoption earlier. While I wrote about the case of Fran Lyon who proved all the experts wrong, especially the expert she had never met but deemed her to be a "risk" to her child, these cases are occurring now in about 70% of all Forced Adoptions. Many of the parents affected have no opportunity to "go public" as the media wont cover the story and the timeline for Forced Adoption has now dropped to 26 weeks. We see cases where parents are accused of "Risk" but could not possibly meet the requirements to keep their child as they could not complete the required courses or assessments and in most cases are not even granted even a Legal Aid Loser to try to defend themselves. They are setting up parents to fail. In my opinion this represents a very serious threat to Democracy.

The UK have what has been termed as a "Humanitarian Crisis" by another Irish colleague who helps families fleeing the UK in search of Justice that they cannot receive at home. Brian Rothery, a retired Journalist has written and blogged about Human and Civil Rights for many years. He has helped hundreds of families and has accommodated many "Refugees" from the UK, all pregnant women, to have their babies in Ireland in the hope that the baby wont be taken for Forced Adoption. In recent years, about 100 women a year flee the UK that we know of. Ireland used to be the destination of choice given we speak English, our reciprocal agreements with Health Care and Benefits, but the CFA and HSE have become more like the UK every day. Even without evidence, we see Gardai being used to follow pregnant women around Ireland 24/7 and Emergency "Care" Orders being granted without any evidence. Even in cases where we have advised parents to engage with the CFA before the birth and allow them to do their own assessments, they have refused as in all cases they have decided that the baby will be deported to the UK. This is not about Best Interests of the baby, this is about economics. It's also interesting to note that the same High Court Judge is used for all of these cases and to my knowledge, has never gone against the HSE or CFA.

It should be clear at this point that Child "Protection" is no longer about Advocacy, by default, every child must be taken away without even following the guidelines in Children First and other Best Practice. An "Ounce of Prevention" doesn't benefit the Industry; it's far more profitable to remove every child on mere suspicion and the Governments being advised by their "Experts" and Lobbyists continue to make it easier and easier to remove more children earlier. The term "Early Intervention" is really just an excuse for more intervention earlier to remove more children. You would think that the children who have already suffered Forced Adoption since 1997, many of who are adults now would rise up and sue the government but no, the governments were careful to close that "loophole" as well by gagging the victims of "Care" and Forced Adoption also.

I think it's important that I mention at this point that the UK is the only country in Europe that allows for Forced Adoption. Forced Adoption is one of the main reasons that Slovakia threatened to take the UK to the ECtHR. Romania also expressed a similar concern. Incidentally Slovakia has been closely following Ireland's social services also as has India and Poland.

During the corrupt Children's Referendum in Ireland, one of the main objectives of the Industry was to remove the rights of parents to allow for Forced Adoption here. The Industry had been gearing up for it long before the Referendum date was set and had even identified many children to be forcibly adopted. We were told that there were "doe eyed orphans" languishing in "Care" who desperately needed a "forever home" but nobody on the Yes side mentioned that the UK was the only country in Europe that allowed children to be forcibly adopted. The story of how these "orphans" had nobody to love them was blown out of the water by a former HSE Childcare Manager Eric Plunkett pointed out that not only did these children have a relationship with their parents, they also had foster carers who had the responsibility of caring for the children. He also stated that adoption was not the best option for these children.

In reality, the push for Forced Adoption came from Dr Geoffrey Shannon whose name appears in many instances of Child "Protection" in Ireland. A few years before the Referendum, my colleague and I had attended a talk given at the Law Society by Geoffrey Shannon, Fergus Finlay and Emily Logan. After the session I had heard Dr Shannon telling Emily and Fergus that we needed Forced Adoption in Ireland for the children in "Care" and that a referendum may not even be required. I also overheard about the necessity for a database of "Soft Information" being kept on the children of Ireland.

The Database has since become a reality without much notice or objection from the public. You would think that Human and Civil Rights Organizations would be up-in-arms that such a draconian database could be established but it turns out that in Ireland we don't actually have any Civil or Human Rights Organizations, just NGO's who are always reluctant to take a position against the government. Also interesting to note the previous associations that many of their staff had with political parties or governments. You would also think that since the Database is yet another failed and recycled idea from the UK, that any politician would have stopped it in its tracks? The UK introduced their database along with Vetting and social workers, teachers, doctors and anyone who came into contact with children could submit their concerns even if they didn't amount to "evidence". A teacher could say that Johnny came to school without an adequate lunch or clothing or footwear. Although this would not be excuse enough for intervention, a sufficient number of "concerns" might lead to intervention.

Despite the objections of social workers who said that filling out 29 pages of information on every child in the UK would be a waste of their time and take them away from actually meeting children, the Government brought it into law. It was only when someone pointed out that the children of Tony Blair, MP's, Judges, social workers and everyone would be included, that they amended it to put in a "Celebrity Clause" to exclude anyone in a position of power having any record of failing their children being recorded on a database where over 400,000 people could access it, probably wasn't in their "Best Interests". The UK eventually scrapped the database and after, Ireland set up its own. Can I point out now that the children of politicians, judges and social workers can be kept on the Irish database? And any database is subject to hacking?

Forced Adoption was of course the brainchild of Tony Blair who came into office with I believe, 28 social workers as members of his cabinet. He told a story of how "doe eyed orphans were languishing in care" and needed a "forever home". Almost the same story was rolled out in the Children's Referendum and almost verbatim years after the UK. The only problem with Tony Blair's plan was that nobody wanted to adopt children from "Care" and only 6% of all Forced Adoptions were children from "Care". Most Forced Adoptions were cases like Fran Lyon who was deemed a risk by a doctor she had never met and received a letter through her letterbox from a social worker she had never met that she was a "risk" to her baby and the baby would be placed for adoption against hers and her parents will. It's also interesting the

Blair Government were paying bonuses for meeting adoption targets of hundreds of millions to councils. When the councils couldn't adopt many children from "Care", they targeted unborn babies to meet their targets and collect the money. While the social workers themselves didn't benefit directly, they did benefit indirectly.

You were lied to about the Children's Referendum. The objective was to remove parental rights altogether so that the State, or more accurately, the Industry, could determine on any basis they liked that a parent had failed in their duty and your children could be forcibly adopted. As the Irish System is almost an exact copy of the UK System, the likely outcome would be that only 6% of children being forcibly adopted would come from "Care" and the shortfall would come from new-borns.

As most countries have strictly regulated Foreign Adoptions, there is a severe deficit of children available for adoption in Ireland and the UK, but only of new-borns. There are many older children "languishing in care" in foreign orphanages who are in fact orphans and in actual need of care but not many adoptive "parents" want to "open their heart and their homes" to older children with severe difficulties. As Russia and other countries have cracked down on foreign adoptions, the demand outstrips the supply and jobs of "professionals" are at stake in the Adoption Industry.

The reason that Russia and many countries called a halt was because 1 in 4 of adoptions break down and many children have arrived at Moscow airport with notes pinned to their coats that their new "parents" have rejected them. There was one case in Ireland covered by the media. Another common reason for the disruption rate in Adoption is that social workers lie to Foster "Carers" and Adoptive "Parents". In one case we discovered that a 4 year old had previously been adopted, rejected and dumped back in "Care". Can you imagine 1 in 4 parents rejecting their children? Why is this acceptable in Adoption that children can be rejected? Rejection is also a big factor in Foster "Care", usually at the slightest hint of trouble, children are shuffled from home to home, why is this acceptable?

One of the reasons for introducing Forced Adoption in Ireland was economics. Rather than paying €50,000 a year per child from age zero to 18, if it costs €100,000 to forcibly adopt children from an earlier age, it's cheaper in the long run, also the Outcomes are better, but only slightly. For the victims of Forced Adoption there is a Primal Wound that doesn't heal and one day it will come back to bite the Industry. It's interesting that Dr Shannon has a very close association with the Industry. He is Special Rapporteur for Children by UNICEF, has been employed by successive governments for conducting reports such as the Deaths in "Care" and many others, he also is part of the Family Law Reporting Project and recently became Chair of the New Adoption Authority of Ireland. His original training is as a Solicitor who specialized in Family Law. In the last few years the former Minister for Children Frances

Fitzgerald and Dr Shannon visited countries in an effort to increase the number of adoptions available to Ireland.

My opinion of Adoption is that it is a form of child abuse. For too long we have clung to a fantasy version of the "doe eyed orphans" who were dumped by their parents. In my own experience I see parents sacrificing everything they have for their child. I see parents not accused of any crime having their children literally ripped from the breast in delivery rooms, I see children who don't want to be in "care" and don't want to be adopted. I see horrendous miscarriages of justice taking place contrary to law on nothing more than suspicion. I see children dumped on the streets at 18 not having any skills to take care of themselves.

The fantasy of Adoption is that the "parent" gets what they want, why contend with a dog or a cat when you can adopt a real child? You will be a hero in the eyes of society having "rescued" a doe eyed orphan who nobody loved until "you chose them". You will be lied to that the parents were absolute monsters and never question the social workers to wonder, if they were such monsters, why aren't they in jail? The sanitised terms used in adoption don't cover up all the obvious evidence that people have been saying for years. Adoption is not an act of heroism, it's getting what you want but the child has no say in the matter. If a "birth parent" (I hate that term) rejected one of their four children and dumped them, there would be outrage. If adoption is supposedly permanent, why are "parents" allowed to reject a child and send them to "Care" or send them "Home"? At best, adoption is supposed to be making the best of a bad situation but the reality falls far short of the fantasy. If one parent wasn't capable of looking after their child, they still have another parent and also grandparents and aunts and uncles more than capable, so why give a child to an absolute stranger?

I had to laugh in Ireland there was a Moral Panic about Gypsies stealing children. I thought the Hysteria was a bit comical in a way but unfortunately was traumatic for the children. I was thinking of the many adopted children in Ireland who didn't look anything like their "parents" and was full expecting that the hysteria would reach such heights that hundreds of children would be removed and hundreds of DNA results wouldn't match. I really can't think of a sillier reason for removing a child than they don't look like their parents. Such things are to be expected in a climate of a Moral Panic but fortunately reason was thrown out the window for hysteria. What was also interesting was that many people took note of how easy it is for children to be removed from their parents, a point I have been making for 7 years. While we are lied to that social workers try working with families and all possibilities are exhausted before a child is removed, we saw 2 cases that prove the opposite is true. Shoot first and ask questions later.

To try to put the whole area of Child Protection in a legal perspective, imagine a Policeman arriving at your door tomorrow and saying they had obtained a warrant to arrest and detain you for an indefinite period because they believe at some point in the future, that you were "at risk" of robbing a bank or killing someone. The whole proposition seems absurd and unjust, but this is exactly what happens to children. Not only that but the children are placed in "jail" where they will likely suffer Post Traumatic Stress Disorder and be at a 10 times higher risk of dying by suicide. Also let's not forget that the "Policeman" (or woman) might investigate and decide that you are not a risk at all and later your child is killed because they didn't see the signs of abuse or neglect. You have all the hallmarks of a system that is illegal, unjust, unbalanced and almost does the complete opposite of what it purports to do. Many of the experts and professionals, they know what I have said here is true, yet this is the system we have and we're stuck with, as the bottom line is that children must be "protected".

The signs all around us point to Democracy being dismantled at every level. We need to be protected from "Terrorists" even though we are far more likely to be killed by Police. Justice is becoming scarcer and more difficult to obtain for the average person. Not that Justice was ever that easy to achieve for those who cant afford it. We see a situation now where the UK want to opt of European Human Rights because David Cameron feels that nobody should be able to dictate to the UK on how to run the country. We have seen campaigns such as the Occupy Movement come and go and protest on a massive scale against governments.

The fact is that we have allowed our (Civil) Servants to become our Masters and we accept the supreme authority of governments to run and control our lives without question. The conditions we see now are the conditions for a revolution to occur. In Ireland, if the Dail is ever surrounded as the Hungarian Parliament was, they have a backup plan to use Dublin Castle in case of such emergency. You have to wonder then why politicians would be so scared of losing control that they would feel it necessary to make such plans. In my own view, I prefer Order to Chaos and Democracy to Anarchy. The division between the People and the Government is widening, Governments are losing control and generally making a mess of things.

The Trickle Down Economy has slowed to a Drip Down Economy and people are suffering from Austerity, mostly imposed by Governments and their Lobbyists. The average person doesn't want conflict in their lives, they are happy to pay the government 70% of their earnings in some cases and just go home every night and tuck the kids in bed at night. They don't want to have to worry about anything the government is doing, they pay these people to do a job but the whole country is starting to fall apart. In other countries the people have no such concerns, they know they can surround the parliament and kick the politicians out and replace them.

Democracy only works when it is For the People, By the People and Of the People. The Irish and UK citizens have long since lost control and the only politicians available to elect is the "Devil you know". Politicians have long since lost their way and Leadership is something that only existed years ago. The Lobbyists and the Corporations are running the show and the Profit Motive drives all economies and governments. We see in the UK vulnerable people being starved to death and being cut off benefits. One woman with no arms and no legs has to appear annually to prove that her limbs haven't grown back and the blind and the deaf have similar meetings every year or risk losing their benefit. One man I read about recently, a war veteran, died because his electricity was cut off and he could not keep his insulin refrigerated.

When they found his body there was a stack of CV's that he had printed out and a list of jobs he had applied for.

You can't have a Government Of, By and For the people if the people are not willing to take an active role. You can't blame a government if you didn't vote. You can't expect politicians to make the right choices if they don't have the proper information to begin with. We can no longer idly sit by and expect a benevolent government to take care of us; we have to take some personal responsibility for the position we find ourselves in.

Governments tell us that there are people on benefits who have never worked a day in their life, this is true. I know many disabled or differently abled people who will never have the opportunity to work. In Ireland during the boom, we had negative unemployment and had to import people to meet the demand. I went into the Unemployment Office in January 2000 and I was the only client there, I was just renewing my card. In 2009 the same office would have so many clients that many had to stand out in the rain. When we actually look at who the scroungers are, in the UK we are talking about 0.7%. When you look at the billions given to corporations in tax breaks and incentives, if they were made to pay their fair share, we could pay benefits of €30,000 a year to the unemployed instead of paying less than the minimum wage and certainly less than the basic minimum which doesn't even reflect the actual cost of surviving, never mind living. At the same time we are squandering a billion a year with about 10,000 people "protecting" 6,500 children in "Care". We have to pay stealth TV Tax to fund a TV station that should be free, and if you pay your electricity bill or gas to heat your home and feed your family instead, you could end up in jail.

I may be painting a very bleak picture here, but that is the reality for many. A lot of families trying to raise children are "Working Poor" and need subsidies to make ends meet. Poverty has even become a reason for taking children into "Care", rather than giving a hand up to families in need, the system spends considerably more and doesn't actually resolve the problems. It's mismanagement of the highest order but the Bankers and unsecured debt owners must be paid, "we wont have debtors written across our foreheads".

The simple fact of the matter is that we get the government we allow. For many Irish and UK citizens, the only time we get involved in politics is when a politician knocks at the door looking for votes every 4 years. And many people don't even bother to vote. A revolution starts when people start paying attention to what the government is doing. I don't believe in violence or believe that violence is even necessary to have a revolution. India accomplished independence with no war but they had the most powerful "weapon" imaginable in the leadership of the Mahatma Gandhi. There are statues of great men (and very few women) all over Ireland who achieved great things with their leadership. The fact is the governments know that the people will roll over eventually whenever they impose new taxes or unpopular laws, and we allow this to happen. By not taking an active part in politics and what government is doing, we get the government we deserve.

In India today, you'll see very poor people coming out to listen to local politicians and people of all ages taking part. This is the case in many countries, citizens participate in Democracy and the Lobbyists and Corporations have less power than communities. I don't see any end in sight to the dictatorship system of governance the Ireland and the UK has had for years. Politicians cannot vote with their conscience and must follow the will of the party. If a politician was instructed by his constituents to prevent the closing of a hospital or army base, he or she would have no choice but to vote as the party wants. This is a form of dictatorship. Morality is doing what is right regardless of what you are told. Obedience is doing what you are told regardless of whether it is right. Blind obedience has never served humanity well, many people at their War Crimes Trial in Nuremberg used the defence; "I was just following orders".

Until the Irish decide to take back their own country I can see no end in sight to austerity and inequality. Democracy is not automatic and neither are Rights, you have to work at it continuously. I mentioned earlier that Rights are Imprescriptible, governments cannot make laws to take away rights, and Rights are inalienable, they cant be taken away or granted, you already possess them and shouldn't need to fight for your rights, sadly though, in reality you need to defend your rights and remind judges of them. A government of the people, by the people and for the people does exist in some countries but unfortunately only in countries where the citizens participate in democracy.

Ireland also deserves a World-Class Child Protection System and this won't be accomplished, as long Justice is not equal for all. The concept of Children's "Rights" under Best Interests Principle means that children suffer and die in the "Care" of the State and the system is not required to Benefit a single child. As long as social workers are at the hub of child "protection", the system will fail. As long as the secrecy of these alternate Family Courts is allowed to exist, the system will act with impunity and protect itself before it protects children. And as long as there is no management and the Profit Motive drives the lack of accountability in the system it can only continue to grow. The government will not be the catalyst for change; the Lobbyists and the Industry will dictate how the system is run. Until the Irish people care about all the children of Ireland, as equally as they love their own and until parents are assisted properly to raise their children and child poverty and homelessness is eliminated, we cannot be said to "Cherish all the Children of Ireland Equally".

Meaningless declarations about Children's "Rights" are not benefitting any child. Having laws that are enforced in secret courts has not resulted in safer environments for children; it has done the exact opposite. And disregarding Nature, Science and Law has not produced the expected results. Sociology and Psychology have not delivered on their promises but rather have caused a degeneration of Society. Until we restore Human Rights and follow far better models, society will continue in a downward spiral. We have the capability and the money to manage our society better, what is needed is for the Public to participate in Democracy.

The fundamental shift back to Democracy could start tomorrow if Judges in these secret courts followed the law to the letter of the law. If you have a situation where a judge can grant an order in less than a minute without hearing any evidence and without the other party represented, it could be fairly said that many Irish citizens are living in Tyranny. A lesson of history has always taught; "There can be no Peace without first, Justice".

Members of the Gardaí "off the record" have contacted my colleagues and me; they just can't get their head around this either, even Superintendents and Inspectors and Sergeants who have been on the force all their working life. Gardaí have even been threatened by social workers who feel they are above the law and, as passionate as many Gardaí are about child abuse and neglect, they feel powerless to intervene in cases. I was told a story of a heartless social worker dragging 3 children kicking and screaming to her car while a young male and female Garda team tried to calm down the social worker who was holding a baby and dragging young boy and teenage girl to her car. They complained to their senior officer and said they were shaken by the event that they described as unnecessary, traumatic for the children and personally found the event barbaric.

Let's be honest, it is barbaric, sometimes it needs to be done if children are in need of protection. The question is though, how often is it necessary? If children are being removed for the "crime" of child abuse and neglect, shouldn't the Gardaí be investigating and part of the process?

It is no longer sustainable in Ireland or any Democracy, to have two different systems and standard of Justice. It is no longer sustainable for Gardaí **not** to investigate Child Abuse and Neglect. It is no longer acceptable to allow Punishment Without Crime and equally to allow Crime Without Punishment. The In Camera Rule is not protecting children; it has been allowed to be used to cover up crimes against children. The slogan, "Best Interests of the Child" does not benefit any child and needs to be replaced as a matter of urgency.

CHAPTER 11

"THE DREADOPHILE"

I was watching Vincent Brown on TV one evening, one of my favourite journalists. He made an offhand comment that there were 100,000 paedophiles in Ireland. To me that seemed an extraordinary number but I accepted on good faith as it had come from Vincent. When I actually did some research I found that there might not actually be 100,000 paedophiles in the entire world. It is a very rare disorder that affects a tiny percentage of men and women. Women? Yes there are female paedophiles also.

First I researched the Psychological aspect and found there is a lot of disagreement. It is classified as a sexual attraction to children under the age of puberty by a person over the age of 16, for a period of more than 6 months. A Psychiatrist or Psychologist can only diagnose it. There is huge disagreement within the field of the symptoms and characterists of paedophiles. Some Psych's say that many tend to be small men and many are left-handed. Over the years we have been fed a Hollywood picture of dirty old men in raincoats.

The disagreements within Psychology are testament to the weakness of the profession as a "Science". There is a lack of consensus and the definition has become so broad that many people are wrongly classified or labelled. The only guide available is the DSM, The Diagnostic and Statistical Manual of the American Psychiatric Association. However, it only takes the consensus of 4 clinicians to have a disorder listed. The latest DSM has been widely rejected even by Associations around the world as it now lists every human emotion as a disorder.

The textbook Paedophile as defined by the Psychologists is a person who is sexually attracted to children and only children below the age of puberty. People who rape children are not always paedophiles; Sociopaths and Psychopaths have an equal desire to harm children or adults. Where

Paedophiles feel it necessary to "Groom" children into having sexual relations, Sociopaths don't ask for permission. Unlike the paedophile, the sociopath and psychopath can and will murder children. This is an important distinction and is necessary to understand how their mind works. Most paedophiles "Love" children and believe that they can have a committed relationship, sexual or otherwise, with the child. For them, in their mind they feel this is "normal" and can't understand why a 28-year-old man cannot have a relationship with an 8-year-old girl or boy. Sexual orientation has nothing to do with Paedophilia; they are either attracted to boys or girls and always below the age of Puberty. For the most part Paedophiles don't kill children; the child is harmed from the rape or sexual contact but only Sociopaths and Psychopaths kill.

Over the years we have seen groups like NAMBLA and even politicians advocating that adults should be allowed to have "Consensual" sex with children. Again, it's important to realize in their minds that for them, this is normal. To understand the problem you have to realize how they think. Of course a child cannot "consent" to sex. A child who has not reached the age of puberty has no concept of sex and most children find the whole concept "Yucky" if you ask them. Children don't engage in sex with each other as boys and girls below puberty generally don't mix very well. There is a natural curiosity in children about gender and things like where babies come from, but to call this "Sexual" in any way shows a very poor understanding of children or puberty. Once Puberty hits, the hormones begin to take effect and for the first time in their lives, they begin to understand "sex" and are now interested in the opposite sex.

I also found in my research that the hysteria about Paedophiles, Child Pornography and the whole hysteria of Child Protection started in the 1976, only 4 years later the hysteria about Satanic Ritual Abuse and Fractured and Recovered Memory, before the 70's, none of these existed as they exist today. I know many people wont believe that SRA didn't exist before the book "Michelle Remembers" and I would urge you to do your own research.

Sociologist Frank Furedi has captured the issue of the Moral Panic of Paedophilia quite well. "If you question the crusade, you are seen as evil" Or perhaps he is absolutely correct in calling it a Moral Crusade rather than a Moral Panic. I have to say I greatly admire Furedi for his courage in taking the scientific approach and asking questions that need to be asked. Few people have this courage, as they will be branded Heretics for not sticking to "Group Think" and the Orthodoxy of the Religion of Child Abuse. Indeed the Moral Crusaders and the Social Entrepreneurs need a cause to attach themselves to, but the question we should be asking is; "Is it actually protecting children?"

"Since the 1970s and 80s, says Furedi, paedophilia has become the last remaining moral benchmark in an uncertain age, the single embodiment of evil. If you question it you are seen as evil". Here again you see how we have strayed from Science, science has always relied on questions, and a theory becomes more robust the more it is challenged. Now Dogma has replaced Theory and Religion has replaced Science.

In almost every story of a paedophile case you read online, the comments are a good indicator of how paedophiles are viewed. "Castrate them" being one of the more popular comments. But does castration actually work? Many countries since WWII have incorporated castration into the punishment of offenders. Mostly this is done by chemical means in the form of a drug rather than how online posters would recommend. But does it work? The fact is that it doesn't prevent reoccurrence. Neither has any other psychological method such as electric shocks to the genitals or Aversion "Therapy". Even despite the evidence castration doesn't work, Russia implemented it in 2014. No doubt they will find that when they let the castrated offenders back into society, they will reoffend. And what is their plan for castrating women paedophiles?

The truth of the matter is that paedophilia is a function of the mind rather than the organs. The organs of paedophiles could be removed and it won't prevent children being sexually assaulted. Jail only works as long as the paedophile is incarcerated but once released, they will reoffend. It's also interesting to note that there are many diagnosed paedophiles who have never sexually assaulted any child. So it seems that everything we know and do to combat paedophilia simply isn't working, so what is the solution?

Why are we releasing people whom we know are a danger to children from Prisons? By seeing paedophilia merely as a "crime", the perpetrator must be released after serving their sentence whether they are a danger to children or not. In a similar situation, we have other predators such as Serial Rapists who are known to be a danger but law enforcement and the Justice System are seemingly powerless to act once they have been released.

In Ireland in the case of Larry Murphy, who was caught red handed in a sadistic rape, was jailed and released early for "good behaviour". Before his release the media were abuzz with stories and newspapers were flying off the shelves. Gardaí vowed that the Irish Public would be protected and even the FBI expressed concerns for public safety. Gardaí were supposed to secure a special budget to have a team of 15 officers watching his every move and one pundit quipped that Larry wouldn't be able to fart without Gardaí knowing about it. On the day of his actual release, Larry went missing 20 minutes after his release into a crowd in Grafton Street.

In the Austerity Program of Fine Gael and Labour, Gardaí faced savage cuts and overtime, which many Garda Members relied on to pay their mortgages, was cut. It was announced recently that Gardaí simply didn't have the budget to investigate every possible sighting of Larry or the many others. Isn't it amazing though that Gardaí seem to have no budget constraints to follow heavily pregnant women around Ireland as they have done many times on behalf of the CFA or HSE? These are women not accused of any crime, who's ability to move or flee is seriously impaired and if one of these women drove across the border to Northern Ireland or boarded a flight to Northern Greece, Gardaí would be powerless to stop them.

By seeing Predators as only being criminals, they must be released. By seeing Paedophilia, Sociopathy and Psychopathy as a Mental Illness, which it is as they are listed in the DSM, it would be possible under current laws to see these people as criminally insane. **People who are criminally insane and a threat to society should never be released from prison unless they are cured of the disorder. At present there are no cures for any of these conditions**.

A few years ago a curious psychiatric case shook the Mental Health Community and received much attention, it didn't generate much interest in mainstream media. It was the case of a man who reported to his doctor that he had recently developed a sexual interest in children that he found very disturbing. The GP referred his patient to a Neurologist who discovered that the man had developed a Brain Tumour that threatened his life. After the surgery the urges for sexual contact with children disappeared after the tumour was removed. For the first time ever, Neuro-Scientists had identified the part of the brain believed responsible for Paedophilia. The significance of this discovery is that one day we may be able to cure paedophilia or at least remove the "urges" by means of Psychosurgery, which involves removing a part of the brain as, used to be called a Lobotomy.

It's important to remember though that paedophilia is extremely rare, important because if we "cured" every paedophile, it simply wouldn't eliminate the problem of sexual abuse of children, not even close.

Getting back to my original question; "Is the hysteria actually protecting children?" The evidence suggests it is actually harming more children and has done very little in the way of reducing the numbers of convictions of sexual assaults against children. If anything, the number of sexual assaults hasn't changed in decades. What has changed is an increase in the numbers of people on the Sex Offender Register, but in terms of actual sexual assaults on children, the numbers remain flat but most of the convictions today are for Child Pornography. Before the hysteria children were sexually assaulted and the offenders were punished. A look at the DPP statistics shows and average of about 39 prosecutions a year for sexual abuse of children. 39 is a long way off Vincent's assertion of 100,000 paedophiles and also a long way of the HSE's assertion of 541 "confirmed" cases a year.

Paedophile Hunters have sprung up all over the place, we now have police officers sitting at computers posing as young girls and enticing men into crime. In the USA we have TV hosts setting up "Sting" operations to encourage men, and it's always men, to break the law even though the majority have never fallen afoul of the law before. While I don't condone the actions of these men,

I also can't endorse Police creating new crimes for the entertainment of the TV public. To put it in perspective, Police don't set up stings to entice people to rob banks or beak into houses. I can see where they entice thieves to steal specially equipped cars but I find it sick and perverted to entice men to have sex with children. Of course we have had police dressed up as prostitutes to control prostitution, but at best this has only controlled the situation and has not eliminated prostitution anywhere. Police are allowed by law to lie to anyone, not just suspects, this has been upheld in many courts. They can have 2 suspects in two separate rooms and walk into the other room and lie and say the other party has made a full confession. I have seen social workers doing this also and attempting to play "good Cop, bad Cop", but never with any success, and social workers are not allowed to lie by law.

As disturbing as it is for Police to resort to underhanded tactics, the tactics of self-appointed vigilantes is far more disturbing. In a conversation with an editor, he said I should write a book about paedophiles and use the words "Vile" and "Evil" a lot as I could sell a lot of copies. I don't claim to have any specialised knowledge of the topic other than what I have read and I believe that authors should only write about what they know or have witnessed. His point was that going against the mainstream opinion in a climate of Moral Panic is not the best marketing strategy if history is anything to go by. I'm not concerned about making money from this book, I don't want any notoriety and I frankly don't care if the book makes money, less than 4% of books actually sell. For me this book is a catharsis, I have seen the human misery caused in these courts and the effects on other human beings I have tried to help. My "Therapy" is to explain what I have learned to others in the hope that this insanity will end.

I am not the first person to claim that we are living in a climate of a Moral Panic and I hope I won't be the last. There are very few books written on the topic of Child Protection that go against the dogma and the Hollywood version of the people on a Crusade to "Protect" children. The only 2 books previously written on the topic were Forced Adoption by Ian Josephs and a very comprehensive book written by Jack Frost entitled; "The Gulag of the Family Courts". Another book I mentioned earlier was written by Louise Mason entitled; "A Mothers Nightmare: My Fight to get my children back". Another famous journalist in the UK has told me that he will also release his book in the near future.

More specifically on the topics of Paedophilia and Child Pornography, a very brave writer wrote a book questioning the hysteria surrounding Child Protection. In her book " Harmful to Minors " Judith Levine explores the myths surrounding child protection. Her main point in the book is that Child "Protection" is actually more harmful to minors in many cases. Simply by talking about paedophilia and questioning the hysteria and figures thrown out by people, she became a target and her message was lost. Rather than debate and discuss, she was branded a heretic for even asking questions or pointing out that much of what we were being told was false. The hysteria about paedophilia was gaining a lot of currency but did not spread until another book entitled "Michelle Remembers" was released in 1980.

Earlier I mentioned that Satanic Ritual Abuse did not exist before 1980, and SRA added to the new myth of the Paedophile being on every corner spread around the English-speaking world like wildfire. Funnily enough, in many countries the hysteria of the paedophile doesn't exist although more countries are strengthening their legislation. In the English-speaking world we began to get hysterical after 1980, however some countries have had laws dealing with paedophilia, very harshly I might add, long before 1980.

The original hysteria began in Times Square in New York when the NYPD Vice Squad decided to clean up the area for a Political Convention that was coming to town. They decided sanitize the area of prostitutes and porn shops. To bolster their campaign they used the media to gain support for their cause. In some of the porn shops there were some magazines of Child Pornography and Police seized on the opportunity. This was the age before the Internet and where most people didn't own computers. In reality, there were only a small number of magazines and a small amount of child pornography that had been circulating for years. Some of the material at the time came from Japan where pictures of nude children had been legal, even up until very recently until Japan fell more in line with the rest of the world.

Japanese photographers travelled the world and took nude pictures of children, which were published in Japanese magazines. In the USA, there was only a small following and most pornography was of adults. In Japan the magazines were more publicly accepted and more widely available. None of these magazines of children were considered "Sexual" in Japan and the children were not posed in "sexual" positions, as you would see with adult pornography. At the same time in Europe for many years, famous photographers such as David Hamilton took "Erotic" images of pubescent children. Up until 1970 there was no hysteria and the works of Hamilton hung in major art museums and famous places for years. David had been a fashion photographer in Paris, much sought after before he used young girls as models, as has been the practice for decades, even today. Many of his models wanted David to take pictures of their daughters in very artistic poses, again, not what you would see in Playboy. He developed a photographic technique in his images that has been copied many times called Soft Focus. This was a result of using large old Plate Cameras that gave a grainy and out of focus appearance. Many photographers today use the same technique on wedding and portrait shots.

Up until the hysteria started in the USA, nobody batted an eyelid, except perhaps the few paedophiles, and David Hamilton's work was available in libraries around the world. Interestingly, today you can buy his books on Amazon and in bookstores, but if you download his images you are guilty of making child pornography. A new dilemma has arisen lately with eBooks, if you buy a paperback copy of certain books which are not banned, you are not breaking the law, but if you download the same book to a Kindle, Kobo or eBook format, you are guilty of making child pornography. In an interview a few years ago, David Hamilton stated that not one of his models had ever later claimed that they had been violated or harmed in any way, in fact many of them now appear at gallery showings of his work. Some of his former models have asked him to take images of their daughters and granddaughters but since the 1980's he has refused to photograph any models. He has lived quite comfortably in Paris and the south of France for years on the proceeds of his work. He has been the subject of Police investigations over the years but has never been successfully prosecuted. His books have sold millions of copies and are still available in many libraries throughout the world but not in the UK or Ireland even though they are not banned.

In a famous case in Australia, a man was found guilty of downloading images of the Simpsons cartoons which were in extremely poor taste. It depicted Bart and Lisa in sexual positions as well as the rest of the cast. The conviction was upheld in the Supreme Court because under Australian laws, the Simpsons depicted real people. I heard of a case in the USA where a father was arrested for taking images of his baby being breastfed in a public park by the baby's mother. The cop though' "Breast & Child" amounted to child pornography, fortunately the judge didn't agree, but under the Adam Walsh Act, the father is an un-convicted Sex Offender.

For years, Art was almost exclusively about Beauty. Women are more attractive than men and young women and children considered the most attractive. If you visit the Vatican and Sistine Chapel, Paris and the Louvre, everywhere you see images of naked cherubs and breasts and nudes. Artists often painted wealthy young girls and the painting given to a man they admired. Essentially, "Selfies" existed for hundreds of years before the invention of the Polaroid Camera or the Smartphone or Tablet. There was no hysteria even in Victorian times when Morality became more fashionable. Granted, children who do this are harming themselves, it may come back to haunt them, but to prosecute, jail and put that child on a Sex Offenders Register for years is something that is far more damaging to the child.

The author of the book "Alice in Wonderland" Lewis Carroll was an avid photographer and in 1873 published nude photos of naked girls. Nobody questioned whether his work with young girls was anything other than creating beautiful art. If you view his work online or see the photos at an art gallery or in a book, you have committed no crime. If you download his work you are "making child pornography" if you email it to someone you are "distributing child pornography". When you look at strict Islamic countries like Iran or Saudi Arabia, young girls do not need to be completely covered but past the age of puberty, women are required to cover every inch of skin and Moral Police ruthlessly enforce Sharia Law. As I said before, I honestly believe that if this hysteria, which is not protecting children, continues unabated, we are only a few short years away from making children wear burqas in case a paedophile might be titillated. The complete opposite of what Saudi Arabia is doing.

As with many things, the pendulum swings too far occasionally in one direction. I wouldn't wish to see photographers being allowed to use under-age models as Hamilton did in the 1970's posing nude. Children need to be protected, often from themselves. But let's look at the Fashion Industry for a moment. The most sought after models are thin girls often around 14 years old. These models are presented on magazine covers, often Photo-Shopped, wearing make-up and selling Sex to sell a product. The idealized version of womanhood is an unrealistic model and many people have spoken out against it, but it still continues today. Even the Barbie Doll has been remodelled in 2014 but is not proving to be as popular as her predecessor has been for the past 50 years.

When you look at the work of artists, and you only have to wander around old cities to see the statues, sculpture and frescos, none of the models are Barbie Dolls. Instead you see models of all shapes and sizes, often women with bigger hips, which used to be the idealized woman. A child is beautiful simply by virtue of the fact that Nature designed them that way. As adults we are supposed to look at children and see them as beautiful, adorable and cute. We are supposed to look **at** children so that we should look **after** children and protect them. It is in our instinct to look at children but this is being trained out of us because we live in fear that someone may think that we are paedophiles. Even if we don't buy into the hysteria, we still protect our reputations because we live in fear of being wrongly accused. If a story appears in the news or on the Internet about a paedophile, the correct response is to over-compensate and show your support for the Crusaders. I have seen this many times with Gays and Black people where people will try to ingratiate themselves and make statements such as I have Gay friends or Black friends when clearly they don't, but they don't want to be seen as not fitting-in with the mob, because they live in fear of being ostracized. But again I have to keep coming back to the question; "Is this hysteria really helping and protecting children?"

You can see the pendulum has swung very far to one side; the danger in this is the pendulum swinging too far in the other direction as we had in the 1970's. The 1970's saw the downfall of Morality in society. We were introduced to hard drugs, a Sexual Revolution and a shift away from Family Values. Single Motherhood was no longer a sin and teenage mothers could raise their children without stigma. Many children grew up without fathers with disastrous results, and Religion fell out of fashion for many. Homosexuality became decriminal-ized, women were burning their bras and society swung the pendulum far to the other side, too far many believe. It was inevitable that the pendulum would swing, people had been repressed for many years by the morality of the Church which refused to give up any ground rather than shifting with the sands of time.

I remember in Ireland in the late 60's and early 70's when the first Irish "Men's Magazine" came out, as a kid I saw a copy of it. Ireland being a very Catholic country at the time decried the magazine from the Dail to every pulpit in Ireland. Essentially if I remember right, there was one photo of a woman's breasts, which would have been seen, as obscene by most people. Another scandalizing event was the introduction of Ireland's first Condom Dispensing Machine at UCD. At the time, condoms were illegal and against church dogma. Women used to go to Newry on the train and smuggle condoms back to the republic. You could buy condoms on Moore Street at a premium price. At one point in the 1950's people were having them delivered by letter from France and condoms were widely known as "French Letters". I also remember a brave woman who wanted to go on Birth Control Pills, which were illegal at the time and the public outcry against contraception was fully supported by our moral media at the time.

When condoms were finally available on prescription only, I remember medical students dispensing prescriptions from inside the gates of Trinity College which was beyond the reach of the Gardaí. I doubt that many younger people reading this will believe it but it all happened in Catholic Ireland. While the Sexual Revolution of the Hippies was taking place in the UK and USA, and parts of Europe, there was no sex in Ireland before the Late Late Show. Of course having 4 kids was necessary to get a Corporation House or even to get on the housing list. For many years half the children of Ireland emigrated and half stayed behind.

For many years up until the mid 1970's, girls were raped or got pregnant and ended up in the Magdalen Asylum or other Mother and Baby Homes, for most there was no contraception in Ireland because of the Catholic Church. Their babies would be taken from them and sold to rich Americans. It would be a scandal of epic proportions in Ireland to see a young pregnant girl on the street. Sex outside of marriage was supposedly non-existent and yet 60,000 babies were born in Mother & Baby Homes and today, the Irish Government will not give these people, many in their 60's, their records to find their family.

In the USA in the late 1970's, the Moral Panic of Paedophilia and Child Porn was picking up steam. What started off as a few magazines in sex shops on Times Square had become a national emergency such was the hysteria. Central to our story is Sergeant Lloyd of LAPD Vice Squad and Judianne Densen-Gerber, a Child Psychologist, who became public figures and whipped up the hysteria to epidemic proportions.

They made more and more outrageous claims and "massaged" the numbers exponentially. Later they would claim that 300,000 children a year are abducted and by paedophiles when the actual figure was around 500 abductions. In Levine's book she said; "The two careened from sea to sea, stoking outsized claims. Before a congressional committee in 1977, Densen-Gerber estimated that 1.2 million children were victims of child prostitution and pornography, including "snuff" films in which they were killed for viewer's titillation. Martin travelled the country orating speeches of evangelical fervour, warning America on one Christian television show, for instance, that paedophiles actually wait for babies to be born so that, just minutes after birth, they can grab the post-foetuses and sexually victimize them. At that 1977 congressional committee, he declared that the sexual exploitation of children was worse than homicide." In reality, child pornography was already illegal before 1976 and many of the black & white images had been circulating for years. Some of the images were of nudists and their children and could not be deemed "Sexual", even by law. The outrageous claims, because they could not be proven in the USA, implicated other countries like Sweden, Japan and the Netherlands.

Many people have preconceived beliefs about other races or countries. What some people perceive about Amsterdam is extremely offensive to Dutch people. Just as the Irish are stereotyped as drinkers but in reality, many years ago few Irish people could afford to drink. By 1980 there were claims of satanic sacrifice and child prostitutes based on a false perception that a small number of streets in Amsterdam were representative of an entire race. They said that in Holland that 50% of all pornography was Child Porn, however, the Dutch Police stated otherwise. The senior detective inspector of Dutch Central Police Investigations Information Service (Centrale Recherche Informatiedienst) Mr M.J.M. Rijk said

"We pressed, more or less, the people in the shops to stop selling child pornography. We said 'we will arrest you if you continue with it because it's forbidden and we wont allow you to have it. We will be very strict in future". And they said, "Well it's only 1% of our turnover and we don't like to have problems with the Police. It's not big business so we will stop".

The simple fact of the matter is that no right-thinking person is ever going to try to make Paedophilia acceptable, an instinct in every human being is to protect those younger than us, especially children. To solve the problem of paedophilia you need to understand it. Many groups of paedophiles have tried to peddle the idea that children are capable of being sexual beings before the age of puberty, some of them serious scientists. I have read some of these studies but I simply can't accept the fact children are even capable of sexual though without hormones running through their body, I may be wrong but my instinct tells me that this is true. Even scientists point out that children have levels of both hormones before puberty, but of course nothing like the levels they have at puberty. Scholarly articles are regularly written on Child Sexuality but I simply can't get my head around the thought of children being "Sexual". Children often behave and engage in behaviours that give them pleasure, but isn't this just normal childhood curiosity? The term "Playing Doctor" existed long before the term Paedophile.

I could bore you with many studies cited but my impression is that whenever someone pops their head above the parapet and asks a question, they are likely to have their head shot off. This is not how Science is supposed to work. Rather than a scientific theory being peer-reviewed, the attack is often based on political motivation and a politician jumping on a bandwagon. In a climate of a Moral Panic, you simply can't have rational debate. The objective is to attack the theorist rather than attacking the argument, this is usually the last resort of a fool. By attacking the theory, the theory is bolstered by the attack; this is the whole point of peer-review.

We see today how medical scientists can easily fall afoul of the law or the Medical Councils simply for asking questions. I have seen in the case of Shaken Baby Syndrome, one of the worst pieces of junk science ever dreamed up, where every Doctor or expert who testifies on behalf of families, has been attacked by prosecutors and Medical Councils. If you don't preach the dogma of an unproven theory then you must be a child abuser or advocate for child abuse. Arguing with these people is a pointless exercise; you may as well walk into a church and declare that there is no God as the congregation will not accept any evidence you present regardless of it's validity. Psychologists call this Cognitive Dissonance but I think calling it a Religion is a more valid term. I stand to be corrected on that but that's how Science works, you have to keep an open mind.

In a case in the UK, a Professor of Criminology, one of the worlds leading experts on child pornography, arrived at work one day to find his office had been broken into and had his computers and files seized by Police. He was suspended and when he arrived home, found that his home computer and files had been raided also but he wasn't arrested. When he complained to Police that he was a registered Expert with the Home Office, and testified on behalf of Police and Crown Prosecution Service, his complaints fell on deaf ears. He stated; "you can't render an opinion on child pornography without possessing it". He was not charged, was reinstated and continues to advise the UK government as an expert. The Police Detective was later elevated to the rank of Superintendent and no action was taken against her.

Incidentally, did you know that the largest collection of child pornography in the world is located in Cork, Ireland at UCC?

A convicted criminal, who burned down a school and assaulted a man and is responsible for the death of a man by suicide, is hailed as a hero by many. Stinson Hunter, whose real name is Kieren Parsons has set himself up as a Paedophile Hunter. He lures men who have not committed any crime and entices them to have sex with a minor, usually above the age of puberty, and videotapes the meeting. Technically, he is not a Paedophile Hunter as paedophilia is defined as a sexual attraction to pre-pubescent children, technically he would be an Ephibophile Hunter as the children are above the age of puberty. This definition would be lost on most people as they don't know what an Ephibophile is and many would struggle to pronounce it. Parsons has claimed that Police secretly support his witch hunting even though the police issued a press release that they want him to stop and have warned him. Still, his supporters have given him over £15,000 to fund his activities. Parsons has also objected to being identified by his real name as he feels he is entitled to anonymity. The irony that he exposes others as a vigilante is obviously lost on him.

In another famous case in the USA, a family took films to be developed at a Walmart. On their return they were arrested and their children taken into "Care". At the trial, the prosecutor said he wasn't going to show the images to the jury as they were the most depraved he had ever seen. He claimed in one photo of a baby lying on it's back with it's legs raised in the air that the child was lying in a "sexual position" in readiness for sex. The judge however disagreed and dismissed the case. The judge pointed out that babies regularly hold their legs raised when their nappies are being changed. The prosecutor was later booted out and Walmart forced to pay a large sum in damages to the family. Curiously though, social services still didn't want to give the children back to their parents but eventually social services lost their case.

As there is no cure for a Moral Panic, you have to wait a while until the Puritans have hanged a number of "Witches" or crushed them to death under heavy rocks before everyone stands up and says, "This is wrong". Individuals wont make a huge difference and as they will likely be made an example of, few people will be willing to stick their heads up. The damage caused to children in these cases is very severe and sometimes will affect them into adulthood. The heavy-handed approach is usually worse than the alleged offense.

We are living in a climate where a father can take his son, but not his daughter to an event in case he will be viewed as a paedophile. An 8 year old girl told me that her grandfather hates her because he will take his grandson "everywhere" but wont come to her dance recital. I read a story yesterday where single people, let's be honest, MEN, cant go to a theme park unless they are accompanied by a child. 15 years ago when I went to the gym, fathers would take their young daughters into the dressing room and in 2003 they dropped the age of girls from 8 to 3 and even then men had to undress in private and no nudity was allowed, you had to put your towel on before leaving the shower. God forbid that a 4-year-old girl should catch a glimpse of male's genitals, but then at age 5 she will taught how to have sex and how babies are born in Sex Education class. I read a story yesterday where a 14-year-old boy raped a girl immediately after a Sex Education Class, presumably, which didn't teach him that rape was wrong.

In a recent survey in the UK recently, 80% of parents didn't want schools teaching children Sex Education at the age of 5. If a 5 year old asks where babies come from, all they need to know is that they grow inside a mommy's tummy. To give them any more information than that is pointless, they don't understand. The term "Age Appropriate" is a good guide to follow. But rather than focus on Sex, we should be more concerned that Adult Entertainment, and I'm not talking about XXX Rated Material, should not be viewed by children. Young female pop stars give children an unrealistic view of the world, that women are objects and that men treat women as objects. Instead of aspiring to study to go into careers and high paying jobs, or motherhood which is an equally noble profession, we are teaching children that they are a Star yet to be discovered. If you turn off your TV and let your child learn from you, their parent, they will thank you later in life. I find it astonishing that we allow marketing aimed at children that is not Age Appropriate. A movie can have a "14 Rating" for a shot of a female breast, but there are no controls of advertising and pop stars "Twerking" in seductive poses on TV?

In the USA, a federal law known as the Adam Walsh Act states that all sex offenders and even alleged sex offenders must be registered, often on the Internet. If you browse these "Sex Offenders" you will see children as young as 5 and their photographs posted online. The hysteria of Sarah's Law, that parents have a right to know if paedophiles are living nearby was written into the Adam Walsh Act. You can't help but notice something very disturbing when you look at these websites; most of the "sex offenders" are boys about 14 years old. The one positive benefit of the Adam Walsh Act is that it has given us a far better profile of who sexually assaults children. **As incredible as it may seem, over 80% of all sex offences carried out against children are by 14 year olds, 70% of the perpetrators being boys.** You would think that this stunning piece of information would be front-page news and lead to scholarly debate as it throws everything we have been told in the past about dirty-old-men in raincoats, right out the window? The vast majority of prosecutions are around the age of 28, this is the same pattern as in most countries, and very few offenders are over 50 and almost none by age 70.

If the vast majority of sex offenders are 14, the age in most cases where puberty occurs, isn't that telling us something needs to be done urgently about educating 14 year olds that it's wrong to sexually abuse younger children? Is the whole hysteria about protecting children actually about children at all? I don't pretend to have the solutions, but maybe if parents and society celebrated puberty in some way as a "Coming of Age" as it is in some cultures, and treated it as normal event to be celebrated by the family? As puberty doesn't come with the same regularity as the Tooth Fairy, shouldn't we be teaching sex education to children on the basis that they have reached puberty rather than teaching 5 year olds who have no concept of sex?

The simple fact is that parents have no rights over their children as they once had before Psychology & Sociology started meddling and going against eons of evolution. If your 14 year old daughter suddenly takes a boy home and has sex in your house, you, the parent will be charged whether you report it or not. By not reporting this horrible crime of sex between 2 consenting children you are guilty of not reporting a crime, but by reporting you are guilty of "allowing" it to take place in your home. Under the law, the parent is always going to be "damned if they do and damned if they don't". Unless of course the "abuse" takes place to a child in "Care" and the matter will be promptly swept under the carpet.

Did I mention that in Ireland that there is no mechanism to report the abuse, sexual or otherwise, of a child in Irish State "care"? You can of course report to the Case Manager but the CFA only investigate the CFA and have never to my knowledge found themselves at fault. Gardaí are not allowed to investigate In Camera cases without the permission of the judge, if the permission isn't forthcoming you cant go to another judge as you could be jailed under the In Camera Rule for saying "anything to anybody". I can attest to this as a corrupt HSE solicitor went "shopping for judges" to jail my colleagues and I for reporting a rape.

Not that we want children having sex with other children of the same age but the question is; "should a child be criminalized for not having control of raging hormones?" If you drive drunk and kill a person you won't be accused of murder and lack of mental capacity will be taken into account. If a child who hasn't learned to master their emotions, has their mental capacity affected by hormones, which is worse sometimes than alcohol, is it fair that they be criminalized for relatively minor infractions that do not involve violence, coercion or threats?

Actually this has been debated in Ireland and many people have recommended that children not be punished in the same way as adults would for consensual sex where the couple were in a relationship and there was no issue of rape. In some ways we are fortunate not to have the Adam Walsh Act and we don't destroy the lives of 5 year olds who are not old enough to even understand what they have done wrong. But we do have problems however, in a case of a 15-year-old boy having sex with a 14 year old girl, the boy was prosecuted for having consensual sex. As they both were willing participants, shouldn't the girl have been prosecuted as well? They were both below the age of consent, so neither could consent legally. It seems in Ireland that only boys can be sex offenders. In an unbelievably bad decision by a Judge, his conviction was upheld. It seems in Ireland that boys are discriminated against because they cant get pregnant; they can however become fathers as a result of a pregnancy. In the case of this couple, if they later marry, she will be marrying a registered sex offender and both their lives will be severely affected. Has any child benefitted from this prosecution? Has any child benefitted from having a law where teenagers are prosecuted for having consensual sex? Will teenagers stop having sex as a result of this prosecution? I doubt it.

In the USA we have a situation where a couple above the Age of Consent can legally have sex and no law is broken. If they decide however to take a picture of the "blessed event" they can be convicted for "Making Child Pornography" and if they text or email to each other, be charged with "Distributing Child Pornography", even though the sex was legal.

We have also seen the situation where "Sexting" teens taking indecent photos of themselves are increasingly being charged with Child Pornography offenses. This creates a situation where the Perpetrator is also the Victim. Even if the "Victim" does not feel harmed or victimized by the "crime", the perpetrator will be charged regardless. There is no question in these cases that the children, or adolescents in many cases did something stupid and made a mistake, but should they have their whole life destroyed for committing a crime against themselves?

What is also interesting is that Sexting is deemed such a heinous crime, that the penalty is more sever than Murder. Essentially if you raped someone between 16 and 18 you would maybe receive a 10 year sentence, if you took a video or photo of the rape you would get a far higher sentence for making and distributing the video or photo from your phone to your computer. Has the pendulum swung too far with this hysteria?

The reason that "Children" between 16 and 18 are criminalized is because the law once saw "Adulthood" at age 16 and changed the law to 18. This changed every other law regarding 16 to 18 year olds. When you consider that a child of 10 can be tried for murder as an adult, and that the "Adult" cant vote until 18, isn't that a good indication that we need to change these laws? You can have sex at 16 but just don't take a picture of it. You can murder someone at 10 and be tried as an adult but you cant take a picture or your consenting girlfriend at 16 or you will receive a stiffer sentence than if you had killed her. Again, we don't want to think about young teens having sex or taking pictures, but the reality is those teens are doing it regardless of the law. The question is, "should we be criminalizing these children no old enough to vote or drink?"

And the 5 year old on the Sex Offender Register? His "Crime" was nuzzling his face into the breasts of his kindergarten teacher. She didn't want to report the "crime" but because of Mandatory Reporting, she feared that she would be jailed for not reporting it. The Law does not allow the 5 year old in playgrounds or any facility where children congregate and he must never visit Disneyland.

We look back at what happened in Salem, Massachusetts in the 1690's and think that these religious fanatics were monsters, brainwashed by religion, but they were not. They were good people who lived in fear of the Devil. The Devil was waiting on every street corner for an opportunity to strike. I have visited Salem many times. Today in Salem, Concord and Boston, the Devil and the Witch Hunters still live and they are still good people with the best intentions. The origin of the witch-hunt in Salem was Child Protection too just as it is today in Salem. Children are removed there today from loving families and children are prosecuted and placed on the sex offender register for committing crimes against themselves, but at least they are not hanging or crushing innocent people, just destroying their lives and the lives of the children they purport to protect. Have we really advanced in 300 years of human evolution?

Where the people of Salem 300 years ago had an excuse, that many of them were under the influence of a fungus on the crops that produced an effect similar to LSD, the witch hunters of today have no excuse for destroying lives. As Social Worker Molly McGrath points out, ego's are not going to be satisfied by helping families in the same they get an adrenalin rush from breaking up a family.

One mantra I have heard repeatedly from social workers echoes the fear of the devil; "I left the home on Friday afternoon and worried all weekend if the children would still be alive when I came back on Monday morning". In each case when I have heard this textbook mantra, I asked; "and did the children die?" which was more of a rhetorical question because I knew they didn't die and were not harmed. I once watched a toddler while the mother talked to her social worker. To keep him distracted, he was playing with coins he found in my shirt pocket and I was teaching him how to count. The mother was in great distress and just needed a bit of reassurance that everything would be ok, as I had said at the start of the meeting.

The social worker couldn't focus on anything but the child and was so worried that the child would swallow the coins. He was already past the point of putting things in his mouth and was already trying to talk. She just couldn't focus on the mother, this was a child "at risk" even though he was sat on my lap and playing with the money on the table. The child was never in any danger but she was so afraid that anything might happen, her fear was irrational. We can't lend any particular significance to this one event or say that all social workers are so irrational but this incident is indicative of social work fear. We are asking social workers to do a job that they will never be capable of doing.

If the child had swallowed a coin, as the babysitter I would have been responsible. The reason I was babysitting is because the mother was heavily pregnant and had mobility issues. The mother enlisted our help because she was so afraid that social workers would take the toddler away from her and her stress didn't help her medical condition and her pregnancy. The social worker was ineffective in helping the mother because she was so distracted by the child who was not in any danger. The problem with social work is that it is not robust enough and focuses too much on non-existent Risk. By trying to be Risk Aversive, it is not dealing with issues and advocacy is non-existent. You can't be an advocate and a prosecutor of families at the same time. You have to focus on advocacy and leave crime to criminologists as most countries do. When child protection is left up to social workers, they want to take every child into "Care" by default so they can sleep at night and know the child will be alive on

Monday morning. The problems with this approach are that many children are taken for no good reason and they are actually at far higher risk in "Care". But if the child dies in "Care", no social worker will accept responsibility.

I am not the first person to suggest that the Gardaí are abrogating their responsibility to serve & protect children. In the Dail on the 24 February 2012, TD Charlie McConalogue asked questions in the house regarding Garda Inspectorate's report Responding to Child Sexual Abuse released in 2010.

Mentioned was a "Turf War" going on between Gardaí and the HSE. Naturally the TD was reassured that this is not the case, Gardaí and the HSE regularly work together in cases of sexual abuse of children. This is the same HSE of course who didn't feel it in the public interest to tell us that 500 children in their "Care" were trafficked into sex slavery. But obviously this is not the case if the HSE can claim to have 541 "Confirmed" cases of sexual abuse of children every year but the DPP only have a handful of prosecutions. The Turf War continues today in 2014 because the CFA don't want Gardaí "confirming" sexual abuse of children, especially if those children are already in State "Care". Once the case becomes "In Camera", the CFA don't want any scrutiny of what happens. You would think that one of the key learning's from Ryan Report would be a robust system of reporting child abuse and neglect to Gardaí but in truth, Gardaí's role in serving and protecting children has been all but eliminated. I don't know if this is a deliberate policy of the Gardaí or the CFA. Where the government have no control over the CFA, they at least have some power and influence with Gardaí.

I have never understood how people can claim that children below the age of puberty are being "Sexualized" by clothing or products. Perhaps in their own corrupted minds they believe that children can be sexual beings even without hormones running through their body? If an 8-year-old girl wants underwear with a "Sexy" message printed on it, what business is it of yours or mine what a child wears under her clothing? Before "Sexualized" clothing was ever available for children, didn't children always dress up in mommy or daddy's shoes or coat and "act out" a scene in play that they don't understand? Children learn by play and walking or trying to walk in mommy high heels or putting on her nurse's uniform is a normal and expected part of childhood. While I cringe at parents who would buy "sexy" underwear for pre-pubescent children, I am savvy enough to mind my own business and not wade into the debate. Sometimes you have to bite your tongue. If the 8 year old want's "Sexy" products, it is likely that the child is being influenced by Marketing. We should be more concerned that she is learning the wrong message from her idols who are probably pop stars and teaching her that she has less value than a man.

In the UK before he became Prime Minister, David Cameron waded into a debate about "sexual" underwear for little girls and likewise in Ireland, France Fitzgerald waded into a similar debate. It caused a media storm in both cases but nobody stopped to ask; "hang on, aren't these kids just playing grown ups?"

What it is really about is "dressing down" children to make them less attractive to paedophiles. In the past few decades we have seen many library books taken off the shelves and presumably burned because people were afraid that paedophiles might look at these books and become sexually stimulated. I honestly believe that we are only a few short years away from dressing girl children in Burqa's until the age of 18 if this hysteria continues. Isn't it also curious that nobody has declared any issue with Boy's being "Sexualized" or wearing "Sexy" underwear? Is it just me or do these people who believe in "Sexualisation" of Children, have an unhealthy obsession with little girls?

Can the Prime Minister or Minister for Children honestly say that a paedophile will become sexually attracted to a child because of their underwear? How would the paedophile actually see what they are wearing under their clothing? It's not really about the children or what they are wearing, it's about governments and the Child Abuse Industry stripping away the rights of parents to make bad decisions for their children. Their concern is really about the stupid mother who would buy such clothing. In their minds it's a safe bet that the little girl will be pregnant before she is 16 and on Welfare. Maybe for the little girl, she feels happier wearing "grown up" clothes and doesn't understand the implications of the word "Slut" or "Ho" that they hear on TV? But I have to ask the question; "If clothing manufacturers made the same clothing for adults in children's sizes, would the Moral Entrepreneur's still say they clothes are too sexy or grown up?"

In a free market economy, manufacturers sell what people will buy, if there was no demand it would not be available. If you ever watched cartoons on TV in the mornings, you would see a wide range of products being marketed to children. Children have no money and yet 60% of the clothing market is children's clothing. Advertisers have been "Branding" products for years and children and young people buy the bulk of these name brands. I once listened to my nephew threaten his mother that if she didn't buy him X brand and Y brand, that he was told in school that this was child abuse and he could report her for abuse and she would be taken away. His mother and I both laughed, I told him that they don't take away bad parents, the way it works is they take away the children of bad parents. He wasn't too impressed but when I explained orphanages and Foster "Care" I think he got the message. I have never understood why governments don't seek to stop all marketing directed at children. As long as we have "Happy" meals and "Fun Size" bananas and sugary drinks, the children grow up to believe all the hype themselves and often find out that the latest trainers don't make you happy.

"Sexualisation" has another aspect to it that has little to do with sex. Many young girls play with Barbie Dolls and have done for 5 decades. I don't think there was a big moral decline as a result. But when you look at children's toys and the advertising that is being marketed to children, you see very disturbing trends of the role models that children are being marketed. Girls as young as 5 are "Twerking" and following an unrealistic model of "Womanhood". This influences the boys as well who grow up to see girls as objects to be judged on their "figures" and the style of clothing they wear. Children watch scantily clad young female singers and believe that this is how life works. Children are very much a product of what they see on TV and their parents are warned that they can't interfere in their child's autonomy as the child has individual "rights" which are paramount to the parents. On one hand you have children placed in uniforms, which are invariably expensive, but out of uniform they dictate to their parents based on advertising aimed at children and what their peers are wearing. It's interesting to note that not every country has school uniforms; in Norway children wear what they like within reason.

I suspect that if children were allowed to wear what they want, that few people would be happy with their choices. Children don't make the best decisions for themselves. But we also see a situation today where parents have little autonomy over their children. We are so brainwashed by the ideology of children's "Rights" and that the concept that children are autonomous beings who can decide for themselves, that parents are afraid of having control over their children. If you discipline your child you can expect to have a social worker show up at the door to investigate why the child was crying. If your child gets a cut or a bruise and you take them to the GP or hospital, you can expect an inquisition to take place.

As a "Free Range Child", I roamed the neighbourhood with other kids in the 1960's. All the neighbours kept an eye on us, and the opinion of a neighbour, of my behaviour carried a great deal of weight with my parents. One day we found some fireworks and took them back to my friend's garden. Most of them had been spent but there was sufficient material that if we scraped enough of them we could make a good explosion. I was aware that I was not allowed to play with matches, mostly because of previous childhood experiments that didn't end well. We decided that we were going to blow up an Anthill to help his father who had made a complaint earlier about "damn ants" coming into the house. We readied all our "ammunition" and bought "safety matches" at the local shop. When I threw the match, a loud bang reverberated throughout the whole community. Nobody was hurt and no windows were broken. There was however a considerable amount of dirt scattered for several meters in all directions.

We ran screaming and crying and hid, trembling with fear from our experience. Our neighbours "squealed" on us to our parents and we were all spanked as a result. We weren't allowed out or to play with each other for a few days, but nobody could stay mad at us "little rascals" and the incident was soon forgotten. It reinforced my belief that I should not indeed play with matches, even "Safety Matches".

If such an event were to take place today, the likely response is that we would all be taken into "Care". You could reasonably expect the Army Bomb

Disposal Unit, a team of Gardaí, barriers around the "crime scene", Psychological counselling and the media reporting through satellite from the scene. When my friend broke a car window playing football, we all got a slap around the ears from the neighbour and a spanking later when our father came home. I used to get beaten on a regular basis in school by the Master for being late or falling asleep. The window was promptly fixed and everybody forgot about it soon after. We were "Free Range" and at the age of 6 I had to look after my younger brother who was a toddler. Nobody batted an eyelid that I was too young and my mother would call when she wanted me. She could go out of range if she wanted in the secure knowledge that I was in no danger and at the time many parents worked and children would be left alone and nobody would call the Emergency Services. Last year I assisted in a case where a neighbour felt that it was dangerous to leave children playing with their toys in their own back garden and called social services. As a kid I got stitched up so many times at Dr Steven's Hospital that I knew all the doctors and sisters (as they were known then) and nobody ever asked me if I was abused. I had an idyllic childhood by many standards but today if I appeared at a hospital I would expect an Inquisition. Funnily enough as an adult, years later I met one of the doctors in Northern Canada and he recognized me.

In the 1960's nobody was operating under a Moral Panic and nobody had ever heard the word "Paedophile". There was always of course the "dirty feckers" that even at the age of 6 you knew well enough to stay away from. A child couldn't walk the length of our street without several neighbours saying hello and talking to us. If any of these dirty feckers approached us, there would be a team of women and maybe a few men if they were not at work, watching our every move and protecting us. You knew as a kid that you stayed away from public toilets, dark alleys and if ever you had any problem, to run to any adult for help. A child screaming in the street would attract instant attention and we felt safe in our own community. If we were getting a spanking for our behaviour, even the neighbours knew why and were not sympathetic to our plight. More importantly, we knew why we were being spanked and we learned that there were consequences to our actions. If anything, it taught me to become a Critical Thinker and to question everything. It didn't turn me into an obedient servant, by learning to over-think situations and not being afraid to ask questions before acting, I learned Impulse Control, which has served me well in life. I don't believe that spanking works as intended, but I see no reason to criminalize parents who feel it is necessary. The threat of spanking works just as well.

Today, people don't know the name of their neighbour and will cross the street to avoid coming into contact with children. We are so afraid of even toddlers that we don't dare look at them. If my parents had abused or neglected me in any way, the community would know about it and intervene. There is no community today like we had in the past, even where there are quiet neighbourhoods where children can play in safety, there is still the hysteria that your child could be abducted by the dreaded paedophile. James Grant of UNICEF was a visionary; he recognized that it takes a whole community to raise a child, just as I was raised.

In hospitals you see doctors and nurses who believe that child abuse is of epidemic proportions. I have even seen where foster carers believe the lies of social workers that the parents abused their child and it wouldn't occur to them that if the parents had committed the crime of child abuse, that they would likely be in prison and have their parental rights terminated. I have seen where doctors are so afraid that they will take a very heavy-handed approach and protect themselves and not the child. In a climate of Moral Panic, people act out of fear and now the fear has spread to the doctors and nurses that on the least suspicion, everything must be reported as child abuse. When I get involved in these cases, I find that I am dealing with very irrational people.

A young mother I was helping took her toddler to the doctor, she worried about a discoloration that appeared in his right ear that would come and go. The doctor suspected that this was a bruise and reasoned that it was abuse. My own training taught me that a bruise doesn't simply appear and disappear so a bruise was out of the question. I advised the mother to take photos and watch it every day at different times. If the child was sleeping on his side, he may have his circulation to his ear restricted or have swelling. If we could pinpoint a cause or trigger we would diagnose it, this is unfortunately what parents have to do sometimes rather that a doctor making the diagnosis. It was not painful to the child when touched, but sometimes it would appear colder than the other ear. The doctor examined the child a week later and said the bruise appears larger than a week before. By this time the doctor was in full "Child Abuse Mode" and nothing other than having social workers dragging this child away was going to change her mind. Until of course I pointed out that the "bruise" was now in the Left Ear and the Right Ear appeared normal.

Child abuse makes us angry, very angry. I have seen doctors storming into a room, arms folded and veins bulging accusing parents of child abuse. I have also seen doctors and staff treat parents very badly when their baby was dying because the doctors had misdiagnosed Shaken Baby Syndrome. I have also heard shocking stories from parents who were treated as criminals when it was time to turn off life support and their babies died before their eyes. When doctors stray away from Medicine and start acting as Detectives, they do a great disservice to their patients. When they wander into the field of criminology, where they have no training or experience, the diagnostic procedure ends and sometimes the patient dies because they have jumped to a conclusion of child abuse. How criminologists and Forensic Pathologists would act differently, is that they would do a Differential Diagnosis. It is not sufficient to simply latch on to the nearest cause without scientifically eliminating other causes.

Once the Child Abuse ship sets sail, there is no stopping it. Even Police shift into Child Abuse Mode and are driven by anger. You can throw Reason out the window at this point and sometimes it takes many weeks or months for cooler heads to prevail. As we have seen in Ireland in the Moira Woods fiasco, there are certain doctors who are more prone to anger and lack Impulse Control and will see every case as child abuse. If no children and no anger were present, as in adult cases, one of the first reactions would be to get a second opinion. In almost every medical case I have involved in, I have insisted on a second opinion but only by a properly qualified and experienced physician. I mentioned earlier the case of a paediatrician who was presented with a baby who was sick every day of his entire short life, and how a judge made a very courageous decision and refused a second opinion even though our experts were very concerned for the life of this child. Such is the fear and anger, that even when presented with the evidence, that it's not really about protecting the child, it's about punishing the child abusers. It's not hard to see then how junk science like Shaken Baby Syndrome, Munchausen's Syndrome by Proxy and how so many parents are wrongly accused because doctors fail to diagnose Rickets or Tissue Scurvy. When the child dies, as has happened many times, doctors, police, judges and social workers are never held accountable. They are literally getting away with murder and even when I have reported such cases to medical councils, there are no consequences for the misdiagnosis of child abuse.

Not everyone is suited to performing child abuse investigations. By having Mandatory Reporting, we force doctors and nurses to become bad investigators and we are killing or harming children by not treating or even diagnosing the correct medical condition to begin with. A proper response would be having a competent investigation at the start. Any doctor who suspects abuse should not report it, what they should do first of all is get a second opinion and perform a Forensic Diagnosis by an expert. If there is no consensus between the two doctors, get a third opinion. If they have scientifically ruled out, bearing in mind that they need the proper qualifications and experience, then they can call Police and not social workers to investigate further.

As panicked and angry as we are with child abuse and neglect nothing can instil our anger like sexual abuse. Without the dreaded Paedophile to turn our anger towards, we would have to find some other feeble beast to demonize. We all want to be heroes and satisfy our egos that we are saving children. We can no longer smile at a child in the street because people might suspect that we are paedophiles. Babies and toddlers are growing up smiling at adults and not having those smiles returned, they are learning that the world is a dangerous place and nobody cares about anyone else.

Fathers have to be extra careful around their daughters almost like in countries where women wear burqas and have to be escorted by other women or male members of their family. Little girls are very confused, they don't have the same rights and freedoms as boys and their "Innocence" is prised as a commodity. Children are growing up well aware of their "rights" but not of their responsibilities, they don't have to answer to their parents as the Law has put "Children First" to the detriment of society. We are seeing a whole new generation of spoiled children who will be very disillusioned when they grow up that their parents are hovering above them and tending to their every need.

We have the power to lock up paedophiles forever on their first offense and never allow them near children again by seeing them as mentally ill. In their anger, many people are unwilling to see paedophilia as a mental illness and the consequence is that predators must be released after serving their time. This is a classic example of how the Moral Panic does not benefit children and why we need to think differently about these problems.

In his very brave book entitled, "Spoiled Generation" Dr Aric Sigman went against the grain of the Children's Rights Mafia and pointed out that parents are not preparing children properly for the challenges they will face as adults. He said that spanking was acceptable as long as other options had been considered. He pointed out that as adults, we will see children growing up thinking that their "Rights" trump all else and whether they were right or wrong, they would tend to be selfish and disillusioned with life. I don't know if I have characterised Dr Sigman's philosophy as I'm paraphrasing his message. Even if you don't buy the book "The Spoilt Generation", he has some excellent videos on YouTube in which he lays out his platform for parenting. Essentially it's not much different from how you or your parents were raised. His message was one of personal responsibility and raising children and being a parent who is not afraid to make unpopular decisions for your child. Children don't need parents as friends, they need someone to challenge them and teach them that life is not a bed of roses and they need to do this with love.

His message is very disturbing to many, what he is saying makes complete sense but completely goes against the grain of the Children's Rights Mafia. Even years before I first heard Dr Sigman on the radio while driving, I have heard many people, even my own mother saying almost exactly the same thing. Let children play without being restricted with too much safety, they will learn better from making mistakes and learn to manage Risk. As Dr Sigman says; "It's better a child falls off a bike at age 8 and learns to manage risk, than having the child reach adulthood and learn by crashing a car". If you make them wear a helmet and tell them they can't go on the road and why they cant go on the road and let them play they will soon learn it's better to be safe than in pain. It's a child's job to learn what the parameters are, and we do a great disservice to children by not allowing children to be children.

I say that Dr Sigman is a very brave man because he goes against the dogma and the pop-psychology, anyone who simply asks questions these days is seen as a heretic and predictably, he was attacked and condemned by the Child Abuse Industry. At no time did Dr Sigman advocate the abuse of children, instead he pointed out that not raising your children properly **is** a form of child abuse. Single mothers are not valued by society and not given the support they need, we are already seeing the consequences of this in society. I have to wonder then how Dr Sigman's children will turn out? Will they have far better outcomes? Given that the outcomes for children "Cared For" by the State have dismal outcomes in 80% of cases, could he do any worse?

Spanking is a very contentious issue, I don't believe in it myself. The legal position in Ireland is that "Reasonable Chastisement" is acceptable. Spanking is not Punishment, and the goal of Chastisement is to teach the child not to engage in certain behaviours. In the human body when a child touches a hot surface, they receive a pain signal making them stop to minimize tissue damage. Pain is the body's reaction to protect the body. It occurs instantly, which is an important point. When a mother says, "wait till your father gets home", the reaction is not instant and this is why spanking doesn't work. In a few hours the child has forgotten what they have done and doesn't associate the pain with the act so is not effective. The vast majority of people in the Child Abuse Industry are strongly opposed to spanking because they feel that children are autonomous beings and want to protect them from experiencing any pain. A person can go through life and not experience the pain of breakups of relationships, but equally, not experience the joy or love that a relationship brings either. The important point being that we "Experience" it because only by living it can we learn. Parents should focus on giving children many different experiences and doing it safely rather than trying to shelter children. They also learn our bad behaviour so in becoming a parent, you need to teach by example. It's not sufficient to tell a child to be good, you have to show them what "Good" is. You have to become a better person than you were the day before and be the role model of how you want your child to be. In school they are taught to assimilate information without understand it. You have the ability to teach your child to understand, to think and not just absorb a set of rules. They need to know the who, what, where, why and how of everything. Years ago I learned an important lesson from a child by the name of Ryan that I have never forgotten. I asked Ryan why he asked so many questions and told me, "because I'm a Kid, that's my job!" Ryan turned out to be a fine young man many years later even though a struggling single mother raised him, as did all her children.

I say that chastisement is not punishment. Punishment is meted out to cause pain or hardship with the goal of revenge, chastisement is done out of love for the child to prevent them from harm. If a child is spanked so severely that it injures the tissues of the body, this is clearly child abuse and is illegal and rightly should be punished. I have seen in cases with social services that spanking, regardless or the severity, is deemed child abuse when clearly it is not. The mere fact that a parent admits spanking and the fact that the child confirms it is not child abuse. They are actually more concerned with the psychological aspect than the physical "damage". In the minds of a social worker, they see a small child and a large parent, a balance of power that is disproportional. I agree that spanking is a very powerful tool to use and should never be used in anger. My objection is that spanking can damage the parent/child bond. I can remember being spanked by my father when I got lost on a busy street. When he realized that I was missing, he was panicked and frantic with worry and the slap I received was nothing compared to the feeling of being reunited. He slapped me then he carried me in his arms and even I could tell from his face and his tone that he was acting out of fear and love. I can't claim to be damaged by the event; I learned a valuable lesson from the experience.

Children are naturally cautious and wary of danger much of the time. Children are not "Careless" they are "Carefree" because they don't realize the dangers involved. The concerns of the social workers are the emotional aspect. The parent being stronger is threatening to use the power they hold over the child and the child cannot fight back or complain. Nobody would reasonably argue that if children were left to their own devices that they would harm themselves or come to harm. So obviously children need constant supervision and guidance, for their own protection. The argument is that spanking emotionally harms the child. As spanking is only applied in cases to correct the behaviour of the child, to prevent them from coming to harm, how can it be claimed that this is abuse? Is it not more abusive and emotionally damaging to a child to allow them to grow up thinking that there are no consequences in life and will they not be disillusioned when life does not hand them everything on a plate as their "Helicopter" Parents did? Granted there are monsters who shouldn't have children and will abuse their child. But actual cases of abuse are quite rare, I say this because during the Children's Referendum, the best the Yes side could come up with is 18 serious where parents had abused their child and were prosecuted. On the other hand, 196 children died and 500 went missing from "Care" in one decade alone. In the 18 cases, each one was testament to a failing system where social workers didn't protect children. The removal of children for spanking where there are no injuries to the child is a far more damaging experience to the child and is not warranted. Removal is far too powerful a tool that is known to cause harm to the child to be used for very minor infractions. Again I say that if child abuse is a crime, then let it be punished as a crime. For these crimes not to be investigated by Police is a travesty of justice.

Aversion therapy works quite well, in experiments with humans and animals, the subject will not repeat the experiment in most cases without a very compelling reason. For decades in schools around the world Corporal Punishment was widely used. Usually it was fairly effective and millions of people who received it didn't grow up to be serial killers. I don't agree with Corporal Punishment either and I'm happy it was abolished but the difference is that teachers were not criminalized for slapping children. Social workers and the Children's "Rights' Mafia want to criminalize not just spanking or slapping, they want to criminalize parents for reasonable chastisement. So a few slaps on the bum with a good "talking to" versus months or years in "Care" for the child, which one do you think that the child would prefer? This is a perfect example of how the hysteria of protecting children is not benefitting children is not working and why the ideology of Children's Rights is wrong.

I mentioned, "wait till your father comes home", I will deal with this in more detail later. One of the most important reason you should not slap or spank your child is that the bond between parent and child can be damaged. On one hand you have a duty to be a parent and make the tough decisions. Children don't need parents as "Friends", the need parents who will guide and protect them. For a mother to adopt a more submissive role and make the father the authoritarian is wrong. Men have as much capacity to love and care for their child as women. While men tend to be more aggressive and active with children, women should not use men in this way. If a child's behaviour needs to be corrected, to be effective it must be done immediately for the child to associate pain with the action. Many parents use the threat of spanking and hold their hand up to a child and threaten them but never actually carry it out. For many children the threat of pain is enough and the lesson is learned. To call spanking a form of violence is a complete nonsense.

Abuse is clearly defined in law and the law has never been a barrier to protecting children. It is far more abusive and damaging to a child to use a far "Heavier Handed" approach of removing a scared child from their parents and siblings and placing them at higher risk with strangers. Especially when it is done unnecessarily. I read a story a few years ago of a Dublin child who received a broken arm from his father. He told social workers he wants his father placed in jail for 100 years for what he did to him. Of course actual cases of child abuse such as this are fairly rare, if this were not true we would be reading far more cases in the Criminal Courts. We would also see that if you asked the majority of children in "Care", they just want to go home to their parents. The horrible truth is that "Care" is child abuse for many children. We talk a lot of guff of children having no voice but if anyone ever talked to the children in "Care", the vast majority want to go home to their parents. I know this because I have talked to many of them.

Perhaps there is a psychological link also when social workers fail in their duty to protect a child in "Care" or in need of "Care"? Where social workers don't want to see any punishment against children, perhaps they also don't want to see any punishment against themselves for their failings? The fact that 196 children died and 500 went missing in a decade in Irish State "Care" and not a single social worker, GAL or judge was punished, is showing us that lack of discipline against social workers who fail, is clearly not working as nothing has substantially changed? Maybe if Ireland adopted the same punishments for these failures as the UK, then there might be a significant improvement? I have never heard any of the "Usual Suspects" or Lobbyists calling for social workers who fail in their duty to be punished in any way.

I have been saying for years that I would love to see a study of Outcomes for children of Psychologists and Social Workers are their children healthier and happier? Do they earn more money than children of Plumbers and Electricians? What about Judges? And Lawyers? I doubt that anyone would study this or get a grant for it. Even if they did, would they get access to such information? The reason I ask is because in the UK the government brought in legislation for a database of "Soft Information" to be kept on all children in the UK, this was under Blair's government. Much to the consternation of social workers who didn't see any value to filling out 29 pages of information on every single child, whether they had come to the attention of services or not, the Database was steamrolled into place and 400,000 people would have access. In the end the database cost far more than the estimate and £42 million was paid out for a database that social workers wouldn't use. It wasn't until someone pointed out that Tony Blair's children would equally be on the database that they had a re-think. They introduced emergency legislation called the "Celebrity Amendment" so that children of politicians, judges, social workers and other "experts" and maybe a few celebrities would not be listed either. But in the end the database was scrapped.

Funnily enough in Ireland, Forced Adoption and a Database of Soft Information was recommended by Dr Geoffrey Shannon an "Expert" on Child "Protection", one of the group of people I usually refer to as the "Usual Suspects" who successive Irish governments pay to help out when a new disaster befalls the Child Abuse Industry. It may have escaped many peoples notice, but legislation was passed in Ireland for a database of Soft Information, even years after it had failed and been scrapped in the UK. I honestly don't know what has happened to the Irish Database, maybe someone pointed out that the children of Dr Shannon, social workers, politicians and judges would be listed on the database?

When Blair came to power in 1997, he had 28 social workers as members of his parliament. One of the first things they did was implement Forced Adoption. This was done under the guise of "doe eyed orphans languishing in Care". Of course what happened when nobody wanted to adopt these children, the government paid bonuses to Councils to hit adoption targets. The UK was the only country in Europe, which allowed children to be adopted against the wishes of their parents. Only 6% of the children in "Care" were adopted and to hit their targets, social workers started trolling records of pregnancies looking for potential "bad" parents like Fran Lyon who became a target of a social worker that she had never even met. Incidentally, did you know that Ireland keeps a database on pregnant women that is available to social workers? With the corrupt Children's Referendum, the HSE had already begun targeting children for Forced Adoption, particularly in Cork.

None of the "Usual Suspects" have ever suggested any child protection measures that hasn't already been implemented and usually failed in the UK. Far better models in other European countries are never implemented in Ireland and as I mentioned earlier, many of the CFA and HSE staff are UK subjects, some of who left under suspicious circumstances. As I also work with colleagues in the UK, some names often appear to pop up in Ireland later. The irony that Ireland follows the worst excesses of the UK and then hires the dregs of the UK system has not been lost on many people.

One dramatic, and positive development in the UK has been the appointment of Justice Sir James Munby as President of Family Proceedings. In his short tenure he has become the most hated man by the Child Abuse Industry. He regularly castigates social workers and even judges whose decisions he often overturns. He has stated that names of failing social workers can be published and has abolished gagging of parents. Unfortunately Sir James cannot hear every appeal personally and many of his colleagues in the Appeal Court still cling to the old ways. In one particular case I had a small involvement in, a newborn baby was taken shortly after birth, the parents had lost previous babies to Forced Adoption.

On our Facebook page I published all of the documents I had been provided by the father and also the video of the brutal removal of the baby. I had earlier published documents and pictures of their case and a distressing photo of the father holding his daughter at the "Goodbye Meeting". Facebook were served by a gagging order by the council and removed the evidence. The father was threatened with jail and in discussions I had with him, he said he was prepared to go to jail for life as he and his wife, had no life. I said I would share the files internationally and the video was even shown on CNN. On appeal, the father was lucky enough to get Sir James Munby and he ordered that the video and information could be published. I have kept the screenshot or the order from the council and will later publish it on a website, along with the video and all the documents.

Sir James began as President as so many others, blindly believing that children were only removed "after all other possibilities have been exhausted" but quickly got up to speed. He has received submissions from many of my colleagues in the UK who also help families. He seems to be coming to the realization, as we have, that the system is corrupt and that reform alone is not going to benefit children. He received a submission from a colleague who has also appeared before him in cases. Sir James took note of what we had said and seems to have taken it on board. In a few of his judgements after, he has quoted my colleague and has made some very progressive Case Law as a result. But Sir James is only one man, albeit a powerful one and the "reforms" are not happening as fast at they should. The Industry fears publicity above all else. When staff leaves councils, they are paid off and are gagged to the extent that they could not testify before Government Boards of Inquiry. Many arguments have been put forward by the Industry to maintain the secrecy of these courts over the years and there is strong opposition to any "opening up" and strong opposition to Sir Justice Munby.

Another colleague based in Germany, Sabine Kurjo McNeill has taken a submission to the EU, which has had a very good impact. John Hemming MP called a meeting in Parliament over the UK Child Protection System and was overwhelmed by the result; almost every country in Europe sent a representative and voiced their concerns about treatment of their citizens in the UK. At the Council of Europe, many of these countries supported Sabine's submission and the topic of Forced Adoption and the UK Child Protection System is very much on the minds of the European Parliament at the moment.

John Hemming MP also supported APS in the Children's Referendum, as he too was concerned that Ireland might allow Forced Adoption. John is also involved in sending pregnant women to Ireland and other countries and has advised mothers to flee the UK. A few years ago I asked him to stop, as Ireland had suddenly taken the approach to bend over backwards for the UK to get these babies deported who were born in Ireland, and returned for Forced Adoption. In the last few years the UK have pursued a relentless policy of following pregnant women all over the world and have no issue with lying to foreign courts to kidnap babies for adoption. It seems that the Industry will fight for any measures to take children and wont be put-off by having to obey the law, even the laws of the UK. In the European Parliament, many of the parents from the UK who testified had been served with gagging orders and threatened with jail if they named the councils or social workers. The were threatened and gagged again that I they spoke out, that their relationship with their children would be terminated. Fortunately many did speak out and at least the truth is now a matter of public record.

David Cameron doesn't like the idea that the European Court of Human Rights should have the power to punish the UK and wants to abolish Human Rights for UK citizens. Surprisingly, groups who purport to protect our Human Rights are largely silent. I have seen exactly the same situation in Ireland where Human and Civil Rights organizations cannot be bothered with miscarriages of justice taking place in Ireland. I know this because I have contacted them about cases. I have also contacted Justice Minister Shatter, who has special powers to intervene under the law and chose to do nothing, even when foreign countries sent their ambassadors to talk with the Irish Government.

It has been a long time since Justice has existed in Ireland or the UK. Where our system is based on the belief that 10 men should go free before 1 innocent man is wrongly convicted, in the illegal Family Courts in Ireland the figure I have used is that 183 children are wrongly removed so that 1 guilty parent is prosecuted. Unlike the UK, We don't have Sir Justice Munby to clean up our mess.

CHAPTER 12

"THE BEST CHILD PROTECTION SYSTEM IN THE WORLD?"

In talking with my editor, it was suggested that I should write a book based on child protection on the UK system, as it was a larger market. I have always felt that this was not necessary as the systems of the UK, Ireland, the USA and Canada are for the most part identical. While there are some local differences in laws and customs, there is no difference in the modus operandi of the social workers, lawyers or judges. As human beings, International Human Rights Law unites us all. There are however some differences between Ireland and the UK in that the UK public and the European public are becoming more aware of the dysfunction in the UK system; whereas in Ireland, the system is actually becoming more secretive while the UK tries to open up its system to scrutiny.

In the UK we have seen in the last year how the President of the Family Courts, Sir James Munby has vowed to open up the Family Court System. In many of his judgements he has been critical of social work and even of his colleagues in the lower courts. In Ireland, we have no Sir James Munby, instead we have retired judges who side 100% with the system. We have a system with lobbyists for the Child Abuse Industry who are incapable of even conceiving that the UK is worst possible model to follow and yet have a very poor understanding of what happens in the system. Their positions are based on an ill-founded faith in a system that even they say is "Unfit for Purpose". They bluster from one failed theory to the next and blindly follow "Experts" who have no expertise or experience.

Whenever the system fails their tactic is delay. When a new horror story comes to light, they will resort to statements such as; "we will add 260 new social work positions", "the Children's Referendum will be held soon", "we will reform the system by removing the HSE from their role of Child Protection", "We will put Children First on a statutory basis". All of these are supposed to "fix" an unfixable system. Fortunately the Referendum to remove parental rights has not passed into law as yet and hopefully never will. I suspect that it will pass into law because if the Supreme Court rules that the Government held an illegal Referendum, the government of the day will just keep having referenda until Ireland becomes the second country in Europe that allows for Forced Adoption.

I don't pay a great deal of attention to new laws being introduced on child protection as I once did. Any government will bow down to the Child Abuse Industry and the Children's Rights Mafia and any new legislation will not benefit children. I don't even hide my contempt for this system any longer. It doesn't matter whether we are talking about Ireland, the UK, the USA, Canada or Norway. I make no apology to what I believe is an abusive system, which harms children and places them at higher risk. Whenever the government introduce new laws, and it doesn't matter which country I mentioned above, the legislation is never going to benefit children. While it may tick all the boxes for Best Interests and it may satisfy the Industry, but the industry is growing and more children are being harmed. More children will be raped, psychologically abused, will die and more children dumped on the streets at age 18.

When laws fail or a system fails, the inevitable result will be removing more rights from parents and rather than giving more power to children, the power is given instead to the State to intervene more easily and making it impossible for parents to get justice. When we were lied to that there was a 'shortage of social workers" and 260 new positions were added, it only resulted in more children being taken on more spurious grounds. More children of course will benefit the Industry. When they say; "Earlier Intervention" they really mean; "More intervention". At the present time, a child dies in the "Care" system in Ireland about every 2 weeks. At the present rate of growth of the industry, it will be a child dying every week in "Care" in a few short years. Of course the number of criminal prosecutions for abuse or neglect will never increase, as the numbers of prosecutions have remained fairly flat for decades. The numbers of complaints to the HSE and CFA have dramatically increased as Social Work becomes a willing and effective weapon used by parents against parents and vindictive neighbours are realizing the damage they can cause with complete immunity.

If adding 260 new positions resulted in 3.7 times more children being removed than the UK on a per capita basis, and without any scrutiny of why this was necessary, wouldn't the solution be to remove 260 or more positions to bring the system into balance? If the CFA and HSE legal teams, in reality private law firms are over-spending without any scrutiny, wouldn't the solution be to replace these lawyers and eliminate their ability to stretch-out cases to maximize their profits? If we were talking about a private company and profit margins were at risk, these questions would be asked, but in the alternate universe of Child Abuse there are no budgets. Court orders have no meaning to social workers on a crusade and nobody is in control of the entire system. When the system fails, the solution will be to add more people, delay, spend more money, delay, take away more parental rights, delay and enlarge the system and the industry.

In his time as CEO of the HSE, Dr Brendan Drumm said that the HSE would be far easier to run without child protection. He also made an extraordinary statement that we were only seeing the tip of the iceberg and that only 1 in 25 cases were investigated. Of course there was the usual head nodding in support of his proposition, essentially that we need to increase the number of children in "Care" by a factor 25 times, but no critical analysis by the media who are supposed to be the Watchdogs of Society, no questions from a single politician to even ask the question of whether we had suddenly become a nation of child abusers. No questions from Gardai who have not seen any dramatic increase of child abuse or neglect investigations.

The system is a sacred cow that is beyond inspection and criticism. If you ask a question, you must be supporting child abuse. If you criticize a single event, you have to be careful not to attack the system. You have to make excuses and not fire a single social worker even when 196 children die and 500 go "missing". It was very impressive to see Deputy Alan Shatter suddenly become a voice for Tracy Fay but not imply that the system itself was indeed the fault. As a former family law solicitor who made a very exceptional living when he was known as Mr Family Law, Alan knew very well how corrupt the system was and has been for years. When he became Minister Alan Shatter, he was largely silent on the issue but did introduce legislation that benefitted the Industry and did little for children. Even during the scandal of the Deaths in "Care" when he was a deputy in the opposition, he was preaching the dogma of the Children's Rights referendum.

When I became aware of the agenda of Forced Adoption in 2010, I also learned about the agenda of "putting the Family Courts on a Constitutional basis", this has been on the cards for some time. Sometime in the future a government will try to sell the Irish Public on a proposition of giving away more of their rights in the constitution to legalize Family Courts. As extraordinary as it may seem, Family Courts are contrary to Human and Civil Rights law and must be opposed. The government lawyers and the legal fraternity know that Family Law is contrary to the Irish Constitution and in their minds gives too much power to parents to raise their child. In reality, no child in Ireland has ever been abused or neglected because Irish Laws were not sufficiently robust to protect them. This was an opinion that was put forward by several Irish Judges and experts during the Children's Referendum. Keep in mind that any Garda can remove any child from anywhere if they reasonably believe the child to be at serious risk of harm, but where Gardai need to establish harm, social workers do not.

Emily Logan who was then Ombudsman for Children made one very telling comment on the notion of Children's "Rights". She said,

"My office has never examined a case involving a conflict between parents' rights and children's rights. And if there is one thing that has become confirmed by the eight years of this office's operation, it is that parents are by far the strongest and most tenacious advocates for children."

Essentially, where we were told that children have no right against their parents, this lie is laid bare by the statement above. There are no cases of conflict between parents and their children. The conflicts arise when the State becomes involved and purports to speak for children. Parents are the most tenacious advocates for their children when the child is denied their rights. When there are conflicts, in the vast majority of cases, it is because the State has abused the rights of the child. When you remove the tenacious parent to vindicate for those rights, you have a situation of the State being both the abuser of that child's right and at the same time the vindicator or the child's rights. Given the choice of who should vindicate for the child, most of us would side with the parent because the parent is acting out of love for their child.

I have seen such a case where a Special Needs child was denied an education even though the child is guaranteed this right under the Constitution and also under the UNCRC, which Ireland ratified into law. The parent being unable to fight for their child was told that if the child was placed in "Care", that they would be guaranteed an education. When the child went into "Care" it was decided that they didn't need an education. The State is not going to fight the State and this is how we were deceived during the referendum. By taking away the right of parents to vindicate for their children and giving that power to the State, it also removes the right of the child. In several cases, one of which was widely published, a young girl in "Care" became pregnant and was taken to the UK for an abortion. The child wanted to give birth and put the baby up for adoption and didn't even know what an abortion was. It was decided in her Best Interests that the baby should be aborted. There have been many such cases in Ireland but you didn't hear about them because the child was in "Care". What the child wants is unimportant, as far as the system is concerned, they will hire a GAL to decide for every child and parents have no say in the matter.

Without knowing anything about the law, ask yourself whether it would be considered justice to have two separate trials for a person under two different Burdens of Proof? Family Law Prosecutions completely go against the grain of what we know of how Justice is supposed to work. How can you be innocent in one system and guilty until proven innocent in another system? Where Gardai investigate, the DPP prosecute, a Judge and/or Jury decide on innocence or guilt and the Prison Service punish, in Family law the same people investigate, prosecute and punish? The difference between Criminal Prosecution and prosecution for Child Abuse and Neglect is that in Family "Justice" you are investigated by two separate bodies and even if the Criminal Justice System finds you innocent or the case does not get past the investigation stage, you are still punished in the Family Court System whether you are guilty or not. This Double Jeopardy is the part that most people don't know or understand. Many people I have spoken with think that when people are accused of child abuse or neglect, that Gardai investigate and the fact is that Gardai only investigate a fraction of the cases.

I have seen lives destroyed and children harmed for almost nothing. The "Cure" was far worse than the "Disease". The operation was a complete success but the patient died. The system is very much like a Doctor whose patients don't get any better and 80% of the time they get far worse. Parents are left jobless from taking time from work to see their children. If you are allowed to see your children for only a few hours a week and had to take time off work, your children would come first. They are left bankrupt by the Law Fraternity and get lawyers who give them bad advice at €750/day in court for a solicitor and €1,500 and up for a barrister as well. We have seen an increase in parents representing themselves as they cant afford the fees to apply for Legal Aid, which Alan Shatter increased in 2013.

In the UK, Legal Aid has all but been eliminated in Family Law cases and there has been a dramatic increase in Litigants In Person and McKenzie Friends assisting them. Numerous people in the UK who have lost their children forever to Forced Adoption have become "Jail House Lawyers" and help other parents, usually at no cost. 87% of the Legal profession in the UK now believe that Justice is only available for the powerful and wealthy. Having assisted a few "Wealthy" parents, I have seen where even when you have the funds, you still can't get a level playing field in family court.

The UK careens from bad to worse with disastrous policies that social workers say are unworkable and rammed in place regardless. They have now set a target of 26 weeks for a child to be adopted from the apprehension to the "Goodbye Meeting". When parents are accused of needing classes or therapy or treatment, they have no hope of achieving the targets of 26 weeks. The "Adoption Tsar" who advises the UK government has no expertise or experience and yet his ill informed and biased opinions are used as government policy. The Children's Tsar recently said that the secrecy of the courts should be maintained because it would lead to children committing suicide, when asked why, she said because I'm a social worker, I know. It seems to have escaped her notice that a child in "Care" is 10 times the risk of suicide.

Martin Narey, a former Prison Governor later became CEO of Barnardos UK. Barnardos UK make a very substantial income from Forced Adoption. Forced Adoptions in 2013 have skyrocketed to 2,400 children. I know many of their parents, many of them fled to Ireland when pregnant. Likewise, the Chair of the "New" Adoption Authority is a proponent of Forced Adoption happening in Ireland. Even with the downward spiral of the UK system, the lobbyists in Ireland still copy many of the failed theories. In 2014, the UK hit a 25-year high for the number of children in "Care", now over 100,000. The goal of the UK Eugenics Plan to reduce the number of children in "Care" by getting them adopted has been a miserable failure with less that 6% being adopted from "Care". Still, in late 2014 the Chair of the Adoption Authority in Ireland is still pushing ahead with his plan for Forced Adoption of 2,000 children in Irish State "Care" if the Children's Referendum passes into law.

There must be a presumption that when the State steps in and decides a parent has failed in their duty and removes a child, that this child will have a far better outcome in life than if they were left with their family. In the UK councils are rated by OSTED every year and most councils have had an "Inadequate" rating at least once in the last decade. In Ireland, there is no scrutiny, no rating of areas, nobody with any power or authority to walk into a CFA office and view files. Of course a few laptops have been stolen with extremely delicate information contained on them but that is another story.

If you go to a carwash and your car comes out far more damaged than when it went in, nobody in their right mind would go back and they would quickly go out of business. If the car wash owners gagged you and had unlimited funds to abuse you and left you bruised and battered by the ordeal, they could probably stay in business long enough to damage most of the cars in town before anyone takes notice. How long before the Irish Public and Media will take notice?

Journalist and Writer John Waters once did a story on; "Two HSE's", one that fails patients waiting on trolleys and another magical HSE that protects children unquestionably and without any fear of scrutiny. It looks like a wolf, smells like a wolf and growls like a wolf it must actually be warm and fuzzy little bunny was the gist of his story. Much of what we believe and are told about the system is a lie. Even when we are given proof to the contrary, we still believe in a sacred cow that can do no wrong. Only a few people are saying that the system is wrong, usually the ones who have actually seen it, and those who think the system works are working on blind faith that it actually protects children. We don't question the 100 or so Children's "Charities" and take a huge leap of faith that they are working to the benefit of children everywhere. If a charity claims that 85% of their donations are spent directly helping children, we accept that beyond question. Perhaps we should be asking if 85% of their donations are spent **on** children? Perhaps we should be asking to see their Balance Sheet and see how much they actually pay their staff and count this as "helping children?" The reason I ask this is because I have seen young mothers in desperate need, if they don't get some financial help their children will end up in "Care". As little as €100 could prevent their children being taken away at a cost of thousands. When these people contact "Charities" they are fobbed off.

These minor problems that sometimes people experience are so "fixable" in many cases. The young mother had her Gas shut off and had no gas to heat the home, hot water to bathe her baby or cook hot food. The reason she had no money was because her baby was sick in hospital for a few weeks and she had to sleep on the floor every night beside his cot, she couldn't afford the bus fare every day back and forth or eating meals in the hospital cafeteria. When he got out she had to give the baby a special diet and buy non-prescription medicines, which left her without food for herself. She couldn't even visit the Community Welfare Officer as she was stuck miles away at Crumlin Children's Hospital with her baby. When her gas was turned off she would have to pay a disconnection and reconnection fee. How much economic sense does it make to spend many thousands on "Professionals" when a few hundred would solve many of these problems?

I was laughed at one time when I suggested that social workers should be given a budget of €250,000 a year to directly help children in these situations rather than taking children into "Care". If a Child Protection Social Worker takes a child into "Care" for a fixable problem like this, which only takes a few hundred, how much has the State and the taxpayer saved? I'm sure a few people would try to take advantage of the situation but I think that social workers are smart enough to know when the are being conned. The Irish State, specifically Alan Shatter, a property millionaire himself, made it easier for Banks that we own, to re-possess homes. When a family need emergency accommodation, the State and taxpayer are responsible for finding accommodation. At the time of writing, there are nearly 1,000 children in emergency accommodation, officially "Homeless". What is also interesting is that there is an estimated 28 "People-less Homes" in Ireland for every "Home-less Person". Perhaps a little management and creative accounting by government would free up some of these homes and place families in these vacant homes and save the taxpayers money? Perhaps the banks could pay back the taxpayer their debt by using vacant homes as emergency accommodation? We bailed out banks and there is no plan to recover the money from these banks. Banks wrote off bad loans of Irish Tax Exiles and ultimately the taxpayer paid off these debts. Why are bank allowed to give loans to Tax Exiles?

Should we have "Charities" and Social Workers bailing out struggling families? No? Problem is that governments have taken away any power for common sense thinking from civil servants. The rules are the rules and must be obeyed. I have seen a ridiculous situation where a mother needed to urgently move from her rat-infested privately rented house in Tallaght because of the risk to her baby and toddler and the community welfare officer throwing every possible roadblock in her way. She was receiving Rent Subsidy in one area, but the rules didn't allow her to move to another area without re-applying to the Council and getting rejected before she could even apply for rent subsidy in her new area. It was essentially an emergency situation as rats had built a nest on her water supply tank. We even had this verified by a Health Official but the official would not go into the attic for "Health Reasons" and sent me in instead to take photos. If the newborn or the toddler had contracted a disease, what would be the cost to the taxpayer, perhaps a funeral for the children? These problems are so easily fixed, but the people involved have no power to change the system.

I would take strong exception to being called "Anti Social Worker", I have no problem however being called "Anti Social worker acting as a Prosecutor of Families". We are asking social workers to do a job that they will never be capable of doing. We are asking social workers to be able to predict future crimes and by not having any scrutiny there is no impetus for change. Until the social workers themselves stand up and stop portraying themselves as the victims, they can't reasonably expect the full support of the public. If the suicide rate of social workers was 10 times higher than other professions I would be very concerned. As long as social workers remain low on the list for suicide but their clients remain a 10 times higher risk, I honestly can't see social workers as being victims. Until the majority of the profession stand up for children instead of themselves I will continue to have no faith in their ability or competence, or indeed the value they supposedly add by their prosecutions of families. While many people recognize the Baby P Effect, that social workers are taking too many children away from families, I am underwhelmed by how people won't speak up against this injustice.

The only Judge in Ireland who is actually in favour of the corrupt Children's Referendum, retired Judge Catherine McGuinesss used the Baby Ann Case in favour of removing all Parental Rights. The Yes campaign dishonestly presented about 18 cases of where parents had failed their children as an example of why parents should give away their rights under the Constitution. It was about as dishonest an argument as you could get. In the Baby Ann case for example, which was about a single mother giving up her baby for adoption but later changing her mind, some extraordinary facts were left out by the Yes side.

Baby Ann was raised for the first 2 years of her life by Foster Carers who wanted to adopt her. After signing the papers, the mother had a change of heart and wanted her baby back. However it was the social workers involved who were opposed to giving Baby Ann back to her mother and fought her parents all the way to the Supreme Court in support of the Foster Carers. While Catherine McGuiness gave an account that Baby Ann was dragged away from the arms of the only parents she had ever known, the truth was that the social workers had "Played God" with the baby and did everything in the power to oppose the parents who had since been married. If Baby Ann had been returned when the mother had asked, she would not have been kept away from her parents for almost 2 years.

It's important to realize that Forced Adoption has always been theoretically possible for unmarried mothers under the Constitution. In reality it hasn't been possible in many cases because the parents could get married to prevent Forced

Adoption. It's also interesting to note that in the Mother & Baby Units, that if a young mother later decided to get married, that the child would still be adopted as the child was considered by the Church and others as a "Bastard Child" or "Illegitimate Child". The "Illegitimate Children's Act of 1933" still makes interesting reading today. In the Baby Ann case, McGuiness was forced to side with the other judges and uphold the Constitution. A decision, which has obviously not sat well with her. But the simple fact remains that if social workers had returned Baby Ann immediately, the case would never have come to court. If it's any consolation to Catherine McGuiness, she should bear in mind that 1 in 4 adoptions "Disrupt" and the children end up back in "Care".

Politicians were reading from the same "Hymn Sheet" and using cherry picked cases that they obviously had not researched, because in debate Kathy Sinnott, John Waters, Dr Gerry Fahey, Maria McMeanmhain and myself, easily pulled their arguments apart. One of the most widely used cases was the Roscommon House of Horrors in which children lived a horrible existence for 11 years at the hands of a mother who was jailed. What's interesting to note about that case is the fact that social workers were involved for 11 years with the family and in the end, it was the children who saved themselves. This case parallels the Baby P Case in highlighting the incompetence and inability of social workers in being unable to determine which children are being abused. The learning's of both of these cases should have been that social workers cannot protect children and should have no role in investigating crime. Both of these cases are used as justification for "shoot first and ask questions later". In the minds of the Crusaders they justify that it is acceptable to harm some children by removing them unnecessarily, just as Dr Phil says; "I would rather see 1,000 children being taken rather than seeing one swing in the wind". Even Martin Narey said that he believes that possibly 2% or 4% of Forced Adoptions are wrongful, but this is the price we must pay to keep children safe. By Narey's estimates, there are 100 or so children wrongly forcibly adopted every year and he finds this acceptable? Is 100 Miscarriages of Justice a year in the UK acceptable?

During the Referendum there was face-painting, balloons, happy children and a carefully orchestrated media campaign by the Government. Everything was planned and PR people were hired a year in advance. Graphic Artists worked for months in total secrecy to build the campaign, there were meetings and consultants who would try to counter the arguments of the No side and the referendum would be announced without giving anyone on the No side a chance to oppose it. Even when Mark McCrystal won his case in court and it was clear that the government had broken the rules and it was clear that the government had been corrupt and had not followed the constitution and the law and were clearly looking for a Yes vote, they still ploughed ahead with the plan. Politicians were standing up in the Dail and trying to justify the illegality and corruption. Even before a No side existed, many were saying that anyone who opposed this was a conspiracy theorist, a nutcase as one man called me and anybody opposed to this legislation was supporting child abuse.

I did an interview with one "journalist" in particular who was clearly looking for some "dirt" and the best he could come up with is that John Hemming MP was the man involved in the "Giggs Super-Injunction" case in the UK had lent his support for a No vote. I also mentioned that the No side had no funding and that there wouldn't be a single poster in Ireland opposing the Referendum. At the start of the referendum only 4% of the Irish Public were opposed, in the end, 42% of Irish people voted No.

Given another month, we would have won easily. On an online poll the No side were going to win by a 2/3rds majority. Even with the support of the Media, who were clearly in favour of a Yes vote, a small group of largely unorganized people turned the vote around. A document I published online entitled "10 Reasons to Vote No" was downloaded by hundreds of Irish citizens, many printed this out by the hundreds and distributed it in small towns and cities around Ireland. In interviews and debates I focused on educating the Public into how dysfunctional and unjust the system was. I figured that win or lose, that I would draw attention to what passes for "Protection" in Ireland and I feel that I accomplished this goal. On my websites and blogs, people started paying attention, among them the Government departments and politicians. They really didn't have a clue as to what was happening in these Secret Courts.

In December 2014, the appeal against the legality of the Children's Referendum is being heard in the Supreme Court. I had hoped that the decision would be handed down before the publication of this book. Regardless of the outcome, the truth is that the State has been abusing the rights of Irish children since the inception of the State. Every day in Ireland, the rights of children are being in Secret Courts and the Irish Public are blissfully unaware that regardless of our constitution, the State does what it likes and has always done. Parents and children only have rights as long as those rights don't need to be vindicated. When the State steps in, children have no rights and no voice and it has been this way for a long time. The only advantage to the State of having the referendum pass into law, is that it would legalize the law breaking they have been doing for years.

CHAPTER 13

FATHER'S RIGHTS

I have always said the Father's Rights Movement have been doing it wrong for years. When father's cry and tell us that they are being denied a right to parent their child, they often come off as whiners and deadbeat dads in the argument. When they say they love their baby and want to be part of the baby's life and upbringing this is not seen as "Manly" endeavour. When I was born many years ago, fathers went to the pub across the street from the Rotunda as God forbid; nobody wanted them in the Delivery Room and holding their wife's hand for support. The right to be present was hard won by men, but not men in the Fathers Rights Movement. It's important to differentiate between Men's Rights and Fathers Rights.

Even in tribes that have followed traditions for thousands of years, men were not involved and were left out of the process. Father's are not valued in the same way as Mothers. Few would disagree with me when I say that babies need their mother more for the first 6 months of their life. Hopefully a baby will be breastfed and have a gentle introduction to the world around them. Father's are critical at this point to take an active role and equally bond with the baby so that the child knows they have 2 caregivers protecting them. But as men are not given 6 months Paternity Leave, the reality is that the men have to go back to work and look after his entire family. Men suffer too having to wake up for feedings and then expected to perform at work the next day. Nobody ever said parenting was easy. When you have to rush your sick baby to a hospital in the middle of the night, wait and then rush off to work, nobody is going to give you any medals.

One day when I was in Cork, I was walking through a lane and I saw a man crying and in obvious distress. After some coaxing, he agreed to join me for a cup of coffee at a cheap take out and told me his story. It was obvious that he was a hopeless alcoholic, not completely hopeless though, he was cleanly dressed and shaved. He told me after his divorce, he was forbidden to see his son, now aged 8 years. He had been walking through town when he heard his son call out to him from the bus stop. Instinctively he ran away from his son as fast as he could. If he so much as talked to his son, waved or acknowledged him in any way, he would be in breach of a Barring Order and would be jailed, again.

I couldn't help thinking how his son felt. His dad was giving him a clear signal that he didn't love him or want to be part of his life. Children don't understand Barring or Protection Orders, they just know who their parent is.

This to me is the crux of why the Father's Rights Movement has never succeeded to gain the public support it deserves. Men have become disenfranchised from the lives of their children, but nobody seems to care. It makes little difference that men are "Battered" and abused by their partners at an almost equal rate to women, we protect the women in every case. There isn't a single Men's Shelter in the world for Battered Men. I don't know if this man became an alcoholic before or after his divorce, I have seen so many men damaged by divorce and many never recover. The biggest injury to men is being systematically carved out of their children's lives. But let's forget father's for a minute, what about the children?

Many years ago as a 21 year old, I became good friends with an inspiring man who I saw as a hero and a role model, his name was Richard Scarisbrick and was English. As a fellow engineer we could have great conversations and he taught me a lot as a role model. One day we stepped into an elevator, or Lift, as they are known in Ireland. There was a very old lady dressed "to the nines" as if she had an audience with the Queen. Richard instinctively beamed a smile when he saw her and said in his wonderfully British accent; "Oh My, my dear you look absolutely divine", the old lady beamed and coyly was able to utter Thank You in her most lady-like giggling tone. My initial reaction was one of shock that a cartoon-like character had come to life but I still managed a Wow!

When the old lady left Richard said; "you know Joe, it doesn't cost anything to be nice to people. I didn't honestly believe what I said, but it was obvious that she had spent many hours preparing herself. A few kind words go a long way". Whenever I have been tempted to be unkind to people I remember what Richard was teaching me. I believe that this exercise with the old lady was more of an exercise to teach me than to compliment the lady. He recognized in me that I was and "angry young man" as many are at that age and that I needed to grow up rapidly to survive in a harsh environment and unforgiving world more than 3,000 kilometres away from home and family.

I also recognized in Richard that he wan an angry man too in his 50's. He had access to his children on weekend every second weekend and I knew not to bother him during that time. Of course I had him every second weekend as he had me under his wing and he wanted to parent me as young adult as most of my friends were of the same age. When I did see him with his children, he was an amazing parent. He would spend 2 weeks preparing for his weekend with his children and had a 3-bedroom apartment that was a home away from home with his children. He didn't feel that every second weekend was good enough and was deeply bitter that even through years of fighting in the courts, this was the best deal he could get. I have also wondered for years how Richards's children turned out.

At the age of 28 I lived with a young woman with 3 children from 6 to 13 for some time. At the time I was also running my own business, which took a considerable amount of my time and resources. Her daughter was 10 years old and one day when I was babysitting while the mother was doing the very considerable laundry for the week, I heard the child crying in her room. As you do, I investigated and she told me that she really missed her daddy. She hadn't known her dad as he walked out on his family when she was 4. I'm not sure whether she missed him or the missed having a "real" family with a dad, even if that dad was a stepdad. I held her hands and comforted her as best I could. I told her that if I was her dad, that I would see her every day, pick her up from school, buy her gifts and would want to be a big part of her life. I was almost in tears at what her "father" had done to her and her family. I told her that her father must be a very stupid man and it was he who was missing a great opportunity to see his beautiful and smart daughter.

A few days later she told her mother what I had said and she understood that I could not be her father. Where her father had taught her that men could not be trusted, I had taught her that not all men are bad and that not all parents are good.

When I reflect on this event many years later and think of what I would do differently today, I would have swept her up in my arms, hugged her and gently kissed her on the forehead and told her that I cared for her deeply, just as her mother did when she disclosed the story to her. Even all those years ago there was the hysteria of child abuse and hugging a child that is not your offspring, especially a man hugging a young girl, was not something that was done. I did exactly that when she disclosed the story to her mother, but only with her mother present. I sometimes wonder if she had turned out differently if I had taken the risk at the time. I often grieve for the children in "Care", who don't get hugs every day from their foster carers and have to wait for a once a week hug from their parents. We had a great time together as a family, especially on Sundays, which was "Family Day", and we would do what any parents would do with their children. Even years later, I am still in contact with the family and the children have children of their own and have always kept in contact with the mother even though the relationship didn't work out.

In the UK every day about 200 fathers are cut out of their children's lives, this is insanity, 4 million UK children are without a father. Many times the fathers are wrongly accused of sexual abuse and Domestic Violence, few are ever charged in a criminal court for these crimes and social workers are involved in every case. I know of fathers who have cut themselves out of their children's lives because social workers threatened to take the children away if they didn't terminate their relationship. Social workers and judges are not prepared to take any risk whatsoever, for as little as a neighbour telling a social worker that the parents have arguments and raise their voices, fathers are severed from the family. Let me rephrase that a different way.

In the UK every day more than 200 children are cut out of their father's lives, this is insanity. We have known for years that children of a traditional husband/wife family have far better outcomes in life. Young girls are better able to relate to young men because they had a father who taught them everything they need to know about men and relationships. Young girls are far less likely to become teenage mothers or engage in sex because they don't have a father to love them and teach them to be a lady. It's telling that daughters dearly want their dads to "give them away" at their wedding because the first man they ever loved, loved her unconditionally and didn't have any ulterior motives. They learn that men and women can be in a loving relationship without sex coming into the equation and that they have a man who is willing to sweep them up in their arms and protect them like a fairy princess. They learn that intimacy, when you need a hug and reassurance, just like a baby, that it is available anytime and you can always count on (or manipulate) dad when the need arises.

Of course it's not just girls who are cut out of their fathers lives, boys are just as in need of hugs and the protection of their father so that they can learn to relate to women and see them as people and not just objects.

It's not a surprise then that youth often go into gangs with their "Homies" if they have not had an adequate parents and not lucky enough to part of the Natural Family with all the aunts, uncles and cousins. "Biology" means a lot, Love means a lot. If there is one truism that can be said about Best Interests, it is that Best Interests doesn't Love any Child. There is a biological need in a parent to be a parent to their child, but equally there is a need in a child to be parented and to have what Nature intended. We all want to be loved and bond with a group. We are "Pack Animals" and tend to thrive as a group rather than being loners, unloved and unwanted. This is against the dogma of Social Work that says the concept of Family is an out-dated concept with its roots in Tribal traditions that are no longer valid in the modern world. Even though the need for our Tribe, our Homies, our Gang and our Family is a strong instinct in all of us and even though the vast majority of readers will agree with this, 50 years of Social Work knows better and wants us to go against our natural instincts. I wouldn't be exaggerating to say that much of Social Work Theory is "Unnatural".

We have seen lately where the definition of Family is being extended beyond the natural concept. We now have Gay Marriage and LGBT couples adopting children. We have women being used as "Gestational Carriers" to carry another woman's Ova that are Artificially Inseminated and implanted in her womb. Surrogacy is creating big problems for Lawyers and Judges who struggle with these concepts. Buyers can select from a catalogue of sperm donors and we create Artificial Families for those who cannot conceive or carry a baby to term.

I have no issue with Gay Marriage as such. I am of the view that if 2 people are in a loving and committed relationship, that if one of them dies, the other partner should inherit their estate as is the normal practice in marriage. I also believe that a couple should have equal protection in matters of insurance such as illness to one partner. It doesn't cost me anything and benefits another person. While the religious view is that marriage can only be between a man and woman, I tend to follow Nature as a guide. I wish that there were an acceptable term to everyone other than Marriage and Gay Marriage because I believe there should be a distinction. I don't feel that using the term Gay Marriage discriminates, the point of the union is to have the same rights and protections as any other couple in a committed relationship. I don't see why LGBT have an issue with the term "Civil Union" and want the same rights as a man and a woman. Obviously a marriage between a man and woman exists for the purpose of having children in most cases. As LGBT cannot reproduce by normal means and the purpose of the union is not to reproduce, it cannot be said to be the same thing as marriage. While I would defend the rights of LGBT to have equal protection as any couple in a loving relationship, I don't believe that they have an automatic right to adopt children.

I don't even have an issue with gay or lesbian couples adopting but with one caveat; as long as one of them is the biological parent and the child has full access to the other parent. For too long Adoption has been seen as a panacea when the reality is that in many cases it is a form of child abuse. The idea of biology meaning nothing does not sit very well with the 60,000 or so Irish people who were forcibly adopted in the mother & baby homes. Some, even at the age of 60 or 70 still want to know who they are. It is only a recent development that we are seeing children who were raised by 2 mommies or 2 daddies with good results, but with a sampling size of far too small a sampling size to know if these children have better or poorer outcomes in life as a result. What is beyond dispute is that children do better when they are raised by a man and a woman. There is no longitudinal data for comparison of Outcomes for children raised by 2 men or 2 women.

We are also only recently seeing cases in some countries where sperm donors are being sued for child support and judges and politicians are left to sort out the legal quagmire of going against Nature. In Nature, homosexuality is normal but reproduction is never an issue.

Too often people will base their opinions on nothing more than; "I know someone who was adopted" but they know nothing of the circumstances of how the child came to be available for adoption in the first place. These personal views, although widely held, are not indicative of the reality of Adoption. As an Irish Judge so eloquently put it, "Adoption is the breaking up of one family to create another". We have entered a new age where Reproductive Technology has exceeded the Law's ability to deal with the new definition of "Family". Where the liberals and the Ideology of Social Work want to broaden the definition so broadly, that the word "Family" can mean anything, they are also weakening the value of Family. Does this actually benefit Children?

There is no shortage of studies that prove that children will always have better outcomes in life in the traditional family. There are no studies whatsoever to say that children do equally well being the product of a surrogate mother, being raised by gay or lesbian parents and more importantly, there are no studies which prove that the offspring of Social Workers and Psychologists have better Outcomes in life. We have seen in many cases of "Designer Babies" where single women can pick genetic traits of sperm donors and not be bothered with fathers being a part of the child's life. Why do we find this acceptable that a child will be raised without a father? Babies are aborted on the basis of gender and health of the baby and the quest for "Perfect Children" is now a reality that Hitler would have given his eyeteeth for with his Lebensborn Program.

Technology is a wonderful thing, I have embraced it all my life and spent years in continuing education to constantly "up-skill". Technology has an equal chance of being misused for nefarious purposes. Alfred Nobel who invented types of explosives and sold them for military purposes also sold his products to Miners and others who would use them for good. When his brother was blown up in one of Alfred's Laboratories, the press wrongly reported that Alfred had died and his epitaph was not one where history had remembered him fondly. He was so aggrieved by this that he set up the Nobel Prize foundation in his name where people are awarded for their contribution to the betterment of Mankind. In recent years the Nobel Prize has been awarded, many believe unfairly to such people as Barrack Obama and Al Gore.

Reproductive Technology has a great potential for good. Genetic Traits in some people can be screened out or eliminated. Conditions that often run in families can be treated early and other technologies such as Stem Cell Research are showing great promise. Equally though the potential is there for misuse. In a recent case in Australia a surrogate mother had twins for a couple. They rejected one baby who had Downs Syndrome and took the other. I don't believe we are too far away from growing babies in a laboratory or cloning human beings, it's already been done with animals.

Many countries have already outlawed surrogacy except in very exceptional circumstances such as a sister carrying a baby. I don't have any issue with that and I don't believe that most people could. However to use poor women in poor countries to be incubators for strangers is a form of Slavery. To sanitize this term to "Gestational Carrier" speaks volumes for the people who need to use sanitized terms to ease their own conscience is an abomination, not against God but against Nature.

I'm not opposed to technology and the betterment of Mankind, I have no religious grounds to oppose anything and I don't buy some of the arguments of the Church, whichever Monotheist brand of Religion supports or doesn't. The simple fact is that children need a father and Biology is hugely important to everyone. Child Trafficking is a problem that is not going away, as long as we see Adoption as a good thing and that children can be moved from one family to another without consequences, then Child Trafficking will always be acceptable in one form or another. In Mexico last year for example, 15 Irish couples were arrested and suspected of trafficking. As long as there is money available to buy children, criminals, whether in government or not, will always take advantage of the situation.

We saw a situation in the UK when Blair wanted to cut billions out of the Child "Protection" budget and gave a sob story of "doe eyed orphans languishing in care that were looking for a forever home". We saw the same story almost verbatim during the Children's referendum. However it wasn't the children languishing or who had disabilities or had been traumatized by parents or "care" that were adopted, only 6% of the children of "Care" were adopted. When Blair's government paid bonuses of hundreds of millions to hit targets, most LA's exceeded the targets by targeting unborn babies. To say that this was not Child Trafficking for Profit by civil servants would be an outright lie.

To prove my point further, what happened in the USA only reinforces my argument. Where the UK paid bonuses per head, the USA paid a higher premium for Black, Hispanic and Disabled children and the demand for White Caucasians went down. Another difference between UK and USA adoptions is that the UK adopters pay large sums to adopt babies. The USA on the other hand paid Fosterers or Adopters to adopt children and they get paid a weekly salary until the child is 18. Many of these children later find themselves being dumped on the streets at the age of 18 by their "Parents" just as they would as if they were in "Care". Many of the children are also traded publicly as commodities on social media and Craigslist, the US version of Buy & Sell. Anyone who would deny that this is Child Trafficking is either lying or delusional, but this is the same insanity that we are being sold in Ireland today. On one hand you have ONE country in Europe which allows for Forced Adoption on the other you have almost every other country in Europe complaining to the EU Parliament that the UK are stealing their young citizens and selling them to desperate couples wanting a baby.

We are being sold a bill of goods. We all love Fairy Tales and Happy Endings but the Adoption Panacea that is being sold to us is a lie. It will not be the children "Languishing in Care" who will be adopted, they don't want to be adopted, they just want to know that they will not be dumped on the streets by their Foster "Carers" at age 18 when the money runs out. Nobody wants the

"Damaged" children who have been shuffled between foster homes and institutions and residential "Care", adopters want babies, preferably at birth. It would be complete idiocy to believe that the children "Languishing" in Irish State "Care" will be adopted at all, unless of course the government has plans to pay big bucks as they did in the USA. If the State has the power in law to remove a baby at birth and forcibly adopt it, I guarantee that this is exactly what will happen. I don't have the gift of foresight and I don't own a crystal ball that has become the weapon of social workers, what I do have is History and I can bet with Statistical Probability that Ireland will repeat the mistakes of the UK and the USA, as they have done for many years.

To return to the topic of father's rights, fathers are tremendously important, but we know that. To deny children the right to be raised by a father is a form of child abuse. It has been estimated that as many as 30% of Irish Fathers don't have equal parenting rights and access to their child. I know one man who has access once a month and has to pay child support. Because he was deemed by a social worker to be a risk to his child, although Gardai never investigated and he was never charged, he has to pay a GAL the sum of €250 a month for an hour with his child in a "Contact Centre" run by a "Charity". This is obscene; this is an abuse of not only the father's but the child's Human Rights. The father lives very frugally in a caravan to save up enough money each month to see his child. Who benefits from this? Wouldn't the money be better spent on the child?

It takes the genetic material of a man and a woman to make a baby; even technology cannot alter that fact. Both parents are important to the child and the child can only learn certain things from males of females. Often when a child doesn't have a father, they latch on to a male figure such as Grand Dad or Uncle or stepfather. We know that these children will have far better outcomes in life and we have real scientific studies to prove this. While we talk about nonsense like having a licence to have a baby, we cut fathers out of children's lives in divorce and make it impossible for fathers to be fathers. As it takes 50% of the genetic material to make a baby, why is it that only 70% of fathers have full access to their children? Why is it that in divorce those fathers usually get the wrong end of the deal and find themselves systematically erased from their children's lives? Shouldn't we be doing the complete opposite and upholding the rights of children to be raised by their fathers? Divorce traumatizes children also, but why should children suffer for the sins of their parents?

As a starting point in divorce, custody and access should be granted on a 50/50 basis and work from there. Child Support should have nothing whatsoever to do with access; poverty should never be a reason to deny a child's right to access to their father. While I don't agree with licenses for babies or Eugenics, I recognise that there are men out there with babies they want nothing to do with, many have multiple children but leave it up to the taxpayer to pay for the child. There are also women who are "Baby Factories" that have babies from multiple partners. I believe if a man has multiple children whom he doesn't raise and support, is guilty of child abuse and neglect and that this crime should not go unpunished. While we don't need States to license parenting, as China has done, we need politicians to legislate so that fathers are guaranteed a right to full access to their child, and we need to do this for the children. This is what I have found lacking in the argument for Father's Rights; we need to put Children First and foremost.

The fact also that this same argument is not used by Children's NGO and Children's "Rights" Groups is testament to the fact that they don't exist to promote the benefit of children being raised by fathers and have planted their flag in the Ideology of Biology being nothing more than a vestige of out tribal roots. We have almost no evidence to support their theories that adoption leads to good outcomes for children, in fact the opposite is true and the real science proves beyond any doubt that children always have better outcomes in the traditional family, just as Nature intended.

In our Constitution the word "Father" only appears once and even then only in relation to our Founding Fathers. The words "Mother" and "Family" are mentioned many times. The architects of our constitution in 1939 were brave men who never envisioned a world where children would grow up as "Father-less" except where the father died and they never envisioned Militant Feminism. For years in Ireland women were expected to give up their jobs and stay at home to raise children. I'm happy that women are no longer burning bras and demonstrating for equal rights. I'm not happy that a woman who stays home to raise her child is no longer valued in society and that a woman must work in order to claim a pension. I'm also not happy that the divorce rate is almost 50% and children are written out of their father's lives. The pendulum has swung too far against children and we need to swing back to legislate for the benefit of children. We need to look at what started going wrong in the 1970's when the concept of Family became unimportant and Society took a downward spiral. We need to follow the guide of Nature and trust our instincts rather than Pseudo-Science.

When there are longitudinal studies to show that the children of Adam & Steve and Thelma & Louise do equally well and have good outcomes in life then I will still be cautious about whether Social "Science" knows better than eons of Evolution and Nature. But for now I'm going to stick with the scientific evidence that children will always be better off in the traditional family. I accept that adults divorce and frankly I would rather see them split up than being angry and taking it out on the children. What I cant accept however is that divorce should ever abuse a child's right to their father.

Why is "Feminist" an acceptable term but "Masculinist" is an unused term? I have never heard of the term Radical Masculinist and doubt the term will ever gain any currency. I understand that the pendulum had to swing in favour of women because for years, women were an under-class and that we needed to have Gender Equality. I'm proud to say I was part of the movement since the

1970's that brought this about. I worked at Women's Shelters long before Ireland opened its first shelter and I'm still a fan of Erin Pizzey who opened the first shelter in the UK.

Today, Erin Pizzey works for Men's Rights and recognizes that the pendulum has swung too far. She also sees that the radicals have co-opted the agenda and their goal is to divide men and women. They have taken ownership of Women's Issues away from ordinary women who don't want to be radicalized and don't constantly blame men for everything.

As I said earlier, Domestic Violence is not simply Man = Bad / Woman = Victim. People who present the issue of Gender Based Violence as that it is "all the man's fault" as I was told 35 years ago, have a very poor understanding of the issue. The real Domestic Violence is about learned behaviour that both the man and the woman learned from their parents and if it was learned it could be unlearned. There are cases of abuse, usually a singular event, that are wrongly classified as Domestic Violence. We can provide shelters for women, prosecute the abusive men and the women will still go out and find another abuser. I know this is heresy to say this but it is the truth, I have seen the pattern repeat itself for 35 years since I started a self-help group for men all those years ago.

I have seen social workers that have a very poor understanding of Domestic Abuse remove children from mothers based on a single event of violence with no substantiated pattern of abuse or abusive relationships. I have seen men who were abused by women and Police arresting men because they believe that Domestic Violence is only by Men against Women. I have seen abusive couples go from one abusive relationship to another with no treatment for either gender.

Domestic Violence is a serious issue make no mistake about that. It harms children who grow up watching this control and abuse and those children will then go on to abuse themselves. By denying that women who repeat this pattern of abuse that they learned from their parents allow that pattern to continue. The definition of Domestic Violence has become so broad that raising your voice or ignoring your partner is considered abuse. 1 in 5 women are not victims of Domestic Violence, this is a popular myth that has gained too much currency and grown over the years. DV is characterized as a pattern of abuse and not a singular event. If a woman is assaulted by a stranger on the street its called "Assault", if the women is assaulted once its called Domestic Violence. If a stranger assaults the woman, her children are not removed. If the woman is assaulted by her partner, even once, this is seen as DV and her children will be removed from her as she is deemed a risk by allowing the assault to take place. There is no distinction made between a singular event and a pattern of abuse. So you see the Radical Feminist agenda is actually working against women.

The issue of Domestic Violence is an issue that invokes a lot of anger in people and rightly so, but the truth is that men are abused by women at an equal rate. I could quote hundreds of studies that show the rate of abuse is almost equal. The rate of murders shows that for every 1000 women murdered by men, women murder 750 men. I was told to believe 35 years ago that the women who kill were defending themselves against abusive partners. The evidence doesn't add up. The figure of "1 in 5" came from a very small study on two US University Campuses and is widely quoted even though the study was not of Domestic Violence of in a committed relationship. It was of students between the age of 18 and 30, which is hardly representative of the general population.

In Ireland 78 women and 10 children were murdered in a 28-year period. To put that in perspective, the odds of a woman being murdered by her partner are roughly 1 in 1 Million a year or that an average of 2 women will be murdered a year, of course 1 is too many. Of these murders about 50% are by their partners or husbands in Ireland, however according to FBI data the figure is 36.5%. In many of the cases drugs and alcohol are a factor and in the Irish statistics these are not taken into account. There are no Men's Groups putting out figures for husbands and boyfriends murdered by their partners and no Men's Shelters to protect them from abusive partners anywhere in the world.

In 35 years of studying this topic we have not learned anything or worked towards solving the problem of Intergenerational Domestic Violence. We could have stamped it out in a generation if there was any will on the part on the Domestic Violence Industry. I have seen Women's Shelters in Ireland being a willing participant to social workers to accommodate women who have not been abused and yet are allowed to stay at shelters. I have seen where social workers lie to women that if they leave their partner and go to a shelter, that they will be given their children back if they lied to a judge that they were abused. Sadly, this is a lie that never sees the child returned and if women agree to this lie, then their children are removed permanently because they allowed the child to witness their abuse even though they could not have prevented the abuse.

Never underestimate the power of good people with the best intentions to destroy lives.

The abuse men suffer is not always in the form of physical attacks. It has become "Standard Procedure" in divorce for the woman to claim victimhood. Divorce is an Industry with big profits for the Legal Profession. Even when the woman has been protagonist in the divorce, men still end up worse off in the deal. A mere accusation against the father means his life as a father is over. Even when there is no substantiation of the claim, the likelihood of the father getting custody of his child is extremely slim. If the mother makes an allegation and the mother herself is incapable of looking after the child, the child will likely end up in "Care". I have seen many cases where widowers lose their children to "Care" and even in the 21st century, men are less likely to be seen as capable of being a sole parent.

The solution as I see it is to make all divorces "No Fault Divorce" and no lawyers needed. As a starting point men should have 50/50 custody and access and again, let me stress that this is something we need to do for the benefit of the children. If a mother or a father refuses access, as they frequently do, this is a form of child abuse and should be punished severely. If social workers refuse parental access, they should equally be charged with the crime of child abuse. Too often children are used as weapons against the other parent, judges can spot this easily but yet there are few consequences for the offenders. Many times fathers are accused of horrendous crimes against their child by the mother and yet these crimes are hardly ever investigated. In one case I advised a man to stand up in court and demand that the judge have him arrested by Gardaí and investigated for the "crimes" he was accused of, which he did and the allegations were immediately withdrawn.

What the radical feminists have **not** done is to measure the effect that they have on children.

The assumption is that women can be better parents than men and the bias has always been in favour of women raising children. In fact Nature has also favoured women over men, women can carry a baby to term and feed them, men cant. But although a woman can raise a child from birth to adulthood, children still need a father in their live if they are to have better outcomes in life. Many children have been raised exclusively by only a father or mother and have good outcomes in life. Many children have been raised by aunts, uncles and grandparents and have had very good outcomes. Where children tend to have poorer outcomes is in the case of Foster Care, which is a disaster for children. The high suicide rate and dismal outcomes are testament to why Foster Care should only be used in extreme circumstances. Kinship Care should be the care of choice but sadly is less than 30% in Ireland. Only slightly better is Adoption but the failure rate of Adoption is far too high. Kinship Adoption has significantly more benefits for the child, but again, Biology means nothing to social workers and with a large demand for babies and toddlers, family are left out. Children whose parents remarry also have significant difficulty with the new "parent".

But are children actually safer when raised by women? As women are often trapped in a cycle of poverty, many women want to work but simply can't afford care for their children. There are few jobs available that a woman can work for the few hours that a child is in school and when babies or toddlers are sick, few employers could manage their workforce on the basis of their employees having to take time off at short notice. I know many single mothers who are highly educated and experienced who are in that situation who want to work, but simply cant, as no such jobs are available. They don't want to live on State Benefit but they don't have any other options. Single Motherhood is not valued and as a consequence their children are marginalized. I have never seen a viable option being offered by Governments, every time their response is to force women into work and cut away at their benefit, in the process, cutting the benefit to children.

As a society, the Irish have become complacent and expect that a benevolent government would solve all their problems. People have become too reliant on running to TD's with petty problems like house transfers and helping them with taxes. Politicians have become too reliant on Lobbyists and the "Party Faithful" for re-election. Democracy as it should exist is dead. You can't have a Government of the People, for the people and by the people if only some of the people participate. Our system of governance is not work for anyone except the rich. We tolerate Tax Exiles, large Corporations making billions and paying no taxes and the corruption that has existed for years hasn't gone away, it just took on new forms. If the way we treat some Irish children is a measure of our Humanity, then it can be fairly said that we lost all humanity a long time ago.

The simple fact is that men and women are not equal and will never be. Both are important in different ways and when men and women are put together as a family unit, the sum of the union is greater than either part. In the Irish Constitution, Family is seen as basic unit of our society. We all come from families whether it's just a mother or a father and eons of Evolution and Nature has designed human beings as a "Tribe" and Biology is hugely important. 50 years of Psychology and Sociology has not given us any great gifts or insights. 90 years of Eugenics and governments meddling around in families has only resulted in massive failure and the quality of society has only suffered as a result.

We need to stop pretending that governments have the solutions and become involved in the political process. We are seeing a massive collapse of Civilization before our eyes, but as many people are not affected by this personally, they deny that others are suffering or frankly don't care. For the "Common Good" has no meaning any longer, because we are divided. Men are pitted against women and "Divide & Conquer" is driving a wedge into society. The Rich are pitted against the Poor, Governments pitted against the People and there is no unifying force for all of us to work together as a Society. We will never have Equality; there will always be rich and poor, highly educated and hardly educated, the "haves" and the "Have Not's". Programs such as Affirmative Action and setting quotas and forcefully swinging pendulums too far in one direction have always met with failure. You can't fix Discrimination with Reverse Discrimination; you can't fix Racism with Reverse Racism.

The more governments impose laws and regulations and criminalize ordinary people, the more people will rebel. Laws need to be enforceable in order to work. If you impose a speed limit of 30kph in a zone designed for 70Kph, most people will not obey it. And if most people believe that the speed limit should be 70, then this is Democracy and the will of the people. Imposing tougher fines on people has never worked and only criminalizes people who don't need to be criminalized.

For all its failures, society was far better off in some ways when the Church ran the country. Crime rates were lower; children were raised in poverty and still went on to have very good outcomes in life. Life was harder but we still survived. Not that I recommend that we all run back to the Church, but when the Church fell into disrepute they left a void that has not been filled and Governments have not instilled any Faith in their ability to manage for the Common Good. There is no "Common" any more, it's "Them" and "Us".

I don't know what the solution is to this problem but I wish to point out that where we lost our faith in the Church, our faith in Government and the Trickle Down Theory is waning very fast. What I do see is that we need to become active in Politics and participate. We need to challenge all the sacred cows and at least challenge everything you read, see and hear. Challenge everything that I have written here and do your own research. It's not a perfect world and human beings are not perfect, we are not all equal and some are more equal than others, but it could be a far better world, a more equal world if we are prepared to work towards that goal together and refuse to be divided.

We need to get back to basics and restore the values we once had, the Family being the basic unit of society and not allow Family to be devalued or redefined by Social Engineers and Theorists with no proven record of success or excellence. Standing by when others are being oppressed and treated unfairly just makes us oppressors. If we can't raise children properly and Cherish all the Children of Ireland Equally", we will surely pay the price in future generations. It is indeed a measure of a sick society when Irish children are starving but we prioritize paying unsecured bondholders over feeding poor children. "We will not have debtor written across our forehead" and will starve children and make them homeless because our Honour is a stake, Is there any Honour in making children suffer for the sins of the rich? I'm not a Socialist or Communist, I believe in Democracy but I also believe that our Humanity is far more important than and our humanity to all the children of Ireland is measured by our actions. I also believe that if Socialism is such a good thing, that the Socialists should move to Socialist countries.

Granting children "Rights" without any consequence when those rights are not enforced or vindicated is a fallacy and does not benefit children. The bureaucracy and rhetoric is not feeding children or giving them a home, it's not ensuring that children will be listened to or ensuring that all children will have equal access to be raised by their fathers. The Bureaucracy serves only the Bureaucracy and does not benefit children. There are few happy stories from the children in "Care" and no success stories from the Child Protection Industry. There are few stories at all because the Industry hides behind the In Camera Rule. Ireland is now the most secretive country in the world because even the UK has made far more effort to inform the public.

If we truly believe in Children's "Rights", we need to accept that Parental Alienation is a real phenomenon where the rights of children are being abused by not allowing them to know their families. Most of us accept that a child has a mother and a father, grandparents, aunts, uncles and cousins. To deny any child this basic right is a form of child abuse. Many governments have already adopted Parental Alienation into law.

Parental Alienation Syndrome (PAS) is not recognized as a disorder by the medical or legal communities and has been extensively criticized by legal and mental health scholars for lacking scientific validity and reliability. However, the separate but related concept of **Parental Alienation,** the estrangement of a child from a parent, is recognized as a factor in some divorcing families. Psychologists differentiate between parental alienation and parental alimentation syndrome by linking parental alienation with behaviors or symptoms of the parents, while Parental Alienation Syndrome is linked to hatred and vilification of a targeted parent by the child.

Far too many of us still believe that Adoption is a good thing for children. We still believe the fairy-tale happy ending even though all the evidence shows the opposite is true. In Ireland we have 60,000 or so people who after years are still denied the right to know about the Genetics, which we now know is hugely important, the right to know if the have siblings and even the denied the right to know if their mothers gave them away or were forcibly adopted. Few of us can fathom the pain of people who spend their life with a huge question mark over their head. Sure, they are grateful that someone raised and loved them, but they want to know why. Is that too much to ask?

With fairy tales we don't want to be confronted with the realities of what happened, it's very painful to see child abuse. We don't want to know the details, even if the victims of Forced Adoption do.

> *"Neither Society nor the adopter who holds the child in her arms, wants to confront the agony of the mother from whose arms that same child was taken."*
>
> *Margaret McDonald Lawrence.*

We prefer to live with the lie because it is more palatable. If you told a 5 year old where babies actually came from they would be disgusted. If you told the average person that adopted babies are snatched at birth, often a few hours old and scurried off to Foster Homes, even being denied the right to be breastfed and bond with their mother, many people would equally be disgusted by the inhumanity of the process, and yet this is the reality. This is the ultimate form of child abuse and the very definition of Parental Alienation and this happens in Ireland and the UK.

Adoption is a wonderful thing for the adopter, they get what they want, and the child has no say in the matter regardless of age. It's no surprise then that adopted children have poorer outcomes in life and that 1 in 4 children will be rejected by their new "Parents", especially if the child has special needs or doesn't want to be adopted. The Adoption Industry resorts to sanitized terms and slogans and justifies in their minds that they have stolen someone else's child. I'm sure many readers know an adopted child and believe in their minds that that the child is happy that they were "Chosen" and "Grew in the hearts of their parents instead of their womb". I'm sure that some adopted children will disagree with me also but I am just reflecting what I have been told by many parents whose children were stolen and what many adopted children have told me themselves.

Unlike adopted children, I can speak personally for the parents not accused of any crime or incapacity to be able to raise their child. I can also speak, having been asked to speak for the many parents who are gagged and cant speak for themselves.

Many people have tried to associate PAS with Paedophilia. They argue that with PAS, that a paedophile has an absolute Right to access with their children. This is of course nonsense. No child should ever be forced to have contact with any person who has abused them; it is an abuse of the child's rights. However the issue that doesn't sit well with them, is that they don't want parents, (let's be honest, Men), having access if the man is "accused" of harming the child even if the abuse is not confirmed. If PA became law, it would also apply to social workers who could no longer abuse the child's rights to know and be raised by both parents. If a person is accused in a criminal proceeding of abuse, I could see access being supervised, but only if the child wishes contact, if convicted, no person convicted of child abuse should have any right or access. It would also raise questions about whether Foster "Care" and Adoption, especially Forced Adoption, is an abuse of the child's rights.

PA is not about parents rights, it's about a child's right of access to both parents. You can see then why the Child Abuse Industry opposes PA, they would have to follow the law and put the rights of the child before anything else.

The Father's Rights struggle is an indication of a sick society. If a father wants to be a part of raising their child, what right does government or society have to interfere with this sacred bond? We should all, if we are so concerned with Children's "Rights", to ensure that Parental Alienation laws are instituted in every country. We need to legislate for "Sperm Donors" whether they went through the legal process or other method. If you create a child, whether by accident or not, you are responsible for that child forever and there needs to be penalties for those who don't comply. It's not sufficient for a fathers name to be on the birth certificate, the father needs to have 50/50 access and guardianship and this is something that we need to do for the benefit of children. Fathers should not have to apply to courts to become Guardian of their own child it should be automatic. This is akin to applying to adopt your own flesh and blood.

CHAPTER 14

SWEET CHILD O'MINE

"Where do we go from here?"

If you watch someone with Obsessive/Compulsive Disorder, you will see them obsessively repeat the same ritual, washing their hands 50 times, locking a door 5 times, or getting out of bed 10 times to make sure they unplugged the TV. If social workers and judges know that the likely outcome of placing a child in "Care" until 18 will most likely result in that child going back to court and have their children taken into "Care", (assuming they don't die first), would it not be a safe assumption to say that the judge and the social workers are suffering from a mental illness?

To say that they didn't know that the child would have a bad outcome in life is to either claim Incompetence or Stupidity. If they didn't know this would happen they are incompetent for not keeping current with all the evidence and horror stories. To keep repeating the same experiment over and over and expect different results every time is either Stupidity or Insanity. Sometimes they like to blame the children themselves and claim that the children were "Damaged" before coming into "Care" and that's why they have bad outcomes. If this is true, then why aren't their parents jailed for child abuse or neglect? Sometimes parents are jailed or prosecuted but in the vast majority of cases, I estimate 184:1, they are not even investigated by Gardaí. It is reprehensible to blame children for the position they find themselves in. People of course make bad choices sometimes, but when you have been "raised" in "Care" and systematically isolated from your family, your choices are few and far between. When you are dumped on the streets at age 18 or earlier and you don't have a person who loves and cares about you, to guide and support you, it's hardly likely you will have a good outcome in life. And yet, this is the insanity of what we are doing to children.

Again, I come back to a question I raised; "if you remove a child from their parents and family on the pretext or pretence that they will have a bad outcome in life, shouldn't that child have a far better outcome than if they were left with supposedly "bad" parents"? I could equally ask, shouldn't that child be 10 times less likely to commit suicide than 10 more likely? If "Care" is not better for children, then why do it?

I could quote studies ad nauseum, which agree or disagree with the value of "Care". One such study recently published states that children benefit from "Care" and is widely used, cherry picked to be used, as a glowing example that "Care" is good for children. What the study doesn't consider is "Outcomes" for children. If the State has paid a million in 18 years to raise that child, a lot more than the average parent could afford to spend, is it not a reasonable expectation that from 18 years onwards, that the child will have a far better outcome in life? Is it not reasonable to assume that the child will at least be alive at the end of the 18 years and beyond?

"Care" is turning out children in 80% of cases destined for prison, prostitution, substance abuse and the morgue, at such a high cost shouldn't these children be Doctors and Lawyers, Accountants, Judges and Social Workers? If you look at the uptake rates to higher education, you find "Care" Alumni at the bottom of the list. This is not just the case in Ireland, it's true in every country where social workers at the hub of child protection. Almost every country in the world takes children into "Care", except that in Ireland, the UK, the USA and Canada, they do it too often and keep the children too long. Although children are removed on the pretext of abuse, very few of these children actually receive any therapy. Instead, about 30% of these children will be placed on Psychotropic Drugs, often at adult doses.

During the corrupt Children's Referendum, Frances Fitzgerald made an extraordinary statement, she said; "some children have a good experience of Care", I cannot disagree with this statement, but the question is "how many children?" I noticed that when I started talking about the horrors of "Care" on my blogs, that the minister's office recruited children, now young adults, to give their success stories. Many of them called me to let me know, and the ones who didn't have a "good experience", didn't get their horror stories published. In true politician fashion, she calmed the fears of the public that everything was fine, sure there were problems but she would sort them out. "Don't feed the elephants in the room".

Minister Fitzgerald also stated that many children are in "Care" voluntarily. Again, this is absolutely true. The problem is though, that many of the voluntary cases, which didn't need to go to court, in many cases the parents were threatened that if you don't hand over your child and co-operate, we will take you to court and we never lose, and you don't want that. There are also cases where single mothers, for example diagnosed with breast cancer, went to get their children back after treatment, and found a fight on their hands. As many social workers have told me, "once a child is in care it's very difficult to get them back", again, no disagreement there. While it is difficult it is not impossible but the hardest part is getting a lawyer willing to fight for the children. If I had a budget of a million a year and a staff of 10 people, I could probably get most of the children back home.

I don't doubt for one minute the sincerity of Frances Fitzgerald or many others, even the "usual suspects" and the journalists and many supporters of the Child Abuse Industry. I believe that they are very good people with honourable intentions who want nothing more than the best system of protection for Irish children. What I doubt is their effectiveness and their ability to initiate the necessary changes that will make this happen. I was overjoyed and cautiously optimistic when Frances Fitzgerald made the announcement that the HSE would be removed from the role of protecting children. I campaigned and protested outside the Dáil with the Lamb and McAnaspie Families to make that a reality.

When I heard the news I contacted Sandra Lamb and told her, she was also very happy. A few years later, The Lambs and McAnaspie Families and others still visit the Boardwalk in Dublin when they can and talk to "Care" Alumni and nothing has substantially changed. Despite the promise of Frances Fitzgerald that all children dumped on the streets would be assigned an After-Care social worker, at best all the social workers can do is hand out a pamphlet or refer them somewhere. Again this week in the Irish Times, Carl O'Brien is warning us of a "shortage of social workers" and many children in "Care" not even having an assigned worker. Maybe Carl if they stopped taking children unnecessarily into "Care"?

There was an increase in the number of deaths in "Care" recently despite the "Independent" Panel's report and recommendations on the deaths of the 196 cases that were investigated. The only thing that has substantially changed is the secrecy; the media should be announcing a death of a child in "Care" on average every two weeks because that's not the reality. If anyone actually counted the deaths from age 18 to 26, they would find the figures even more disturbing. They are not lying to you, they are just not telling the whole truth. "No news is Good news"

Rather than Reform the organization, Frances & Co took the same 4,500 staff, gave them a new name and a new budget and added a few more people from the UK. That's not Reform, that's called "Rebranding". Throughout history, it has always been best practice for people who have been part of the problem, to not allow them to be part of the solution. We didn't allow bankers to be part of fixing our destroyed economy, why allow the people who have destroyed the Child Protection System to be part of the solution? As I said earlier, a Minister for Children or Justice is not allowed to know what happens inside the courts. While they want you to believe they are in control and they know what is going on, the truth is they would be breaking the law if they did, this is a ridiculous situation.

Nobody in the DCYA or in upper management at TUSLA or the CFA have any knowledge of anything that happens in a Family Court. The system is a big ship with no captain and the senior crew cant go below decks to talk to the passengers or the staff, it's against the law. This is why everything you are told from the people in charge is a lie. They can't talk to children in "Care". Although HIQA do inspections of "Care" homes, they don't inspect the system. It is also policy of HIQA to hire social workers as inspectors. In the UK they have OFSTED who have the power and the duty to inspect the services themselves and many councils receive an "Inadequate" rating every year. In Ireland we needed 30 Irish citizens to protest outside the Dail for a year, hoping that some opportunistic politician would jump on our bandwagon before someone finally agreed that the service was inadequate.

When Frances Fitzgerald first took office as Children's Minister, I suggested to her in an email that she throw her hands up in the air and say; "look folks, I didn't create this mess but I'm sure as hell going to fix it", she chose instead to side with the system. She knew that the former Minister Barry Andrews went through hell trying to sort out the mess. Barry was a good man with the best intentions, but despite being fobbed of by the HSE who told him to mind his own business, his faith in the system never failed. He toured Ireland and talked to social workers everywhere, other than talking to the Lamb Sisters and the McAnaspie Family and a few others, he didn't talk to children in "Care". He did talk to one young lady who told him a few horror stories and also told him about Tracy Fay, whom she knew. Any manager knows that when you ask why people who are failing at their job, they will always say we need more people, power, time and money. When you give them more people, power, time and money, their failures will be even more spectacular.

Today we are still being fed the "Shortage of social workers". If you pay attention to the media you see the same stories being rolled out the last time we had a "shortage". Hundreds of kids in "Care" are without a social worker and GAL, caseloads are unmanageable, not all cases are being investigated and the constant drip-feed of information that will lead to "Problem – Reaction – Solution". My prediction is that if more social workers are added, that it will result in more children being taken into "Care" for even more spurious reasons and in a few years they will be saying the system is unmanageable and there is a shortage of social workers. History has a habit or repeating itself.

Good social workers are worth their weight in gold, they also tend to be far less likely to take children into "Care". They don't see their role as prosecutors of families because from hard experience they know the damage they can cause. What we are given instead, is students and recent graduates being unleashed on families, many are kids themselves and Child Protection is seen as an entry-level position to get their foot in the door. With all the fervour of youth, they are like young soldiers going to war and see their Managers as

Generals or Ayatollah's as the case may be. The good social workers leave within a year, the turnover in Family Services is the highest within the profession. Social workers learn quickly that they are doing an impossible job, a job that they are not trained for and the only tool they are given is a vaporous "Science" with vague guidelines. They are not given a crystal ball and when they leave the home on Friday afternoon, they wonder if the child will still be alive on Monday. The worst thing that could happen to the social worker is that the child could die with their parents. If the child dies in "Care" nobody is responsible. The system will not stand by them when the child dies and the system only protects the system.

If you send a Plumber out to do Brain Surgery the result will be predictable. This is what we are asking social workers to do, a job that they will never be capable of doing properly. Even the good social workers with years of experience know the job is impossible. I have been told that Child Care Managers occasionally go on a drive to take more children. They are managing a machine with input and output. Kids "Age Out", children die, judge's hand children back to parents and there is a continual drive to keep the numbers up. I know this because social workers have told me. When more fosterers are trained up or the Foster Agency needs more money, the pressure is on the manager to take more children. Some social workers can decide for themselves to take a child, often out of anger and often illegally. Many of them have to call their manager and get permission. The Manager almost never gets to meet the children they make decisions about. It would be exceedingly rare that a judge would meet any child, rather than have to face the child; they rely on GAL's.

If we have a situation in Ireland as the one I witnessed for myself, that a judge hearing only one side of the story without the parents being present, can remove 3 children without hearing any evidence in the space of 1 minute, then we have a serious problem with Irish Justice.

If we have a situation where social workers can remove the wrong child from an innocent family for months, we have a serious problem with social work and justice.

If we have a situation where people who have no legal right can remove children illegally and Gardai are unwitting accomplices and judges willing participants, then it can fairly be said that some people in Ireland are living under Tyranny.

If you have a secretive system where Human Rights Laws have no meaning and people are gagged under threat of prison then we need the ECtHR and the ICJ intervening and asking Irish Human and Civil Rights Groups why they are not paying attention. And we need penalties for those who abuse our human and civil rights.

If the Irish Government is convinced that following the worst possible model then let them publish evidence that our system is better than other countries. Let them also publish the fact that foreign governments have expressed concerns over the treatment of their citizens.

If we have an insane system where judges keep repeating the same mistakes over and over again and expect different results every time, and where those judges are prepared to protect their own reputations rather than protect the children they have sworn to protect, then these judges need to be held to account for their deaths, the deaths by suicide, the rapes that they are enabling and not allowing Gardai to investigate, then the whole malpractice of Family Courts must come to an end and be replaced with a system of One-System-of-Justice-For-All.

It's time to put away the sacred cows and false prophets and see this system for what it really is. Where we have averted our eyes and kept the faith, but the system is not getting better, it's just getting bigger. People need to ask questions and get honest answers about the reality of this system. If only 1% of what I have said is true in this book, we should be calling for Ryan Report Two to see if there is any validity to what I have written here. For years we believed the State looked after children in the Catholic Intuitions only to find out that children were being harmed at a higher rate and didn't have the protection of their parents. The situation today is even more dire.

Historically, the Irish State have never done Child Protection very well, what makes people believe that the situation is any better today? The evidence is all around us, dismal outcomes, children "missing" from "Care" and being trafficked into prostitution, the 10 times higher suicide rate of a child in "Care", the homeless youth that Focus Ireland wrote about over a decade ago, and regardless of the best intentions of the "Care" Industry, we are turning out an underclass of citizens who would have been better off left with their parents.

Years before social work and psychology, Ireland had the National Society for Prevention of Cruelty to Children (NSPCC). Instead of social workers we had the "Cruelty Men" who took children away from alcoholics, damaged and dysfunctional people. Parents were charged and jailed for abuse. The children were sent to the religious institutions and many, like my father and my aunt, turned out well. I have no doubt that things might have turned out better had my grandfather been a better father.

At the age of 90 my father was still trying to parent me, it never leaves you. He told me that human beings were not perfect and we didn't live in a perfect world. I agreed for the most part but told him that we have a responsibility to improve the world and that we need to speak up in cases of social injustice and inequality, I learned this from my mother. We don't or shouldn't need to speak up for the rights of people as Rights are something you already possess. In a perfect world you wouldn't need to fight or vindicate those rights. If Ireland was perfect then you wouldn't need Appeal Courts, Supreme Courts or Civil and Human Rights groups and activists to step up when those rights are being abused.

Status Quo is something we should not be satisfied with, unless there is continuous and meaningful improvement we are just moving backwards. In an environment of total secrecy and with no scrutiny, there is no opportunity or incentive to improve. The problems of the Child Protection Industry are symptomatic of a greater problem in society. What I learned 35 years ago working with both men and women in cases of Domestic Violence, is that Control, above all else is the problem. Governments are battering their citizens and instituting more laws to criminalize its citizens. The EU hand down about 3,000 new laws and regulations every week.

In America you have a situation where they have the largest number of people in prison in the world. 1 in every 30 or so American citizens is in jail, on probation or has a criminal record. When laws fail the usual response of the government is to make tougher laws, stiffer penalties that inevitably fail. People are waking up to the reality that our system of Government and Economics is failing. The rich are getting richer and the wealth is not trickling down, as it should.

In my last job in Ireland I was working from January to July to pay the government taxes and the rest was mine. I accept that we have to pay a price for the Greater Good and I have no issues paying for the children of single mothers for their health and education. Our economy is built on a house of cards that trickles down to our fellow citizens who in the future will pay my pension and my health care when I become ill or too feeble to look after myself. In recent years we are seeing the results of the Spoilt Generation that Dr Aric Sigman wrote about. It's not about the Greater Good any longer. Greedy and selfish people are destroying our economy and civilization. Lehman Brothers and Fanny Mae are just the tip of a very big iceberg. The public have become disillusioned that many have to work 40 hours a week and still cant afford rent and food, for many there is no disposable income.

If you live in a society where you work 40 hours a week and you need rent subsidy or food banks, you can only call this Slavery. For the Irish government to make it easier to repossess homes and then for the Irish Taxpayer to have to pay for families to feed, clothe and house them is ridiculous, a waste of taxpayers money. To pour billions of taxpayer money into untenable banks and allow banks to sit on empty homes that we paid for is beyond ridiculous. We have by some estimates 28 or 76 People-less Homes for every Home-less Person, I don't care what the figure is. How is it possible that we bought the banks by bailing them out but we don't own them? And have no control over them? Is there even a plan for the banks to repay the money that we poured in?

In banks offshore, there is Trillions of money sitting there and not trickling down. In Ireland we have "Tax Exiles" and major corporations making billions but not paying the same percentage of tax as a person on minimum wage. We have politicians taking bribes; quite legally I might add, by having corporations make campaign contributions. This is not the result of a pendulum swing too far in one direction; it's a symptom of a sick society that makes greed socially acceptable. The Greater Good only benefits the rich and powerful.

I have seen where social workers and GAL's have systematically isolated children from their parents to the point that the children no longer wish to see their parents. It is done with threats and intimidation, not for the benefit of the child who will be dumped on the streets at age 18, but for the social workers to prove that they were right all along. Egos get bruised easily and the weapon of choice by social workers and GAL's against parents, is often the child. By using flawed methods to take the child, essentially nothing more than suspicion in most cases, the are not willing to accept that they themselves have harmed the child by removing them. In order to maintain their ego, they often lie and exaggerate to keep that child as long as possible.

This is a battle against parents, child abuse makes us angry and the revenge is taken out on the parents. If there were a competent investigation to begin with, no anger and no egos would be involved. If a parent maintains their innocence and refuses to cooperate then they must be guilty. Judges side with the social workers because they believe that the social worker is there to help and can't understand why a good parent would not cooperate.

Social workers are so in fear of making a mistake that they want to take every child, once they have the child their goal is to keep the child and they are not above lying and exaggerating to keep the child. Can you imagine a Policeman investigating, then prosecuting and then punishing? This would be unthinkable in criminal courts, there are checks and balances along the way. Police investigate and their role is complete after they hand the file to Prosecutors. Prosecutors can decide where a prosecution is in the public interest and decide against prosecution. Judges are supposed to judge without fear or favor and if there is a likelihood of a long sentence, the accused has the option of letting 12 of their peers decide on their innocence of guilt. The judge has no part in punishment other than deciding on a fair punishment but doesn't carry it out. The Prison Service has no role in investigating or prosecuting or judging, they simply carry out the sentence.

Compare that with Family "Justice" where the same people investigate, are largely responsible for prosecuting and are part of the punishment. How can this be legal and lawful? Unlike the Director of Public Prosecutions, who can decide whether to go ahead or not with the case, in Family Law the "Prosecutors" only job is to win against the parent. They are lawyers in private practice who have a responsibility to make money for their law firm. They get paid for prosecuting and get paid nothing for not prosecuting, every parent is prosecuted or they don't get paid, the DPP gets paid regardless. This is one of the important checks and balances missing in the Family Law System, the "Prosecutors" prosecute everyone and it is in their financial interest to make the prosecution as expensive as possible. Also the standard of lawyering in Family Law is extremely poor and many parents can't get a fair trial from their own lawyers who are also incentivized to stretch out the case and make it as expensive as possible.

Some judges love my colleagues who act as McKenzie Friends; we have no vested interest, are not getting paid and want the case over and done with as soon as possible. By working together as a group, we come to court prepared with Case Law and we only accept cases we can win. My colleagues don't lie, bring in hired guns that we know will perjure themselves, we don't threaten the other side to stretch out the case, we are at a severe disadvantage at not being given full disclosure of documents and exculpatory evidence that would vindicate those we help. It's not difficult to see where the system is highly incentivized by money and is adversarial, the more adversarial the more money to be made. Against a budget of €10 million a year for legal, they have managed to stretch it to €30 million for the last few years which would indicate to me that the Government has no control, has no clue about what happens and by allowing rogue solicitors to use children as a commodity to make money, obviously are not on the side of children but have sided with an Industry of Child Abuse.

As a matter of urgency we need to remove the lawyers, the lawyers who seemingly don't need to bid for their contracts every year and have become a fixture in these courts. The only way to restore justice is to scrap these family courts and abolish the 'In Camera Rule'. Let Gardaí investigate, the DPP prosecute, the judge decide and the social workers only be allowed to advocate.

We have been lead to this precipice partly by Social Work and Psychology. For years governments relied on these faux "Sciences" to make law and policy. Rather than having Sociology develop into a real science that relies on repeatable experiments, we have experiments being repeated that rely on the theorist. We have seen governments build housing estates that even Police wont enter and we have seen this not just in Ireland, but the same experiment being repeated over and over for many decades in other countries and learned nothing from the experiment. Attempts at control of the population always end in failure. In the USA in the 1930's, women deemed to be of lower class were sterilized, last week in India 30 women died because of botched procedures almost 85 years after the same Eugenics program began in the USA. Contrary to what some believe, Eugenics is an American invention and didn't start in Germany in the 1930's with the Lebensborn program. If we fail to learn from history we are doomed to repeat it.

I can see a situation in Ireland and the UK where parents are going to need a licence to have a child. Some proponents argue that you need a licence to own a dog. Of course you will have to take classes from a Children's NGO and social workers and pay big money first. We have seen in the UK where it has become illegal to hire the 16 year old girl next door to babysit your children, is

Ireland far behind? The young girl needs to be trained by social workers and then vetted by social workers and police, all at a cost of course which would bring up the price of a 16 year old babysitter to £20 an hour so she can pay for the courses that cost £80 and hour or more. If you don't comply you can have your children removed for putting them "At Risk" and fined £3,000. Is any of this actually benefitting children?

Or are the net beneficiaries the Child Abuse Industry? Parents and people who want to volunteer for a School Play have to be vetted as well and take a 4 hour course from a social worker to volunteer for as little as a 1 hour show. Wouldn't it be better perhaps if we taught girls and boys in school at the age of 12 how to properly care for a baby and hopefully learn that giving birth and looking after a baby is the hardest job you will ever do in your life? And maybe they will learn that they shouldn't be having sex at 12? It's an extremely odd situation that we have now, especially in the UK. We have councils giving birth control such as contraceptive implants to 12-year-old girls in school without parental knowledge or permission, but isn't this considered "Grooming"?

We are sheltering the "Innocence" of children by removing any hint of "Sex" but then teaching them how to reproduce at age 5 in Sex Education? Make no mistake about it, the ideology is that your children are not "Yours", they are property of the State and all parental rights terminate the moment you cross the threshold to a school or a hospital. We were sold a package of Children's Rights to decide but the reality is that social workers, guardians and will make these decisions about children and the child's voice will not be heard in court. I have seen in the UK where parents were not allowed to attend their child's football match by a school unless they have been vetted. What we have is an Industry of hysterical people running around in fear and anger "protecting" children from mythical predators, and in the process harming them.

What people failed to understand in the Children's Rights Referendum is that Irish parents had the right to vindicate for their children against the State. This was never a licence to abuse any child despite what some dishonest reporters claimed. If the referendum passes into law, parents will have no rights. The State has always been allowed to step in and no child has ever died or been harmed as a result of inadequate laws.

The Referendum was about making the State the de facto parent and reducing parents to caregivers. It effectively took away the rights of children also, read it for yourself, the State decides that you have failed in your duty and does what it wants. The reality is that the State has always done what it wants but you don't hear about any of these cases because of the In Camera Rule. My overall message and my arguments when campaigning against parents giving up all their rights, is that historically, the State is the worst parent possible. States cannot raise children and will never get it right. The whole point of the referendum was to take away the rights of parents to vindicate the rights of children. Essentially every child in Ireland would be "cared for" by the State but only some of them would be in "Care" in foster or residential institutions. If your 12 year old daughter became pregnant, it would be the States decision to take her for an abortion, as has happened to many girls in "Care". This has been happening for years to children in "Care" and if the referendum every passes into law, the State will decide in every case where there is a dispute with parents. Disputes between parents and children's rights are extremely rare, in her 8 year as Children's Ombudsman, Emily Logan has never heard of such a case. More than likely the decision will be made by a recently graduated social worker with no children of their own and no life experience. Because of the secrecy of the system not many people are aware of what has been happening. We say that in the Church Institutions we didn't know this was happening either but shouldn't one of the key learning's from the Ryan Report is that we should be keeping close tabs on the System?

Many judges spoke out against the Children's Referendum, we didn't need it and it wouldn't help Irish Children. I don't know of a single judge who was in favour of the referendum other than retired judge Catherine McGuiness. However in many of their written judgements, and bear in mind that Family Court judgements are not written, judges have been quite scathing about a dysfunctional system and how a dishonest government and Child Abuse Industry are trying to remove parental rights for more control over family. To say that the constitution puts the rights of parents before the rights of the child is a lie.

Justice Adrian Hardiman in his 2006 judgment in the landmark Baby Ann Case said.

> *"It would be quite untrue, to say that the Constitution puts the rights of parents first and those of children second. It fully acknowledges the "natural and imprescriptible rights" and the human dignity of children, but equally recognises the inescapable fact that a young child cannot exercise his or her own rights. The Constitution does not prefer parents to children. The preference the Constitution gives is this: it prefers parents to third parties, official or private, priest or social worker, as the enablers and guardians of the child's rights."*

Aye, there's the rub. It doesn't sit well with the ideologues, that parents should decide for their children. Social work, has decided that Family is an out-dated concept that has its roots in tribal tradition, no longer valid in today's reality.

I spend a lot of my time reading Family Case Law and while I could probably write another book on the topic, I will leave you with just one more from the UK.

Hedley J in Re L (Care: Threshold Criteria) (Family Division 26 October 2006) in which, dismissing the Local Authority's application for a Care Order, the learned Judge said:

"Society must be willing to tolerate very diverse standards of parenting, including the eccentric, the barely adequate and the inconsistent. Children will inevitable have both very different experiences of parenting and very unequal consequences flowing from it.

It means that some children will experience disadvantage and harm, while others flourish in atmospheres of loving security and emotional stability. These are the consequences of our fallible humanity and it is not the provenance of the State to spare children all the consequences of defective parenting."

Governments in their quest to control society, by using the flawed "Science" of Sociology are spiralling further out of control, it's not working. The worse society becomes, the more control they apply and the inevitable result will always be failure. Sociology and Psychology have their value when used as a tool to help families. When used as a weapon against society it has always resulted in failure.

As Social Worker Molly McGrath-Tierney has said, "**the Intervention IS the problem**". In my own belief, the further we stray from Nature, the worse the situation becomes. Maybe the best solution for Ireland and the UK would be to follow far better models around the world? How did we ever live before social workers? How is it that so many countries don't even have social workers and yet, children thrive? Is anyone brave enough to speak out against the dogma and ideology and risk being shot down?

Perhaps if someone years ago had the courage to stand up in the Religious Orders and say that **this is wrong**, then maybe we wouldn't have seen Ryan Report? Victims did stand up and were quickly shot down and dismissed. For all we know, maybe many brave people may have spoken out but in a culture of secrecy and dogma, were shot down and silenced. Today we see a situation in the UK where social workers are gagged and paid off when leaving councils and hundreds of millions have been spent to prevent them speaking even to courts and tribunals. I only know of 2 UK social workers that refused "Hush Money". I have to wonder if the same has been done in Ireland? Although I hear from social workers regularly, nobody wants to go on the record and even admit to the problems within the system, which is becoming more like the UK system every day.

On the Balance of Probabilities, what would you say the possibility is that among 4,000 staff of the HSE or 4,500 of the CFA, that no social worker has ever made a serious mistake and was punished? Can anyone cite a single case in Ireland? Not that I want to play the blame game, but there are always consequences to our action. In cases in the UK I frequently report social workers to the HCRC and doctors to the GMC but in Ireland there is no such mechanism to report social workers. I find it astonishing that in the deaths in

"Care" of 196 children, that not a single social worker was responsible or held accountable. Also the fact that the Gardai, HSE and Government hid the fact that 500 children went "Missing" from "Care" and again, it was nobodies fault. What I find even more astonishing is that a panel of supposedly "independent" people investigating these deaths didn't assign blame to a single person. I laughed a few months ago when someone told me that the CFA have an "Intelligence Unit", obviously they have nothing to do with management of the system.

I hope of course that this book will have some impact. I don't mind if it's decried as "Hyperbolic" or whatever insult people care to throw at me. I want people to have the debate and to keep talking about it until we fix it. I want for children to have fathers in their lives, even if the father is a hopeless alcoholic, I think he can pull himself together for an hour or two, maybe long enough that his child knows that he has a father who loves him, even if he is not capable of raising him.

Child Abuse make me angry but not to such a point that I cant think clearly and rationally. I cant claim to have any qualifications that make me an "Expert" on the topic, but I have no issue in saying that I am far more qualified by experience than any politician and unlike judges, I have met the children and heard their views on the matter, even children as young as 3 who so eloquently can verbalize their horrendous experience first-hand, unlike the judges who get a 3rd hand account from people whose incomes depend on children being taken away.

I make no apology if I use figures such as; "A child in Care is 6 times more likely to die", if the child was removed for their protection, shouldn't that child be 6 times **less** likely to die? I have fairly represented the figures as honestly as anyone could do the research when the government wont give accurate information. A UCD study has already pointed out a child in "Care" is nearly 10 times the risk of suicide, but other than this being published in one newspaper, it has not lead to any flurry of debate or concern by government or the public to find out why this is the case. At a press conference in Dublin I cited this to the yawns of the Irish Media. And you have to wonder too why Children's NGO's are not incensed by this? Surely these people who are at the coalface of Child Protection would be breaking down the doors of the Dail and the CFA and demand action? Nothing, not a sausage as my father would have said. Every time a child dies in Ireland because of a vehicle collision or dies of a horrendous disease, you will read about it in the newspapers or on TV. Why is it that when a child dies in "Care" that you don't hear about it?

Have you noticed also how the 100 or so Children's NGO are always talking about "Rights", just as the UN has done since James P Grant of UNICEF died? They are supposedly on the front lines and constantly telling describing a tip of an iceberg that most of the problems in child protection is bad parents, so why doesn't the Crime Statistics of the Gardai and the DPP echo their concerns?

How can you have 541 sexual assaults of children a year but so few prosecutions? Is child abuse and neglect not a crime worthy of Police investigation?

Or is the truth that "Charities" are not really all that charitable to children and not working for their benefit? Sure we get the odd story of how tough it is for charities, need more money, children are "at risk", but I don't see any of these "Charities" opening soup kitchens or food banks? What I do see is a lot of bureaucrats running around the country with slick presentations and giving speeches, just as the UN have done for years. I see people on TV and hear them on radio preaching the dogma of "At Risk" and using all the buzzwords that leave the public believing that these people actually know what is happening to children in Ireland. I am not impressed by what they say, I find it more telling what the have not said and more importantly what they have not done.

A few years ago I stood in a quiet council estate in Brighton/Hove with a young woman whose baby had been taken for Forced Adoption. And when I say quiet, the silence was eerie. It was summertime and children should have been playing outside. In the yards of the residents, nearly all single mothers, were unused children's toys. It looked like the aftermath of genocide. She explained that all of the babies and toddlers had been taken from the mothers and placed for Forced Adoption. It was a time when Tony Blair was paying bonuses to Local Authorities to hit targets for Adoption, and hit their targets they did. It wasn't the children of "Care" that were adopted because nobody wants "damaged" children of "Care", the wanted babies and the social workers wanted to hit their targets for bonuses. I later learned that 11 local social workers were struck off and given large sums of money with their gagging orders. On the same visit not too far away in Horsham, the LA were having a big party with face painting and balloons to get more children adopted. Children were paraded around as "doe eyed orphans" "Languishing in Care" and in search of a "Forever Home". Only a mile away, parents were protesting with posters and banners that their children were taken away, while being ring-fenced in by local Police and not allowed to go near the party where their children were being sold to the highest bidder. If these parents were such criminals who deserved losing their children forever, why weren't they in Prison?

We need to stop this ridiculous obsession we have with Paedophiles, its not helping children. The law as it currently stands is not working; no paedophile that has ever sexually assaulted a child should **ever** be released into society. There is no cure for paedophilia. By seeing paedophiles only as criminals and not also mentally ill, we are releasing people from prisons knowing full well that they will reoffend. It's not just paedophiles that harm children, we need to focus on psychopaths and sociopaths that are Serial Offenders, your child is just as likely to fall victim to Predators who unlike paedophiles, will kill. The insanity of allowing a predator back on the streets, knowing full well that they will reoffend cannot continue. If you sexually assault a child and you are over the age of 18, you should never be allowed to assault again. Nobody who is a risk to society should ever be **allowed** to be a risk.

The rhetoric of "castrate them" isn't working because sex is a function of the brain and not the sexual organs. Instead the rhetoric and hysteria protecting children, it's harming them. We need to turn our anger into positive ways of preventing the problem. We also stop need to listening to people purporting to be experts, other than convicting innocent people, they have done nothing to solve the problem. They whip up hysteria to fund their own witch-hunts and in nearly 50 years have not prevented children from being sexually assaulted.

No, there are not 100,000 paedophiles in Ireland, there are however many children around the age of puberty who will sexually assault. As we have seen from the Adam Walsh Act, 80% of all sexual assaults against children are by 14 year olds, this is why we need to focus on Puberty for children and giving them a proper sex education to help them and prevent them from becoming sex offenders. Or we could take the approach of the USA of criminalizing 5 year olds and posting their image on Sex Offender Websites.

We need to start celebrating Puberty as many cultures do rather than hiding under a rock and treating sex as dirty. We need to be asking the "Professionals" and "Experts" why they are lying to us about "Dirty old men in raincoats" and exaggerating the extent of the problem for their own gain. Since they haven't improved the situation in years, we should stop believing that they have all the answers; they certainly don't have the solutions.

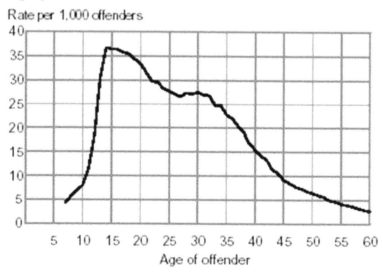

Source: US National Center for Juvenile Justice

It's important to realize also, that in this graph a large number of people accused, as "Sex Offenders" are not sex offenders at all. A 5 year old nuzzling the breasts of a kindergarten teacher is not capable of sex and has not committed any crime but is included in these statistics. A 14-year-old girl taking indecent pictures of herself and sharing them has harmed nobody but herself, she is still charged with making and distributing child pornography. A 16-year-old boy in a loving and consensual relationship with a 14-year girl is hardly in the same league as a 28-year-old man raping an 8 year old. Giving longer sentences for sex crimes to children than they would if they had violently assaulted the child is a reflection of the hysteria we have, and a reaction to the anger we feel to child abuse. It's also a reflection of how we talk **about** children but not **to** them. Nobody seems to be willing to have that conversation or do any serious study of Child Sexuality from the age of puberty to 18. We prefer a more Puritanical approach of "hear no evil, see no evil" and any scientist who would seriously study the topic would be branded a paedophile and a heretic. Perhaps if one person at the Salem Witch Trials had the courage to stand up and urge people to investigate the matter further, they wouldn't have murdered their own people. Criminalizing children as they do in the USA is wrong, I hope we learn from their mistakes or we are doomed to repeat them.

If some people believe that I have defamed Sociology & Psychology in this book, I respectfully disagree. As my esteemed colleague Ian Josephs has said many times; "If you are part of a wicked organization that does wicked things and you do not speak out, you are just as guilty". While Ian often goes on to say that; "I'm sure there were 'nice' prison guards at Auschwitz", I can only say that I echo his views. In an industry devoid of any scrutiny, it would be a very exceptional case that anyone would speak out.

In the Baby P case, the story would never have come to the attention of the press if it hadn't been for one social worker who went public with her story of the dysfunction 6 months before Baby Peter died. There were hundreds of Baby P's since Peter's death but the new regime of gagging and covering up has taken over. Social workers quit Child Protection mostly because they are not allowed to do their jobs and are doing an impossible job to begin with. Nobody can predict future crime and social workers should never have a role in the detection of crimes of child abuse and neglect. However, as Ian points out, unless social work admits its failures rather than playing the victim, it is fair game to defame the entire profession. I know some very good social workers but very few of who work in Child Protection. The dregs of the profession and the recently graduated are running the show, with disastrous results.

In countries other than Ireland and the UK, only the best are given the role of child protection, as it is a role where social workers have the duty to advocate for children rather than prosecuting their parents. The Spanish social workers I have met enjoy their jobs and for the most part are respected. In Ireland and the

UK, they are vilified and have become the most hated profession. No social worker in the UK can claim fairly that they are "Damned if they do and damned if they don't"; they are "damned" when they fail in their duty and a child is harmed of dies because of their incompetence. They are struck off because of lying and failing to do the job that they are paid for. In Ireland it has become evident that hated and vilified or not, no social worker will ever be "damned" or suffer any consequence for their failures even when their client dies.

If I have portrayed the role of Psychology and Sociology in a bad light, again I make no apology. While Psychology can be a marvelous tool for helping people, when used as weapon against families it is one of the most dangerous and destructive weapons imaginable. Psychology has been a product that has been over-sold for years, especially in courts. To present Psychology as a Science is a fraud. It is the only branch of Medicine where an alleged illness cannot be proven to exist and where no Psychologist can ever claim to have "Cured" a single patient ever. The Psychiatric "Illnesses" are not mentioned in any Medical Journal and Psychologists have had to write their own book, the DSM, which even Psychologists themselves have rejected the latest version which lists every Human Emotion as a Mental Illness.

Psychology by a skilled therapist can be life saving but when it is dishonestly portrayed as a Science, especially a science used to destroy families and children and by using non-existent illnesses, it is nothing more than a weapon against society. Psychology is nothing more than subjective opinion and is not robust enough to be used in courtrooms. Many psychologists have spoke out, far more than social workers speaking out against their profession, but until the vast majority rescue their profession from the charlatans that have hijacked it, the value of Psychology will be reduced to Fortune Telling.

Equally Sociology, which relies heavily on Psychology, is increasingly being seen as being of little value. There are many Sociologists whom I admire and respect and their work is of great value to society, but mostly these are Sociologists who are involved in Research and are not afraid to stick their head above the parapet and ask uncomfortable questions, these are the real scientists. The more dangerous Sociologists are the Social Work Professors who are horribly out of touch with the realities of real life and have sequestered themselves to Ivy League Towers and bluster from one failed theory to the next. They sell their products of an education to unwitting students. Real Science does not rely on a Theorist to exist. If Social Work is ever to be seen as being of value to society, you need to accept that Social Work is not a Profession of Excellence and has no track record or history of successes. You need to stop teaching gullible middle-class girls that Sociology and Psychology knows more about Parenting than eons of Evolution and Nature. I would probably start by screening out the undesirables at admission.

I say to Judges, that you couldn't pay me enough money to do your job. I don't have the Wisdom of Solomon or the patience of a saint. Although many judges in higher courts have castigated their colleagues in the lower courts, they have not done this in public. While I can understand the frustration of judges with the system, I cannot understand why you allow it to continue. The quality of Mercy is not strained; it must be given freely and without fear or favor. Equally, when judges themselves allow miscarriages of justice to take place, especially in District Courts, they have perverted Justice and reduced the Quality and Mercy of Justice to the level of what took place in Salem 300 years ago. Judges are equally human and fallible and as angered as anyone else at child abuse and neglect. Judges have allowed charlatans to pervert the course of justice to the point that we now have two Systems of Justice, how is this possible in a Democracy?

- How can a person be innocent in one court and guilty in another?

- How can a person be Punished Without Crime?

- Can you give a Legal, Scientific & Moral value to Best Interests of the Child?

- Is it ever acceptable to grant an Ex parte hearing for an Emergency Care Order?

- If the child is the Primary Concern, how can it be justified to remove a newborn baby from it's mother and abuse the human rights of the baby to bond and be breastfed? Why punish children for the alleged sins of their parents?

- If you have ever allowed a Section 12 to be executed without hearing the evidence of the Garda who invoked it, and their "compelling reasons", then you have committed child abuse.

- If you have allowed the Prosecution to "stretch out" cases for months to make more money you have abuse the child you purport to protect.

- If you have denied a father a right to see their child and be part of that child's upbringing, you have abused a child by removing their father.

- If you have allowed a Legal Aid lawyer to **not** put up a vigorous defense for a parent, you are guilty of perverting the course of justice.

- If you must insist that an "Expert" be brought in to make a decision, then the parents and not those in the system can only choose the expert. Clinical Psychologists have no expertise or training in Forensic Psychology and nobody less than a Forensic Psychologist should ever testify.

- There must be a presumption that if a child needs to be removed from one parent, that the other parent or extended family should be granted custody and paid the same rate for Foster Care as a stranger would get. To remove a child from their home and not place them with their immediate family is child abuse. No excuses or objections from social workers opposed to Kinship Care are acceptable. Siblings should never be separated except for very compelling reasons. Family does not need to be assessed or vetted unless there is evidence and compelling reasons for doing so.

- Children should never be removed without a competent investigation having demonstrated evidence of abuse or neglect. If a crime is alleged, then Gardai must be immediately called to investigate. There shall be No Punishment Without Crime, but equally, there should be No Crime without Punishment.

- Judges should insist on Gardai investigating all cases and not leave these investigations to recent college graduate social workers.

- Rather than taking children into "Care" by default, the emphasis needs to be preventing them going into "Care" in the first instance. For parents affected by this and their children, I can safely say from 7 years of experience that the Punishment is far worse than the Crime. Removing a child should only be done as a very temporary measure and only ever done on the basis of evidence and not mere suspicion.

In Justice there must be a presumption of innocence, I have seen far too often where the starting point is presumed guilty without anything more than suspicion presented as "evidence". I have seen where the reasons change from the ECO to the ICO and then FCO constantly change as social workers fail to prove their case and keep clutching at straws. I have see children supposedly removed by Gardaí under S12 of the CCA but the Garda not confirming this to the court or stating their "Compelling Reasons" and the danger being established as required by law.

To Irish Politicians, I say that as a matter of great urgency we need to replace the "Best Interest of Children" with a far higher standard. To use nothing more than a slogan that has no legal, scientific or moral value and that is in no way measurable or demonstrable is no longer acceptable. For years we have heard the excuses of the system and the industry and we need to stop allowing people who have been part of the problem to be part of the solution. The proposition of pouring almost a billion a year into a system and an industry without any scrutiny is no longer tenable. To continue spending a billion a year on "professionals" and not directly on the children has proven to be a false economy. The more staff added and the more money poured in, the bigger the problem becomes.

The concept that a Minister for Children is not allowed to enter a family court is absurd; the Child Abuse Industry is a big ship with no Captain at the helm and is bound to run aground sooner or later. Even the Department for Children and Youth Affairs have no idea what happens to these children in "Care", have never met them and have no idea how they came to be in "Care".

We don't need another referendum to "put Family Courts on a constitutional basis", we need one system of Justice for all and we need the public and the media to scrutinize the system regardless of the objections of the people who are part of the problem and not the solution. The In Camera system is not justice and only exists to protect the system and prevents it from scrutiny. No system should be allowed to hide behind the secrecy when the secrecy exists, supposedly to benefit the child. The case of Barry Andrews not being allowed to know how many children had died in the system is indicative of a system gone mad. The In Camera Rule exists to protect children, and not the system or the State.

To Children's NGO's, I say we need to stop pretending that Children's Rights actually benefits any child. We need "Charities" to stop Empire Building and selling "Services" while pretending this benefits children. Charities should not receive any money from Governments and should not be multi-million Industries with many employees. It is not to the benefit of Children's "Charities" to keep propping up a system doomed to fail. The "Best Interest of Children" Principle is not working and is no more than a slogan. If Children's NGO's want to work for the benefit of children the BIP must be scrapped in favor of a higher principle of "To the Demonstrable and Measurable Benefit of the Child" and NGO's need to ensure that the benefit to children is demonstrated in every case. If charities exist for the benefit of children, then you need to plant your flag in favor of children and not the system.

To Doctors, Nurses and Paramedics, stop harming children by believing the nonsense that child abuse is of epidemic proportions. The number of criminal prosecutions does not support the proposition that many children are harmed. You job is to diagnose and treat, not to play detective. A diagnosis of child abuse is one that only a properly trained Forensic Pathologist or Biomechanical Study supports. Shaken Baby Syndrome is nonsense and is not supported by Science. Munchausen's Syndrome by Proxy is nonsense and the original theorist is responsible for the deaths of many parents who were wrongly accused. Rickets is of epidemic proportions and if you do not accept this, you risk killing your patient or worsening their condition. Many doctors have destroyed the lives of many of their patients and many have died as a result of doctors refusing to properly diagnose their patient once they have latched on to a conclusion of child abuse.

If a parent insists on a second opinion this is not child abuse, this is Good Medicine. No doctor who suspects abuse should ever put themselves in a position of Judge, Jury and Executioner. Until now there has been no penalty for doctors who wrongly arrive at a conclusion of abuse but the tide is changing. I have personally reported doctors to Medical Councils and Boards and will continue to do so as long as doctors are harming children with misdiagnosis. First, do no harm. You are not a detective and the primary concern should be a Differential Diagnosis to rule out other causes. Your patient's Health and not their Welfare is not your concern.

To Gardaí, you have the duty and the privilege to Serve & Protect the citizens of Ireland. The Irish Constitution does not differentiate between adults and children. It is your sworn duty to protect children as well as adults. I would urge Members to study the Child Care Act very carefully and understand it. Section 12 gives the power to any member, without even needing to consult superiors, to enter any structure and remove any child if they reasonably believe the child to be at risk. For too long, this section has been misused as a Fraud Upon the Court by social workers that have no such statutory right to invoke a S12. For too long Gardaí have not had a role in investigating and intervening in crimes against children. I believe that the management policies of abrogating the role to social workers has gone on too long and in the process has harmed many children. I don't wish to point fingers, but the behaviours of Gardaí in the role of many cases where children have been abused or have died, has been a failure of Garda Management and policy. By "passing the buck" to social workers has proven to be a miserable failure. If child abuse and neglect is a crime, then let it investigated as a crime by trained and experienced Garda Officers who have a statutory duty to investigate.

To the Minister for Children I say that when Frances Fitzgerald took the role of dedicated Children's Minister, within a few days of her taking office I wrote to her advising that she should announce; "Look I didn't create this mess but I'm sure going to fix it". She didn't take my advice and children are far worse off today because of the actions of her Party. Like Barry Andrews before her, she should have seen that she is not in control and refused to take any blame for a mess she has no control over. Instead she followed the lead of Barry Andrews and sided with the system. The "Usual Suspects" who are responsible for the current mess guided her and if history teaches us anything, it teaches us that those who are part of the problem should never be part of the solution. You should also know that you have no right under the law to know what's happening and that you can't control or manage the situation if you have no clue as to how this system operates. The system is based on one of the worst possible models as the rest of the world now sees the UK. Every country in Europe is currently before the EU Parliament and has expressed grave concerns about the treatment of their citizens. We don't need 2 different systems of Justice, we need 1 system for all and if children are ever to be protected, it will not be when social workers are at the hub of child protection. If Child Abuse and Neglect is a crime then lets start punishing crime, in the meantime, lets stop punishing innocent children by removing them from their families to the benefit of an industry.

To the Department of Children and Youth Affairs. I have counted hundreds of visits on our website from Mespill Road. Our website has been attacked and successfully hacked on one occasion. I realise that you are operating in a deficit of information, as is the Minister, but I have a solution. In the future I will publish a website, I will show you videos, audio recordings, Psychology reports from Hired Gun "Experts" who perjure themselves and yet, are used again and again by the CFA. I will publish cases in great detail and let the public decide for themselves whether the child should have been removed. The public have a right to know what is being done in their name. I will publish some of the documents on LiveLeaks and/or WikiLeaks and assist any Media researchers or journalists who are willing to cover these stories. So far you have only heard one side of the story and you still have the option of pleading ignorance that you don't know what is happening.

To the Child and Family Agency, please read the paragraph above.

To Social Workers. Ask yourselves why Child Protection social workers have become the most hated profession today. If you are protecting children, one of the noblest jobs anywhere, why are you so hated and vilified? Attempts to improve the image of Social Care, such as hiring Max Clifford, have met with failure and the slogan of "Damned if we do, damned if we don't" is being exposed for the lie that it is. The fact that no Irish social worker has ever been damned has not escaped the notice of the public. When SORU finally established their Fitness to Practice Committee, my colleagues and I have about 100 cases for them to investigate.

While many Irish social workers like to disassociate themselves from their UK counterparts, we know that the system is becoming more like the UK every day. We have seen the failed theories being instituted slowly by "Experts" who despite their best intentions have little idea of how Child Protection works, or in this case, doesn't. In every profession there are rogues and incompetent people. Until the profession stands up to the rogues and the managers, the public will see no value and see social work as a failure. Social workers need to throw away the Crystal Balls and stop channelling spirits of a Pseudo-Science. You can no more predict future Outcomes for children than I can the lottery numbers.

Hiding behind the secrecy isn't working. Sending eager young graduates out as crusaders to destroy families has been a disaster. You can't be a Prosecutor and an Advocate at the same time as the roles are incompatible. The only way out at this point is for social workers to stop being Prosecutors and do what your colleagues do in other countries, which is Advocacy and not Prosecution. In other area of social work practice, people go to social workers to help and advocacy, in Child "Protection" parents run in fear that their child will be taken. Parents have nowhere to turn in a crisis and anyone they ask for help will "turn them in" to the Authorities. When parents ask for help they get prosecuted instead. Social workers are lying to themselves that children are better off with strangers and then when the system dumps these children at age 18 they become targets for social workers who see them as "damaged" and likely to have their children removed, in fact 60 times more likely.

We need to stop pretending that "Care" is good for children or even that children will be at less risk in "Care", the evidence speaks for itself. The only reliable scientific way of measuring the benefit to children is Outcomes. Biology counts for everything and only family can raise a child to where that child will have a good outcome in life.

This madness of social workers being prosecutors of families instead of advocates has to stop. The only countries in Europe that allow social workers to take a child away is the UK and Ireland, who always blindly follow the UK's lead. The only country in Europe, which allows for Forced Adoption, is the UK and every country in Europe except Ireland has expressed great concerns for the Sledgehammer Approach used by the UK. Ireland can no longer claim to be different from the UK, we have seen the shift to the UK style in recent years and the inevitable result will be a collapse of the system, another Ryan Report that will expose the system for what it is. Where the system has counted on secrecy for many years, the system forgets that victims of these interventions cannot be gagged as adults. Even where the UK tried to gag children in "Care", they have spoken out as adults even though a law was introduced to prevent them from speaking.

Children grow up and remember how they were treated and will seek redress just as they did with Ryan report and the Redress Board. The more victims the system creates, the louder their voice will be. When the system finally crashes, social work will be the target of the public's anger just as the clergy took the brunt, I believe unfairly, as it was the Government and the NSPCC who were responsible for placing the children in "Care" to begin with. Today, I see bad managers who are responsible for the current mess, all of whom should have been replaced in the shift from HSE to CFA. I see social workers acting in anger, young people fresh out of college with no life experience and eager to prove themselves, I see a great divide in the profession where social workers acting as advocates for their clients and have no duty to prosecute, but they themselves are brought into disrepute by the rogues working in Child Protection. I see social workers being asked to do an impossible job that they claim to be capable of doing and failing miserably.

In my own experience I have a great respect for 2 social workers that worked alongside my parents, one of them for many years. In my father's final year of life, a wonderful man worked with the family while he was in hospital and advocated for my father, first and foremost. I also have wonderful memories of a large lady who worked with my mother when she worked as a cleaner in the local Health Board. She would enter the house and plop herself firmly between my mother and father on a sofa designed for 2 people, which was quite an accomplishment. Even in her retirement, she would visit the house and still get on the phone to ensure that my parents had everything they needed. In her philosophy, my parents had worked hard all their lives and were entitled to whatever "entitlements" she could squeeze from the council or government.

My mother had Alzheimer's for 5 years and spent most of that time in the care of my father, who by this stage was legally blind and in poor health himself.

The social worker ensured they had a Medical Alert Pendant to call for help, a Stair-lift to get my mother upstairs, a special shower to bathe my mother and 2 wonderful ladies that were "Home Help" to visit every day. The family did what we could for our parents, but without the help of this wonderful social worker, the lives of my parents would have been impossible. My mother would have needed to go into a home and it would have cost the State far more money without her intervention. Imagine for a moment how poor the lives of my parents would have been if the social worker had taken an adversarial stance instead and prosecuted my father or decided that he was incapable of looking after her? And the cost to the State? This is the real value of Social Work when social workers are advocates.

What a shame that the noble profession of Social Work has become the most hated profession. I have seen so much good work being done by Advocates and so much damage being done by Prosecutors. It's no shock that the turnover rate in child protection is so high and the dregs of the profession work at Child "Protection". It's no shock to see people leaving as soon as they can find another area of the practice, social workers are being asked to do an impossible task that they will never be capable of doing. The System doesn't love any child and is acting out of fear and anger and revenge, and of course Profit. Until social workers stand up for their profession and rescue it from the few who have hijacked it, it is fair that the public tar everyone with the same brush.

To the private law firms acting as Prosecutors for the CFA and GAL's, I can say that I have honestly never met such dishonest people in my life. I have carefully documented many cases and when Ryan Report Two comes around, I will present all the evidence.

To parents, don't allow yourself to be guilt-tripped by fashionable styles of parenting that come and go out of fashion. Your instincts will guide you to do what is right and what is necessary to successfully raise your child. Your child doesn't need you to be a friend or a maid, they need you to teach them and prepare them for living independently. They need to know that you are there for them, even if they don't know they need you. They will not remember how much money you spent on them later in life but will cherish the time you spent with them. You want to protect them and sometimes they need to be protected from themselves. Children are not care-less, they are care-free, and they don't realize the dangers around them. They need freedom to make mistakes for themselves and by wrapping them up in cotton wool; they will never learn the skills they need to learn to protect themselves.

Your instincts about your child are far more important than the subjective opinion of others who don't know your child as you do are who are not connected by bond of love. Your instincts about other people's children have no value. While others feel they are helpful, only you love and understand the child. Trust yourself and give yourself permission to make mistakes, you're doing a good job. Some children will become the next Einstein's but we also need shopkeepers and candlestick makers. The best thing you can do for your children is get together with other parents and get involved in politics so that your children have a better future than us. Don't allow anyone to take away your parental rights and let your children feel loved. The only poster that appeared for the No side during the Children's Referendum said; "If you tolerate this, your children will be next". Your silence is your consent. If you tolerate this injustice to other people's children you have chosen the side of the oppressor and have no right to complain when it happens to you.

In this final paragraph, I have laid out my stall for you and you can choose to believe or not what I have said. I declare now that I have no vested interest in the topic of Child Protection, I do not earn a living from it and my life won't change at all whether the Children's Rights Amendment passes into law or not. I fully expect some ridicule from those who make their living in the Child Abuse Industry; I would be very surprised if they did not. For me this is not about attacking a system or vilifying who have the best intentions and the best interests of children at heart, it is about building the system that children need and will benefit from. I'm sure that many will feel vilified and attacked, but that is not my intention. Sometimes there is no easy way of breaking bad news to people but a responsible person in my view is someone who will say what needs to be said. If egos are hurt, that's too bad but your ego is not my concern. We need to step back and look at this rationally and responsibly. If need be, we need to sit around the table, put our differences aside, agree to disagree and commit to building a better system for the benefit of children. We need to have the serious discussion without anger or fear and work together to accomplish a common goal. I don't pretend to have the solutions but I have offered a few here that are worthy of debate. I could write volumes more on this topic but I feel I have covered the most urgent needs. I have had a very unique experience in the past 7 years of researching this topic and I have shared what I have seen and heard as faithfully as I could. I didn't write this book for academics or for parents affected by this who already understand, I wrote it for the ordinary person who has no knowledge of how the system operates in the hope that the Public will be the catalyst for change. I thank the readers who have reached the last paragraph for your kind attention. Now you know what happens in the Secret Courts.

Lightning Source UK Ltd.
Milton Keynes UK
UKHW051941111019
351361UK00025B/508/P